THE BOOK OF IMAGES

ALIAS

authorHOUSE®

AuthorHouse™
1663 Liberty Drive
Bloomington, IN 47403
www.authorhouse.com
Phone: 833-262-8899

Published by AuthorHouse   05/20/2023

ISBN: 979-8-8230-0899-0 (sc)
ISBN: 979-8-8230-0898-3 (e)

Library of Congress Control Number: 2023909681

Print information available on the last page.

Any people depicted in stock imagery provided by Getty Images are models,
and such images are being used for illustrative purposes only.
Certain stock imagery © Getty Images.

Scripture quotations marked KJV are from the Holy Bible, King James Version
(Authorized Version). First published in 1611. Quoted from the KJV Classic
Reference Bible, Copyright © 1983 by The Zondervan Corporation.

Scripture quotations marked AMP are from The Amplified Bible, Old
Testament copyright © 1965, 1987 by the Zondervan Corporation. The
Amplified Bible, New Testament copyright © 1954, 1958, 1987 by The
Lockman Foundation. Used by permission. All rights reserved.

Scripture quotations marked NASB are taken from the New American
Standard Bible®, Copyright © 1960, 1962, 1963, 1968, 1971, 1972, 1973,
1975, 1977, 1995 by The Lockman Foundation. Used by permission.

Scripture quotations marked NIV are taken from the Holy Bible, New
International Version®. NIV®. Copyright © 1973, 1978, 1984 by International
Bible Society. Used by permission of Zondervan. All rights reserved. [Biblica]

This book is printed on acid-free paper.

INTRODUCTION

The purpose and life of every man is determined by who he listens to and draws spiritual guidance from[1] (Proverbs 4 KJV). Man's innate desire and instinct is to be connected to a higher being.

Before the fall of man, God communicated with humanity directly without the use of other mediums of communication. When God approached Adam and Eve as usual to talk to them, they hid themselves because they had sinned against God. Our fallen nature separates us from the Father. "And they heard the sound of the Lord God walking in the garden in the cool of the day so the man and his wife hid and kept themselves hidden from the presence of the Lord God among the trees of the garden" (Genesis 3:8 KJV).

God is always willing to talk to His children, but because of our sinful nature, we cannot withstand the presence of God. "For what partnership can righteousness have with lawlessness? Or what fellowship can light have with darkness?" (2 Corinthians 6:14b KJV). Adam and Eve hid themselves from God even when He had not yet banished them from the Garden of Eden. After the deliverance of the Israelites from the Egyptians, God strove to talk with the Israelites directly from Mount Sinai, but they were terrified. See Exodus 19:1–24 (KJV).

After the fall of man, God's informal mode of divine communication with Adam and Eve in the Garden of Eden

---

[1] Proverbs 4.

ceased. To fill the vacuum, other channels for spiritual inspiration, guidance, and revelation through His prophets and angels to humankind began to develop. These included signs, body language, dreams, and visions. The most common medium of communication between God and man are dreams. In Genesis 20:1–7 (KJV), God spoke to the King of Gerar, Abimelech, in a dream to warn him off Abraham's wife.[2] Nothing would have made King Abimelech recognize the divine element to that dream except the knowledge that dreams are a mode of divine communication.

God and nature attempt to communicate with humanity regularly, but as a result of man's fallen nature, these messages often go unheard. Many do not understand the language of dreams. Even plants and animals try to commune with humanity, but man fails to understand them as well. King Solomon, son of David, was one of the men of old who understood the language of birds.

This body of work sets out to explain the meaning of various dream scenarios to assist a dreamer in understanding the language of dreams and aid them in communing deliberately with God.

---

[2] Genesis 20:1–7.

TYPES OF DIVINE COMMUNICATION

Vision. A vision is a trancelike, supernatural experience that conveys more clarity than dreams. It is a conscious manifestation of connectedness to the divine. It can present itself as an apparent motion, picture, image, or mental representation of events or abstract worlds. Although some individuals can have visions at will, involuntary visions are more common. Visions occur when a divine force subdues the physical senses to communicate with the inner spirit.

A vision could be a direct message from God or other divine entities. They overpower our physical senses to display pictures, images, or events in order to communicate a message. During a vision, the seven senses are stimulated. The senses of sight, taste, smell, touch, and hearing are heightened. The human consciousness and brain can then perceive objects formerly unnoticed. A vision can occur unexpectedly, although rare people can anticipate and control their visions.

Visions are more common in young people than dreams. Joel prophesied that, in the last human civilization, young men will see visions, while old men will dream dreams (Joel 2:8 KJV).[3]

Dream. Dreaming occurs during a sleep state, when an inner spirit entity transits from a physical body into the dream world. A dream is the past, present, and future—the continuous life experience of an individual. One major difference between a vision and a dream is that, in dreams, heavy symbolism is used to communicate.

---

[3] Joel 2:28.

1

As such, wisdom and deep understanding are required to interpret dreams. This is why Joel prophesied that old men would dream, while young men would have visions. Their wealth of experience, due to age, guarantees them more wisdom to decode the heavy symbolism. One must be in a sleep state to have a dream experience.

Dreams are a means of communication between God, divine entities, supernatural powers or aliens, and human beings, through the use of motion pictures, images, objects, sounds, and other higher mediums. A dream is a true-life experience that could reveal to humanity a possibility of their past, present, and future lives.

Prior to the fall of man, from the Garden of Eden, Adam did not need to fall asleep to gain access to the dream world or spiritual realm. Adam and Eve could live in both the dream and physical world effortlessly. Their physical consciousness and inner human, or spirit being, coexisted simultaneously and harmoniously.

In other words, because the physical body and soul, or spirit, of humanity existed in harmony, humans could live in several realms of consciousness simultaneously. Humans did not require meditation, rest, or other forms of flesh subjugation to enable their souls to transit or project into other abstract worlds.

Adam could worship God with the angels in heaven while his physical body remained tethered to the earth. This meant that he could connect his spirit self to heaven. When God would visit Adam in the Garden of Eden, Adam could discuss with Him with ease, as naturally as two men sharing a coffee.

During the transfiguration of Christ, Jesus's disciples were privileged to glimpse the existence of a supernatural, parallel plane. It existed alongside the physical but was formerly shielded from their gaze. They witnessed entities from a separate world seamlessly while awake (Matthew 17:1–4 KJV).[4]

The fact that Christ had to be transformed, shining like the sun and even a change of raiment, before his divine visitation further illustrates how distinct the spiritual realm is from the physical.

After the forerunners of humanity sinned against God, humanity's privilege of direct communication with the Creator was cut off. Although God could not behold evil, He still wanted a relationship with the humans He created. This is why indirect means for spiritual connection came into being. The conduits available to humans for supernatural communication, including dreams, visions, and prophecy (Joel 2:28b KJV).[5]

Every individual is endowed with a unique means of communing with God. The gift of divine communication may present itself through physical hearing, visions, divine inspiration, naturally occurring discernment, or perception. Some people can even easily connect to scripted waves of thoughts already existing in the universe or from divine entities.

The dream-life experience is a vastly accessible means of communication, available to diverse entities. As documented

---

[4] Matthew 17:1–4.

[5] Joel 2:28b.

in the Bible, God regularly used dreams to speak to His children.

> Hear now My words, If there is a prophet among you, I, the Lord, will make Myself known to him in a vision, and I will speak to him in a dream. (Numbers 12:6 AMP)[6]

> But God came to Abimelech in a dream during the night and said, "Behold you are a dead man because of the woman, whom you have taken as your wife, for she is another man's wife." (Genesis 20:3 AMP)

> But there is a God in heaven who reveals secrets, and He has shown King Nebuchadnezzar what will take place in the latter days (end of days). (Daniel 2:28 AMP)[7]

Dreams are a universal means of supernatural communication whose access is not restricted or regulated. Therefore, it is an open channel, which any spiritual entity may use to communicate.

Prophecy. This is the foreknowledge of future events, intended to uncover hidden things. It cannot be known by natural light of reason. In its strictest sense, a prophecy is a divine light by which God reveals things about the unknown future. This knowledge must be given by God because

---

[6] Numbers 12:6.

[7] Genesis 20:3, Daniel 2:28.

it concerns things beyond the natural power of created intelligence. And it is usually given for the benefit of others.[8]

A prophecy can manifest as a dream or vision. Many prophets chosen by God use either medium to relate with God and the angels. To discern the mind of God and understand His thoughts or will concerning others is the gift of prophecy.

Wisdom. Some individuals, through perception and divine inspiration, communicate with God and divine entities. This medium of spiritual connection is powerful, sacred, and focused on bringing the knowledge and wisdom of God to humanity. Through this medium of communication, the Holy Bible was written and revealed to humankind.

People of God, via the inspiration of the Holy Spirit, penned the revelations that formed the Bible today. It takes wisdom to unravel the deep mysteries of God and share that understanding in a way that a regular person can comprehend.

People of God endowed with this unusual gift usually dream dreams. God reiterated this in the book of Numbers when He said, "If there be a prophet amongst you, I will reveal Myself unto him and speak to him in a dream" (Numbers 2:6 KJV).[9] This verse buttresses the spiritual significance of dreaming.

Any individual chosen to serve as a prophet at the Ministry of Wisdom must dream dreams. Some people of God may see visions, a mental picture of a past, present, or future event, but lack the wisdom to interpret it. Many churches today are blessed with men and women who see visions.

---

[8] Catholic Encyclopaedia, https://www.newadvent.org.

[9] Numbers 12:6.

Although a lot of the past and future of others is revealed to them by the Holy Spirit, occasionally they lack the wisdom to give guidance on next steps. Every church needs old and young people with the gift of prophetic wisdom to go about interpreting visions and bringing God-minded solutions to problems.

DIFFERENTIATING BETWEEN WISDOM AND KNOWLEDGE

Knowledge is a familiarity, awareness, or understanding of any information, which can be acquired from inquiry, memory, education, and practice.[10] It is the ability to understand something due to study or past experience of it. When we read the Bible, we identify God's patterns of behavior and gain insight on the past.

Knowledge creates an awareness based on experience, which helps in guiding future behavior. The Bible was written for reproof, correction, and instruction. This is why studying the Bible helps Christians know what is acceptable to God and what is not (2 Timothy 3:16–17 KJV). Different parts highlight the knowledge of God being revealed, from generation to generation. The application of this knowledge, to achieve desired results, is wisdom.

Wisdom cannot be acquired. It is a divine endowment from God to assist humans in converting knowledge for practical use. Wisdom is therefore the application of knowledge. An individual may study mechanical sciences but lack the practical skills to fix a faulty car. For best results, we should acquire knowledge through personal effort and ask God to give us discernment on how to use that knowledge to serve Him and humanity (1 Kings 3:9 KJV).[11]

---

[10] https://www.wikipedia.org.

[11] 1 Kings 3:9.

PAST-LIFE EXPERIENCES

The mind is the invisible agent of human consciousness and self-awareness. The human mind lives on eternally; it cannot die. As a result of the soul's revolving consciousness, every event that happens to the soul is stored in the subconscious mind. When the mind loses its place in the intelligent body, it becomes unconscious.

Whenever God raised the dead and gave them a new body, their old mind would be returned to them (Matthew 27:52–53 KJV). Without the old mind in a new and intelligent body, the new man, in the new world, would not remember the past. The past of every soul is stored in the mind, and when such a soul is given a new body, in the embryo, the old mind takes its rightful place in the new body.

To live on earth, Christ took a new body in the womb of the Virgin Mary, by the power of the Holy Spirit. But the mind occupying that fetus was the immortal mind of the Father. In His early childhood, the mind of God, in baby Yeshua, could not manifest because baby Jesus wasn't yet self-aware.

At the age of twelve, Jesus began to grow in knowledge, wisdom, and understanding of Himself (Luke 2:40–52 KJV).[12] This demonstrates that twelve years is the age of self-awareness and spiritual responsibility. At that age, we ought to understand who we are.

Each individual is born with a unique personality and

---

[12] Luke 2:40–52.

divine purpose. "Before I formed you in the womb I knew you, before you were born I set you apart" (Jeremiah 1:5 KJV).[13] Jewish custom proposes that every person is a product of the past. So it is common practice for the Israelites to probe the Akashic record or history of their children at birth. In Genesis, God said to Rebekah, who went to inquire from God about the children warring in her womb, "Two nations are in thy womb and two manner of people shall be separated from thy womb."[14] This shows that God already knows our personality prior to conception.[15] Christ knew this truth when He asked His disciples who they thought He was (Mark 8:27–30 KJV).[16] In other uncensored verses of the Bible, Christ revealed to His disciples that John the Baptist was Elijah.

If you consistently have dreams of doing something in a particular place, they are flashbacks into a past life. You could see yourself fighting great wars or doing something superfluous, extraordinary, spectacular, unusual, or strange to this present era or civilization. Whenever such dreams occur, history is about to repeat itself in your present life. There is something special that happened in the past you are expected to draw lessons from to overcome a similar situation in the present.

The kind of dreams an individual has about the past reveals the kind of person they were. Some people who dream of themselves in wars were military men in their past life.

---

[13] Jeremiah 1:5.

[14] Genesis 25:23.

[15] Jeremiah 1:5.

[16] Mark 8: 27–29.

People who have dreams of affairs with women have scores to settle with women. Those who are constantly chased by enemies, especially unfamiliar persons, have some scores to settle with the past. Whatever hurts or haunts us in the dream is directly linked with the past. Our past dreams are a pointer to what good or bad we have done in the past that requires repentances and God's mercy to waive it for us.

It's wrong for us to continue to do the inappropriate things we dream about in our present life. If we usually commit murder, fight, or commit adultery or fornication in our dreams, it is unadvisable to continue living that way physically here on earth. When we have bad dreams revealing the past, it's very important we pray against it and endeavor not to involve ourselves with such in our present lives.

THE PRESENT AND THE FUTURE

In the words of King Solomon, "and that which has been done is that which will be done again, so there is nothing new under the sun" (Psalm 15:16 KJV, Ecclesiastes 1:9 AMP).[17] Time and events repeat themselves. Every event is linked to time, and time obeys the 360–degree rotation of the earth, where the earth moves around and returns to its point of origin. As time travels around the globe, histories are made, and events of the past tend to be repeated. Present events in our world and in our lives are often products of past events. The earth and humanity are not new. "One generations goes and another generation comes, but the earth remains forever" (Ecclesiastes 1:4 AMP). Civilizations and humanity have come and gone, but the earth remains a place to always be inhabited by man. "For the Lord who created the heavens (He is God who formed the earth and made it; He established it and did not create it to be a wasteland, but formed it to be inhabited)" (Isaiah 45:18 AMP).[18] The problem of our sinful world lies in our past-life experience on this same earth. The earth has always been there for man, but man comes here and goes.

The principle of reaping what we sow has the same connotation as the principles of past and present (Galatians

---

[17] Psalm 115:1.

2 Corinthians 9:6.

Ecclesiastes 1:9 (AMP).

[18] Ecclesiastes 1:4.

11

6:8–9, 2 Corinthians 9:6 KJV).[19] In our present life, we are reaping the fruits of our past-life experiences. The way we live at present is planting the seeds of our future harvest.

Every individual's life is preordained by the time they are born; this includes where that person is born, career choice. and length of time to be spent on earth. Our entire life experiences and lessons are already known by God.

It takes the grace of God for any human soul to be born again to the earth, receive another chance to live a good life, and retrace their steps to a loving God. This is why dreams are important. God communicates with us, revealing our past and showing us a way forward and how to draw closer to Him. When this generation ends, God will use our present life to recreate us again in another new world in paradise or on earth. When that time comes, who we shall be will be known by the life we are living now.

God will take away the memory of our present life experiences and make us a brand-new creature. Some people will come back to this earth or some other worlds. However, not every human soul transits to other higher worlds after here.

At the close of this civilization, God will open our eyes to all that has happened under the sun, and on that account, all men will be judged (Ecclesiastes 12:14 AMP).[20]

Timing of dreams. There is no particular time for dreaming. They can occur at any time, particularly low-level dreams, which are dreams experienced on ordinary planes or earth surface or within human space sphere. In the words

---

[19] Galatians 6:7.

[20] Ecclesiastes 12:14.

of King Solomon, to everything under the sun, there is a season or time appointed (Ecclesiastes 3:1 KJV),[21] and this includes dreams. All dreams have timelines for their physical manifestation.

The moment any individual is born through a woman's womb or by scientific intervention, the files of their destiny begin to unravel from birth until they die. These files contain the records about an individual predetermined by God. Tribulations or trials, events that can bring a person to the limelight or humiliate them, and all the information we need to guide us back to God are encoded in our spirit being.

As individuals, we may occasionally perceive impending events without dreams. Mind reading and odd body signs can help us perceive that something good or bad is imminent.

When God created man and established his abode on earth, He appointed guardian angels to be responsible for our well-being and stewardship. However, from the first man created, Adam, man was also given the gift of free will at maturity to decide without interference from God or the angels. All God demanded from man in return was to love Him, keep His commandments, and follow His directives endowed through visions, dreams, and prophetic words in order to succeed (Deuteronomy 11:1 KJV).[22]

Once sin entered the world through Adam, all men became destined to die and be separated from God forever. By sacrifice, through the birth, death, and resurrection of Jesus Christ, man received the privilege to be reborn anew on earth and make amends. True to the futility of man, as he

---

[21] Ecclesiastes 3: 1.

[22] Deuteronomy 11:1.

ages, he forgets the Creator and indulges in destructive habits. Where we are determined to live life according to the dictates of our flesh and human desires, we tend to fall apart. On the flip side, when man listens to God and follows His statutes, the hosts of heaven rejoice.[23] When we devote ourselves to our walk with the Lord by studying our Bible and listening for the voice of God in dreams, it gives our guardian angel the right to fight for us.

The universal law of life dictates that you only reap what you have planted. Therefore, when souls are reincarnated, the fruits of their past life become manifest in the present life. There is no forewarning when the fruits of the past for good or evil come knocking. Events occur spontaneously, depending on the grace available to that person.

However, where events are revealed in a dream, judgment is ongoing to determine whether the fruits will be manifest or not. That soul has been given a chance to plead for leniency or forgiveness. Most dreams we might experience as an attack are exposing uncompleted judgment.

By His sacrifice, Christ created the opportunity for the pull of the past to be nullified. If any man be in Christ, he is a new creature; old things have passed and all things have become new (2 Corinthians 5:17 KJV).[24] To receive this gift, all man needs to do is believe in Jesus Christ (John 3:16 KJV).[25]

---

[23] Luke 15: 10.

[24] 2 Corinthians 5:17.

[25] John 3:16.

TYPES OF DREAMS

Repeated dream. When a particular dream is repeated more than once, it denotes great emphasis on the seriousness of the message from the source. Although repeated dreams may not play out exactly as the first one, the central symbol or object of interpretation remains the same. The message also remains the same. It's like rephrasing information in a different way.

A repeated dream sends a strong warning to heed the message passed. In African tradition, parents or older relatives, when cautioning a child, would call their name repeatedly and ask, "How many times did I call you?" This passes across the severity of their message. Dreams can be repeated for the dreamer's benefit and warning.

Continuation dream. This type of dream occurs when a dreamer wakes up in the middle of dreaming, and when they go back to sleep, the dream continues. There is pertinent information that must be passed across. Sometimes such a dream experience is bizarre or nightmarish, but the dream will usually refuse to go away until it concludes. Dreamers may will themselves to have continuation dreams when the events in the dream were enjoyable. This kind of dream is a very important experience for the soul, and the dream must conclude on its own. Continuation dreams can extend over several days before coming to an end. Whenever a dreamer has a continuation dream, it means such an experience and communication is part of that dreamer's destiny.

If the content of the continuation dream is war, attack, adultery, robbery, and so forth, it's a strong indication that some agents of dark forces are bent on fulfilling their mission in your life. Where a dreamer experiences a frightening continuation dream, the dreamer ought to change their lifestyle. The dreamer should indulge in spiritual exercise like praying with meditation to bolster the inner spirit against imminent danger.

Passed-on dream. Information received in a dream might not be meant for the dreamer. These kinds of dreams are called *passed on* or *transferred dreams*. A message or revelation can be given to another party to extend the information to the intended party. The reason a transferred dream might occur is where the intended party has strong emotional attachment to the situation a dream would reveal. For example, a revelation that your trusted wife is being unfaithful or an imminent death of a loved one.

Spirit beings can induce dreams to a dreamer in order to reveal certain secrets. Some of the dreams we have are intended for other people. Whenever a dreamer receives a message intended for another, it is their duty to pass it on; otherwise, on the last day, we shall give account of it. We must not hide other people's dream, either out of fear or spite. Pray with them and seek wisdom from God to handle it.

Cleansing dreams. As we go about our daily activities, scrolling through social media, traditional media, and even our negative interactions with people, our souls can get burdened with the weight of these negative emotions. Through cleansing dreams, the soul expunges corrupt materials by creating dreams that help it to self-cleanse. If an individual consumes a lot of pornographic movies or exposes themselves to depraved sexual fantasies, the soul can create a dream experience to expel those feelings.

Cleansing dreams can be likened to our physical body excreting; one eats to his fill but must expel waste products of that food by way of urinating, defecating, or sweating. It is not what goes into the mouth of a man that defiles and dishonors him but what comes out of the mouth; this defiles and dishonors him (Matthew 15:11 AMP).[26]

Playback dream. When events in our immediate environment alter and influence our dream experiences, it's called a playback dream. Suppose you fall asleep close to a television set in an action movie, and while asleep, you find yourself shooting guns and jumping out of buildings. Our natural body is susceptible to suggestions. Incidents that we experienced while half-asleep could play back to us in dreams.

To have a true dream, we must allow our physical body to thoroughly shut down for sleep. One of the tells of a playback dream is that they occur in a noisy environment or a polluted place. While He lived on earth, Jesus Christ would go to a secluded place where he could quietly commune with God and nature. "But Jesus Himself would often slip away to the wilderness and pray [in seclusion]"[27] (Luke 5:16 AMP).

Reminiscence dream. A lot of dreamers completely forget their dreams when they wake up. Sometimes the events of the dream suddenly flash back into their mind after a while. When this happens, it is called a reminiscence dream. Memory plays an important role in the life of a dreamer, and if your flashback dreams are inactive, you will always forget the content and message of your dreams.

---

[26] Matthew 15:11 (AMP).

[27] Luke 5:16 (AMP).

STAGES OF DREAMING

Dreams have different levels or degrees through which a dreamer can travel during sleep to have a dream experience. There are many realms through which we can sink through or travel upward when we dream.

First-level dream stage. Dreams experienced in an earthly atmosphere (i.e., your immediate environment or surroundings) are first-level dreams. First-level dreams mimic ordinary human or earthly activity. Dreams experienced on this plane communicate information about our immediate environment.

When dreaming on the first level, the dreamer remains tethered to the physical world while their soul travels along the astral plane. Events in the physical realm can influence first-level dreams, including sounds or images. Dreams experienced in the first level are usually fantasies, illusions, and a reflection of our immediate environment or state of mind. Adventurous or cleansing dream are examples of first-level dreams. Sometimes you can see hidden things and receive understanding of things you're unaware of in the physical realm. Whenever we use our inner bodies to experience something outside this earth, we tend to be more powerful and active. The level of a dream is dependent on how deeply the dreamer sleeps.

Second-level dream stage. At this stage, the physical body detaches completely from the physical realm, and the spirit person assumes control over that person. When dreaming on this level, the physical body relaxes completely and renews itself to face a new day. During second-level dreaming, the physical body is completely unconscious and unaware of anything happening around them. Next, the soul, which is the actual consciousness of the dreamer, takes over and begins to explore other dream worlds.

In reality, the human being does not go into void unconsciousness called sleep. Every human body is comprised of two entities, the soul and physical body, which interchange autonomy. When the physical body is tired from a day's work, it rests or sleeps; at this point, the soul or inner consciousness takes over, and vice versa. This interchange of human autonomy creates an equilibrium and balance between the soul and the physical body. To maintain a healthy soul, the body must be in good health and get adequate rest. When we don't care for our physical body or spiritual health, it affects the twin entity adversely. For instance, without proper rest, one might feel depressed and tired, or when a person is facing emotional turmoil, it may display itself as a physical illness. The physical body is the temple for the soul. As such, every individual must care for their soul and physical body equally.

The soul is the entity that houses our personality. It was breathed into man by God and returns to Him after the physical body dies. "You are dust and to dust you shall return"[28] (Genesis 3:19 KJV). The soul is immortal … and the dust returns to the ground it came from and the spirit returns to God who gave it (Ecclesiastes 12:7 KJV). Death is not the end of conscious life; it is only the separation of the body and the spirit. "Do not fear those who can kill the body but cannot kill the soul, rather fear Him who can destroy

---

[28] Genesis 3:19.

both soul and body in hell" (Matthew 10:28 AMP). When the physical body dies, then we can say that the soul is resting; it lives on in another realm. The destruction of the soul means separation from the life of God.

Without the physical body housing the soul of a man, the soul would be resting or sleeping. Christ spoke of physical death as sleeping. "Our friend Lazarus has fallen asleep, but I am going there to wake him up" (John 11:11 AMP).[29] "Whatever your hands find to do, do it with all your might; for there is no activity or planning or wisdom in Sheol (the nether world, the place of the dead) where you are going (Ecclesiastes 9:10 AMP). This verse aptly illustrates that the soul is powerless without the physical body. It is only after God gives a soul a body to reside in that it begins to function as a living being.

The dead in Christ can't function without a physical body, so God will provide a fresh immortal body for their soul to live on in heaven. When the physical body comes to eternal rest, the soul of man lives on in the astral world of dreams.

The second level of dreams is the astral world of dreams. Dreams that occur at this level are revelations already revealed in the realm of the spirit. Majority of souls do not have control over dreams; rather, our guardian angels direct our souls to the kind of dream experience it needs. In the realm of the spirit, a soul is like a newborn baby in need of guidance and protection. Just like babies are cared for and guided by their earthly parents or guardian, the angels of God guide the human soul in the realm of the spirit. Without

---

[29] John 11:11.

guidance in the realm of the spirit, a soul may be harmed by malevolent forces.

Occasionally, there are mature souls who are self-aware while dreaming, and of their personal volition, they can control or direct the events of the dream world. Even their guardian angels have limited control over their dreams. These souls are mature in spirit; therefore, we should desire to grow our spirit self to aid us become self-aware in dreams and make it easy to communicate with God. It's difficult for a soul to know they are dreaming.

Anyone who begins to gain awareness of themselves while dreaming is growing in spirit. Over time, that soul will master the rules and laws that guide the spirit world; the soul will be able to disappear, become invisible, fly, walk on water, shape shift, read minds, possess improved hearing, and so on. In fact, certain limitations in the physical body are nonexistent to our soul in the dream world.

Third-level dream stage. As explained under the second stage of dreams, the soul of every individual is that unique but intangible personality; it cannot be seen or touched.

There are deeper secrets or revelations that a soul can't gain access to in the second-level dream stage. The soul needs to sleep at this stage to get access to certain revelations. The experiences in this level of dreaming are vital and confidential.

During this experience, the physical body should not be disturbed because it can cause shock or loss of consciousness. If such a dreamer is woken during this stage, they will be disoriented and unaware of their surroundings until their soul has fully returned to them. The distance the soul can travel in this realm of dreaming may take modern means of transportation several years to achieve. All dreamers have to be cautious when waking up from third-level dreaming.

Top secret and classified information are revealed in the third-level dream stage. It is at this level that God speaks directly to humankind. The dream experience at this stage carries divine messages.

In Daniel 2:13–30 (KJV), King Nebuchadnezzar had a strange dream. His carnal mind discerned that it was a divine communication, although it was strange and he could not understand what it meant. Prophetic visions are experienced at this stage. All the prophets, particularly Daniel and John, who wrote the book of Revelation, received divine inspiration while in the third-level dream stage.

Fourth-level dream stage. This is a near-death experience. At this stage, the soul has surrendered itself to God in order to explore another world. Dreaming at this stage is incredibly rare. It occurs strictly by divine intervention, where God wants to reveal something to the dreamer. At this stage, the dreamer can even travel to heaven or hell. Without proper protection, dreamers at this stage may be pronounced dead. Many persons who are pronounced clinically dead on earth are actually on fourth-level dream stage.

COMMON TERMS HELPFUL TO A DREAMER

1. Transfiguration. In Christian teachings, the transfiguration is a pivotal moment, a point where human nature meets God, the temporal meeting eternal, with Jesus Christ as the bridge between heaven and earth. The disciples viewed a demonstration of God's divine nature and glory covered up in the form of a man. Thus, transfiguration is the exaltation of the true nature of the spiritual over the physical. It is a conscious out-of-body experience to manifest the soul or inner man hidden within the physical body.

2. A vision is a conscious communication of divine message or revelation of events via motion picture or images. A vision can be experienced while awake or unconsciously during sleep.

3. During a prophetic utterance, the five senses or mental body of an individual are taken over by the spirit of God to inspire, reveal, and pass messages that could be oral, visual, images, or motion pictures about the past or future events.

4. Dreams are the most common form of communication between God and man. They occur when we lose our physical consciousness or fall asleep. The experiences of our inner man or soul are all regarded as dreams. God communicates with us regularly through dreams. In dreams, there is heavy

use of symbolism, imagery, or dream languages peculiar to that person and their environment. Divine messages in dreams are either for personal instruction, chastisement, or the benefit of others. Dreams are established and simple, and not much spiritual energy is expended.

The other forms of communication with God—transfiguration, vision, and prophecy—are spiritual gifts reserved for people who are called to serve God's people, the body of Christ, and the larger society.

Anyone can dream dreams; however, the other channels of divine communication are gifts of the spirit. The power of transfiguration is reserved for individuals with a vibrant spiritual personality. Before his crucifixion, Jesus Christ transformed into His true nature and was visited by the prophets Elisha and Moses. His disciples bore witness to this miracle (Matthew 17:1–8 KJV).

The art of transfiguration is the manifestation of your spiritual nature using a physical body while retaining your consciousness—the ability to exist in another spirit world with your consciousness and physical body intact.

At the resurrection, it's the soul or inner spirit of man that receives an eternal heavenly body and ascends with Christ to heaven. When we die, our physical bodies perish. "And just as it is appointed and destined for all men to die once and after this [comes certain judgment]" (Hebrews 9:27 AMP).

Jesus ascended into heaven in His physical body. "He was caught up as they looked on, and a cloud took Him up out of their sight" (Acts 1:9 AMP). When King Aram of Syria sent his soldiers to arrest prophet Elisha, his servant was very afraid. "Then Elisha prayed and said, Lord please open his eyes that he may see. And the Lord opened the servant's eyes and he saw and behold the mountain was full of horses and chariots of fire surrounding Elisha (2 Kings 6:17 (KJV). "And [in reverent fear and obedience Enoch walked with God and he was not [found among men] because God took him [away to be home with Him]" (Genesis 5:24 AMP).

The ability to disappear is another form of transfiguration. When a physical body disappears, it instantaneously transforms into tiny molecules that are invisible to the naked eye, travel at the speed of light, and can penetrate any physical matter or building. The kingdom of darkness has converted this sacred spiritual exercise for their own use. Witnesses also practice shape shifting with their physical bodies. Their soul can astral project into other creatures and take possession of them. They utilize the power of the occult to practice these activities without divine permission.

The powers of transfiguration and disappearance have been revealed to angels, but the right to use these powers is reserved for God alone. Misuse of spiritual practices is deleterious and could lead to serious consequences or an untimely death of the user.

In an earlier definition, we confirmed that a dream could be part of our past, present, and future life experiences, communicated to us through motion pictures and images. The meanings of symbols, images, motion pictures, and so on appearing in dreams vary across cultures, races, ethnicities, nationalities, and human civilizations. There is no universal interpretation for objects or images witnessed in dreams. For example, the snake. While some cultures perceive snakes in a dream as a bad omen, to some others, it is looked upon with reverence as a divine visitation. Below we highlight generic dream experiences and their meanings to help build a dreamer's vocabulary and expand the quality of their dream life.

INTERPRETATION OF IMAGES

Aback: Aback in the dream means retrogression in business or in life expectation, setback or distortions in your current endeavor. Some examples include the following:

1. Repetition of class or course in the school, training, or internship program
2. Failure in exam, test, or interview
3. Straight line; queue in orderly position
4. Postponement of opportunity or appointment, blessing, or delay to receiving an appointment
5. Danger, war trouble, accident, ugly situations
6. Back seat
   - 6.1 Back seat in the church, religious gathering, or meeting signifies stagnation in your spiritual life. It shows backsliding or complete demotion from a top or present position to a lesser position and spiritual emptiness.
   - 6.2 Back seat in the car means to be in a less privileged position or playing second fiddle in a place of exaltation.
   - 6.3 Back seat in a place of work or unusual seat lesser than the previous one the dreamer previously occupied signifies job demotion.
     - ➤ Running back: It symbolizes deliverance from danger or returning to a point of origin. Running back from unknown place or other planet means returning to the

physical world that is to awake from sleep. It also means a turning point, wake-up call, physically waking up from sleep, or state of unconsciousness.

➤ Face back: This means a disconnection—a breakup, for example. Having your face turned backward to a friend means quarrel or separation. Seeing a dead person in the dream facing back also means disconnection.

➤ Age: Becoming younger in the dream means the beginning of life cycle and progression.

Abandonment: If you dream about being abandoned by your family, friends, or spouse, it symbolizes possible separation or disappointment resulting from death, marriage, or traveling, and it can also mean neglect. If you are abandoned under the rain or in a natural disaster, it means death or grievous situation that could lead to death or loss.

Abattoir: An abattoir is a slaughterhouse for animals. Animals in the dream represent living souls or entities. Dreaming of abattoir is a sign of initiation into occult or unholy covenant with demonic agencies (e.g., witchcraft, land gods, and marine spirits).

Abrogate: To abolish by authoritative action, to set free an individual.

Abstain: Intervention from above to resist a temptation or refuse to yield to an evil inclination.

Abundance: Abundance means prosperity and success, but the symbolism used determines the area of that abundance. Life and green vegetable plants are signs of prosperity, including animal produce.

Access: A divine privilege to gain knowledge or be initiated into a spiritual class or circle. It's also an admission or invitation of a human soul or astral body into another realm, dominion, kingdom, or spiritual circle. Whenever a human soul gains access at any point of entry to a secured place, they automatically become a member or part of that place.

A human soul having access to a witchcraft organization signifies that the human soul is being held there for trial judgment or sacrifice. If someone gains access to a prison yard or is held in a police cell, it suggests a trial judgment in the realm of the spirit.

The places you gain access to reveal your personality and show inroads or places you are connected to, and you are capable of making inroads there. In most cases, you could become part of that place or related to that place in the course of your life span.

You could get the permission to look into other worlds but will not be granted access into that place. It means it's for your knowledge only; you are restricted from entering that world because your time is not due or you are not qualified to go there.

Acquire: To acquire things in the dream is good, but they must be valuable goods. The goods you acquire reveal the nature of things coming your way. Acquiring a car in the dream may not translate to a physical car on earth but could signify increased anointing power to your soul. Not every property acquired in the dream world translates to physical property on earth. Some acquisitions represent your economic life and your spiritual advancement in the astral world. Most people live in fine houses and drive good cars in the dream world, but physically they have none. Whatever you acquire in the dream can be translated to something here on earth. These things are yours, and it reveals who you are, but you must put in the work, time, diligence, and spiritual exercise to translate them.

Acquisition reveals expansion, progress in whatever you are doing. A minister of God may acquire property in the dream, and it means establishment of more churches or members. To acquire something in the dream is difficult because you don't require money to do so; rather, your reserved anointing or your wealth stored in the spirit or your goodwill is required to acquire things in the dream. Nothing is free on earth, and in the spirit realm, it must cost you something to get anything. When Jesus told His followers to store their treasures in heaven where moth and rust cannot affect it, He was telling them to use their goodwill or wealth to bless people in exchange for savings in heaven, just the way a nation's central bank has foreign reserves in the World Bank for international trade.

To engage in international trade, a country's central bank must keep her money in foreign currency in the World Bank. You can't use your local currency to purchase goods and services in other countries. Additionally, a country's local currency must be converted to a foreign currency for international trade. Likewise, physical money is useless when trading in the spiritual realm.

The future and destiny of all creation has been determined by God from the foundation of the world (Ephesians 1:4 KJV). Everything that we will ever own manifests according to the progression of time in our earthly journey. Whatever we enjoy on the earth was already apportioned to us by God from the beginning of creation. All the good things we are doing in our present world to God and humanity will be allotted to us as treasure in the bank of heaven for our next transition to the new world to come.

When you see yourself acquiring wealth or properties or living large in the dream, it means your wealth is stuck in the spirit realm and may never manifest physically on earth. It is better the good things of life manifest in your physical world than in the spirit realm. Witches and wizards who live in the best houses in the spirit realm and fly on an airplane do not have a common bicycle on earth. This is because they practice a concept at variance with the laws of God; they prefer to be rich in spirit and poor on earth. But in Christendom, we prefer to be poor in spirit and rich in the physical world. "Blessed [Spiritually prosperous, happy, to be admired] are the poor in spirit [those devoid of spiritual arrogance, those who regard themselves as insignificant] for theirs is the kingdom of heaven"[30] (Matthew 5:3 AMP, 2 Corinthians 8:9 KJV).

Prior to the crucifixion and ultimate sacrifice of Christ, the Israelites brought sacrifices of rams, doves, pigeons, and more yearly to sacrifice to God for the forgiveness of sins. These objects represented in the spiritual realm the sinful man in need of forgiveness from God. The ram sacrificed on

---

[30] Matthew 5:3 (AMP), 2 Corinthians 8:9.

behalf of the Israelites did not appear as a ram before God; rather, it signified the human soul. On the flip side, animals in the spirit realm can be used to represent a human being in the physical world. This is how evil forces of witchcraft can present an animal to represent a human being to their coven for sacrifice.

Things in the physical are symbolic in the spiritual and vice versa. For instance, a simple offering of bread, biscuits, banana, and fowl in the physical world will represent a very big feast in the kingdom of darkness. This is akin to the miracle of Jesus Christ transforming five loaves of bread and two fish to feed over five thousand people. A witch who wishes to initiate you through food might disguise maggots, millipedes, or irritating things into a very appetizing meal in the dream. Some meals we partake of in the dream might appear harmless, but they could be poisonous or nauseating objects projected by evil men.

Acquit: Acquit is divine mercy or forgiveness, to regard someone blameless for their past sins. It also means intervention from God to free the dreamer from satanic chains or witchcraft manipulations.

Acting: The actors and actresses you're involved with in a dream scene have a similar destiny and character trait as the dreamer. It also means that the actor a dreamer associates with in the dream will possibly share common life experience and personality.

Actor/actress: If you meet or see an actor or actress in the dream, it means you'll encounter a public figure or a celebrity or someone you hold in high esteem. But if you mingle with them as friends or colleagues, it means you'll be an actor/actress or a public figure. It's advisable for a dreamer to learn the biography of actors and actresses they meet in the dream. Learning the life experiences of these actors can encourage or guide a dreamer on their path to greatness.

Public figures you meet in the dream are your contemporaries of same profession and life experience. Most great people constrain themselves by hiding in the crowd without knowing who they are. So when you find yourself among dignitaries, please know that you're a great person. It's better to find yourself among the company of great people than evil people.

Adage: When you hear an adage in the dream, the interpretation is simple. It means it's a generally established truth that you could interpret yourself or ask elders or someone to tell you. Adages are coded human wisdom hidden within a story or witty saying.

Adaptation: The ability to easily adapt to things or situations shows harmony or a resilient spirit. For instance, if you fall into water and easily adapt to the temperature or start swimming, it indicates an affinity for that activity. You can't adapt to what you don't agree with or understand. If you fall into water and struggle to swim out, it's because you are not part of it. There are people adaptive to air; they could fly physically and pilot an airplane, but in the water, they will struggle. It is advisable for a dreamer to practice what he/she is adaptable to in the dream.

Addict: When a dreamer sees themselves addicted to bad behavior in a dream, it signifies that the person has infected their astral body with that behavior. Dreaming of addictions is a direct warning from God to desist from such addiction immediately. When an astral body starts mimicking or mirroring behavior in the spiritual realm, that person is in bad shape and in need of salvation.

If you see yourself in the dream addicted to a lifestyle unfamiliar to you, it is a reflection of your primitive nature. You have that character trait in your soul but have not manifested it, or witchcraft may have imposed that addiction trait to that person. Some addictions are due to evil manipulations, to make their soul manifest bad character traits to the extent that the person's physical body will manifest it unconsciously. For example, if a woman sees herself prostituting in the dream, it's a strong sign of evil manipulation. It might also mean the spirit of prostitution has possessed that woman.

Most revelation of addiction is either a warning to desist from such addicted tendencies or a clear case of evil manipulation to charm that person to misbehave. Most children and young people are in these problems. You could see a well-behaved girl eloping with her boyfriend to a hotel or a good young man becoming a drunk or suddenly a street boy.

Address: An address means direction, guidance, or a solution. In a dream, one might be given a clear address to see or visit a place on earth. In most cases, this indicates the solution to a problem. That sort of address is untraceable in reality because it doesn't exist in the physical; it is merely symbolic. A dreamer should take note of the address or solution because it is important.

If you find yourself dreaming of your place of birth or a place you grew up in, the dream is trying to reveal the present state of your life. When the location is your first place of work, the dream is about your work life and experiences. When the address shows the dreamer in an unknown place of work, the dream is referring to a new place of work. For instance, you see yourself in Lagos, and you aren't there presently; it means you will get a work or job outside where you are presently, and the activity you see yourself doing shows the kind of event that will happen there.

It may be construction, business, and so on. When the address is abroad, then it's a foreign transaction or contact to get connected to a business or an event that will change your life. Places and events associated with dreams only reveal where and what will happen and not the actual place you are now.

Whenever you have that kind of dream, start praying toward revelation for it to be fulfilled and begin making contacts toward that direction. If you have friends, start chatting with them and open your mind to opportunities within or outside your friendship circle.

Administrator: If you dream of being an administrator in any field, it is a noble thing. This means your life is organized. It shows self-control, and you are in a position to take charge or command powers. It means you are in order in whatever you are presently doing. However, if you see an administrator, it means your file in any office or in heaven is currently being attended to. Whenever you have such a dream, please consult your pastor or prophets to guide you against seizure or delay of your blessings.

Admiral: To be an admiral in the dream means you are a great messenger of God. It doesn't mean physical army or navy. Such a person has a high calling to deliver people and defend people, and such a person will do well in human affairs. They are an authority themselves and can command angels of God to render them help. Such a person is a part of the army of God and shouldn't be tampered with. Admirals in the realm are in charge of wealth, mineral resources, world trade, and business, and they protect the wealth on earth.

If you meet an admiral in the dream, consider your problems solved; it means God has blessed you and has given you a portion to inherit. When you find yourself as part of this heavenly navy, you are either a wealthy person or someone empowered by God to make others rich. When the navy arrests you in a dream, your wealth will suffer.

This interpretation is intended for those who are not physically in any nation's naval force. Naval officers in the spiritual realm are peace lovers and orderly. They are not angels of war but keepers and protectors of wealth, the world economy, and the welfare of people.

Whenever a naval officer sees themselves in the dream with a uniform, they should carefully check the rank on the uniform. They also need to carefully observe all the events surrounding their dreams. Seeing yourself in your place of work or in your uniform reveals something about your profession, especially concerning promotion or demotion.

Adolescence: When you see yourself in the dream younger than your present age, God is turning back the hands of time to show you something vital when you were at that age. Be very attentive to every scenario you find yourself in. They contain lots of lessons to assist you in solving problems. If you see yourself older than your age, God is revealing a future event that could change your future for good. A reduction or increase in age and appearance is symbolic. It is important to remember the surrounding circumstances of such an experience.

God can turn time back a thousand years or forward to reveal hidden secrets or bring clarity to the future. Looking younger in the dream could mean renewal of life or change of life story. On the flip side, it may mean youthful vanities or a lack of self-control. When you dream of yourself as an old man, it shows wisdom, possession of leadership qualities, or endowment as an oracle of God. Most young men or children you see are carrying the gift of being God's oracle.

Adoption: Adoption in the dream signifies a caged soul or shows the person is in bondage or manipulated by dark forces. Any dreamer who has such a dream should seek urgent deliverance by the grace of God.

Adultery: An adulterer in the dream represents the spirit of whoredom surrounding the dreamer. Such a dream serves as a warning not to succumb to seduction; otherwise the dreamer risks losing the blessings of God.

Dreaming of adultery shows worldliness, vanities, or the reason for a blockage in your business. Evil men, witches, and the kingdom of the occult use whoring demons to take away people's blessings in the dream. The moment they succeed in sleeping with you, your blessings are gone. These demons can infect people with diseases that have no medical solution, the spirit of whoredom, or a flirtatious lifestyle. There are people who are inflicted with weak erections, incurable sexually transmitted diseases, and flirtatious lifestyles because of the activities of these demons who try to have sex with dreamers.

If you encounter them and they didn't try to seduce you, then it is a revelation and not an attack. Some women are sent by evil people to target and destroy lives. Many men of God have fallen victim to their wiles because they are cunning. They use church members or coworkers to orchestrate their evil plans.

These dreams act as a trap. It is bad to have sex in your dreams. This is why it is necessary to abandon a carnal lifestyle, to be able to discern and withstand the wiles of the enemy. These evil forces could also use filial attachments to cause you to stumble. A thorough spiritual cleansing through prayer and fasting is necessary.

Adventure: The astral body likes to go on adventures just like the physical body. The soul can travel backward or into future. Although they commonly visit astral worlds within close proximity, their guardian angel must be with you. There are some places where malevolent spirit beings can capture you or harm your soul.

When you see yourself in dangerous places like shrines, evil altars, or wandering, it shows evil manipulation, and your soul needs immediate deliverance. When someone calls your name before an evil altar or summons your soul there, God can reveal it by taking your spirit there on an excursion to see the hidden things. "The secret things belong unto the Lord our God but those things which are revealed belong unto us and to our children forever, that we may do all the words of this law" (Deuteronomy 29:29 KJV).

Whatever is revealed in the dream to you is known and powerless, or its solution is given. Whenever evil is exposed, it has been foiled. The revelation of evil shows that God has intervened and has given you the solution to overcome it.

Adversity: Difficult times in dreams point to immediate hardship. It is a direct message. When you are living in abundance or are well to do and rich, and you dream of hard times, there is likely trouble ahead. Appeal to God in prayers to relieve you of the difficulty.

Be cautious when doing business, in your career or any situation that could lead you to suffer. But if you are already enduring hardship and you see yourself in adversity in a dream, that hardship will soon come to an end.

It means that the merciful Father has transferred the physical time of suffering on earth to the realm of the spirit so that the physical days of hardship will be shortened.

Jesus said, "And except those days should be shortened, there should no flesh be saved; but for the elect's sake those days shall be shortened" (Matthew 24:22 KJV).[31] Take note that if you're already experiencing hardship and you dream of hardship, the period of suffering has been reduced by the mercies of God; otherwise, it is foreboding or a sign of sinister situations in your economic life.

Advertisement: It reveals an established or decided situation. Adverts could be written on print, motion pictures, billboards, or posters. Every advert must be displayed in some way.

---

[31] Matthew 24:22.

A poster in a marketplace means that your endeavors are about to get public acceptance or patronage. Be careful to observe the content of the advert so that you can understand the main objective or symbol of the advertisement. The content of the advert is the main symbol or object for interpretation.

Anything revealed in that manner in the dream is known by everybody tuned into the realm of the spirit, and it cannot be changed. The birth of Christ came with strong signs and adverts in the sky. The heavenly bodies, including the angels of God, made a public advert about it, which was confirmed by the three wise men from a Persian mystical order who visited Jesus and His mother in the manger. However, Jewish scholars didn't take notice of those signs.

If the advert indicates the burial of an individual, then there is danger of death. Evildoers could kill a soul and publish a burial poster in the spirit realm, complete with dates and venue. On that date, the person may die suddenly without intervention from God.

Public places, particularly markets, are a powerful witness and agreement point for events and situations. To gain the most traction for your business, try advertising it in marketplaces, churches, or schools, with strong prayers to gain public witness and agreement. The moment the advert or announcement gets into the public psyche or gains widespread acceptance, such a trend is difficult to reverse.

Advice: Advice in a dream is a direct message from the divine. A dreamer must pay close attention to the content of the advice and the appearance of the adviser. Satan or demons could pose as advisers to deceive a dreamer.

Be cautious of the appearance of the adviser, including the color of their clothing and mannerisms, as these help indicate the origin of the adviser. When it is an unfamiliar person, the advice could be from a divine entity. On the other hand, if the face is familiar, your guardian angel has taken on that appearance to advise you.

The category of familiarity is key to a dream's interpretation. If your late father is used, the advice is sincere and should be taken seriously, unless during his lifetime, your father was insincere, unreliable, and inconsistent. It indicates that you must be careful or wise; an evil entity might be using trickery to gain your trust. Whenever a person appears to you with advice in a dream, take the person's character traits in reality to determine the manner of seriousness you should attach to the dream. The advice must be representative of that person's beliefs in reality.

This is why strange images or persons are better because they are from far or unknown worlds, and their message or advice is direct. When experiencing divine entities, they are not talkative and can change their appearance at will. Every divine being from heaven has light in their eyes. They are tall, can be either male or female, and are fair or attractive to look upon. They dress in white or flowing robes, and they do not follow the latest fashions. If their color isn't white but green, then that spirit is from the worlds within.

Airplane: This indicates the astral power of motion within the astral world. The earth has a strong magnetic energy that holds everything to its position in the ground, but there is boundary between earth and outer space. The higher you ascend, the less the pull of earth's magnetic force.

In the realm of the spirit, the earth we march upon is strong, holding everything to him, including humans from the earth kingdom. We can easily run, walk, or move our body in light speed on the ground or slow motion but can't fly up in the dream. People who can fly up in the dream are super beings that command powers above and below.

Flying in an airplane or seeing someone flying means the person will surpass all obstacles to achieve certain height in their endeavor through the turbulence of life. Without being given the power, anointing, or access, you can't fly up because it's a different world from the earth. We have been given power to possess the earth, plunder it, and walk around both spiritually and physically, but not everybody is permitted to use the space to travel.

Experiencing one's self piloting an airplane in the dream indicates importance. That person possesses power, authority, access, anointing to command the astral world. Such person's powers go beyond the earth forces. The person could be the king of air space, commander of air forces or the astral world. Space in the dream is another world inhabited by powerful spirits. There are spirits that can stop our prayers, and so to fly an airplane across their world is a special privilege from God. If you found yourself aboard an airplane in the dream, you are enjoying special favor and protection from God. Any individual flying or boarding airplanes or piloting them is a spiritually powerful person. When they come to a realization of their true selves, they can do powerful things and become messengers of God.

The activities you engage in while dreaming can reveal a lot about your personality. If you can transform into an airplane or you pilot one, then you are a chief messenger, a leader of great people. You are the forerunner of God, a great prophet, and can't be harmed by earthly powers. They are above earthly things. People like that are carrying the souls and personalities of celestial beings. Some persons in this category turn out to be inventors, scientists, or clergy.

In Africa, when people fly, they call it witchcraft, but unknown to them, those people are powerful by nature. People who practice witchcraft adulterate the practices of God. They might be able to take the form of an airplane, but it is risky because if they are denied access or when power jams their signals, they could crash and die. If you are granted divine access to fly or pilot an airplane by God, you will never crash. The air space in the realm is very powerful and dangerous; earthly spirits can't fly up there. Demons can only drag a flying person down with a strong magnetic energy but can't fly up. You must have a permit or divine authority to fly up. Those witches who fly do so in limited space with great care. There are stories of witches who used birds to fly before crashing into the ground and turning into full human beings. Those who use diabolical powers to navigate the spiritual realm take a lot of risk.

Before planes were ever invented, people already had dreams about them. The Wright brothers had a revelation about planes, but the physical manifestation took time and resources to achieve. There are some things I have personally seen in the spiritual realm that haven't physically manifested. Whatever you see in the dream world is real and can be translated on earth.

Afraid: Fear in the dream is caused by vibrations. When someone's astral body cannot withstand the vibration of another astral entity, it will cause fear. Shock as a result of vibration causes fear. Fear in dreams is also a sign of danger.

Whenever the astral body senses danger or is afraid, it sends signals to the physical body to cause the person to wake up. If you wake up abruptly as a result of nightmare, fear, or shock, don't stand immediately. Try to stay calm, take deep breaths, and pray in your heart while lying down. Shock in the body can disconnect the soul and the physical body and cause unconsciousness. Some severe shock may cause seizure of blood circulation, cause the heart to beat erratically, and result in a stroke.

When a soul is spiritually charged or loaded with much anointing or the aura of God's glory, he/she can withstand and resist shocks or demonic attacks and command them to flee. But a person who is carnal minded, without spiritual backing or a strong praying life, is like chaff of wheat tossed into the air.

Afternoon: The astral world is dominated by the afternoon. When we dream, the time of day we see in the dream is only a reflection of light from outer space. In the beginning, God first created light by separating it from darkness, He called the light day and the darkness night (Genesis 1:3–5 KJV). The difference between night and day is the ability to see. The light represents morning and afternoon, and the darkness represent night. Each twelve-hour cycle runs for twenty-four hours and makes a day. Night and day are equal to one day.

Dreaming of nighttime indicates bad things are about to happen. Darkness conceals things, and evil thrives in the dark. Anything shown in the dark is mystery. The purpose of dreams is to communicate or bring illumination, and these events takes place under the light. Light means life.

Age: If your age is shown to you in the dream, you are privileged to experience the manifestation of the prayer of David; "Lord teach us to number our days so we may apply our hearts to wisdom" (Psalm 90:12 KJV). The manner in which the age is revealed is important; if it is shown on your forehead, that represents your life span, and the knowledge should not be shared with others. There is great wisdom in the revelation of age. If you are younger than the age shown to you in the dream, then something great will happen on the birthday that corresponds to that date. It may not be death but an event that will change your life, and the dream is intended to forewarn you of it.

The revelation of your age may be used to measure the time of an event when it's written on the palm, belly, or torso. Take notice of where the age was shown. If your age is told to you or announced to you in the dream, then you are privileged to know it. It's a clarion call to repent and to prepare your ways or to start doing your mission on earth. If the age is younger than your actual age, then it is pointing at events that happened at that age and is very important in your journey.

Advocate: When you find yourself arguing in a dream, consider it a defense against a predestined decision. Most situations and events are already agreed or decided in the dream world, and whenever you find yourself agitating against such circumstances, then it means rejection of that event or a divine intervention to stop that event from happening.

You can advocate for somebody in the dream; it means God is using you as a vessel to intercede for that person. Whenever you wake up from that sort of dream, please thank God and pray against that circumstance.

"So Jacob was left alone and a man wrestled with him until daybreak. When the Man saw that He had not prevailed against Jacob ... Then He said; Let Me go, for day is breaking. But Jacob said I will not let You go unless You declare a blessing on me" (Genesis 32:22–31 KJV). Whenever you see yourself striving against an angel of God, then you must hold fast until you receive your blessing or deliverance. Such experience is good because its takes a conscious soul to advocate. An individual who is in bondage cannot advocate or stand up for themselves. If you are in bondage to a particular lifestyle, behavior, or addiction and you dream about yourself interceding against it, this shows freedom is near and a chance or willingness to give up.

A prostitute dreamt of herself in a hotel where people were drinking and smoking, and she began arguing with them, after which she woke up. It shows her soul is tired of that life. It's a strong warning from God to stop or prevent an ugly event associated with that lifestyle. Argument or disagreement is rejection of a thing.

Aggressor: To be an aggressor in the dream is very good. Aggressive people possess a fighting spirit to resist any force that attacks them, and they are usually well prepared and self-conscious. Whenever you are in a dangerous situation and your instinct is to fight first, you have the soul of an aggressor.

Aggressors are fearless and difficult to harm. Because they attack first, they catch the enemy off guard. When an evil entity attacks first and you only defend, the attack may leave a lasting mark, impression, or harm on you even after the entity has fled. It is just like a physical wrestling match. The person who gives the first debilitating blow has the upper hand. Even though you defend yourself and eventually attain glory, that first blow will leave certain pains or injuries on you. This is why some people suffer from ill health or trouble that, though it does not consume them, leaves them filled with bitterness. "Therefore put on the whole armor of God so that you may be able to stand up against the schemes and strategies and deceits of the devil" (Ephesians 6:11 KJV). Always be prepared spiritually to defend yourself against evil.

When you are praying against enemies, be aggressive. Don't be afraid or let them throw the first punch. Over time, reacting in this way will train your astral body to be aggressive in the spiritual realm. Some dreamers are so full of cowardice, to the point that their irrational fears have weakened their astral bodies, and they can't stand the spiritual warfare. "Whatsoever is bound on earth is bound in heaven and whatsoever is loosed on earth is loosed in heaven" (Matthew 16:19 KJV). Additionally, you can imagine yourself as an aggressor in the dream with different weapons to have at your disposal—guns and a knife.

Agree: An agreement signifies harmony, settlement, and so on.

Airstrip: Sign of traveling or a visitor from afar. Air hostesses seeing air hostess is a sign of traveling far. If you become an air hostess, it means you are called to serve people.

Anything associated with air is good, and if you are a member of the crew, it shows you are a great person called to serve and lead people to greater heights.

Air force: These are good angels in charge of the heavens. They grant access to people in the air space. Every prayer and assignment to God passes through the air space to connect the heavens. The air force has good angels and unclean angels too, especially in the air space between earth and the first heaven. These angels are clean, though out of control. Most satanic assignments or evil incantations are channeled to the ground—plants or vegetation, animals or the sea—but prayers or assignments done to God go up or pass through the air space. The air force spirits are very powerful.

In Daniel 10 (KJV), the Bible talks about an air space spirit called the prince of the kingdom of Persia. He did not allow the answers to the prayers for understanding to reach Daniel for twenty-one days, until Michael, one of the chief celestial princes, came to help the angel out. If you encounter an air space spirit or beings in your dreams, please observe what they are doing and their appearance. They all appear religious and good, but their actions or activities will tell you whether they are for or against you. It also means your case file is under review.

Due to the activities of air space spirits, the answers to the prayers of the righteous are stuck. It will take an angel of war to release your answered prayers to you. These angels are also close to the earth, like the spirits that live in water.

Alarm: Alarms in the dream signify an awakening of knowledge. After an alarm is sounded, the activities that follow give enlightenment. Alarms also expose the devil's game and have the power to chase evildoers away. An alarm is a tool of revelation, and its sound calls the dreamer to be alert or wary of danger.

Alarms are instruments that call attention to the dreamer. If the dreamer is a trader or a public person, dreaming of alarms works in their favor. It signifies that an event to elevate and popularize the dreamer is around the corner. It can also attract good luck and favor to the dreamer.

Album: The gift of an album is profitable to a dreamer. It is a prepackaged revelation of the past or future.

An album shows the biography of the dreamer or others. It's a collection of social interactions with people and life events. Seeing your album in a dream is a revelation of your life story. The contents of the album are the main object of the message.

When a dreamer views an album in a dream, it indicates that he/she is fully in charge of their destiny and should make guided decisions to harness their greatness. On the other hand, if the album shows you a woman, she is meant to be your wife or play an important role in your life. Your album reveals your history, your present and future life journey, and unveils your true personality and your established destiny. Remember to keep it secret; don't share it like earthly album. It's for your personal spiritual development.

Alcohol: It connotes the spirit of whoredom and immorality. Whenever you witness yourself drinking in the dream, it's a warning to avoid bad company that influences you into drinking. If you formerly indulged in alcohol physically on earth and you see yourself drinking in a dream, it's a strong warning to stop or minimize your alcohol intake. When you don't drink in reality but drink in dreams, you must pray against the spirit of alcoholism. Most drunks or habitual drinkers became that way due to manipulation by evil forces to ruin their lives.

On the other hand, if people offer you gifts of alcohol in a dream, it means an event, celebration, or other ceremony.

Alien: All alien beings are divine and supernatural and manifest in dreams or reality in various appearances. They do not speak much, but their appearance is dazzling, particularly their magnificent eyes. Whenever a dreamer encounters aliens, it connotes a divine blessing. This is because they rarely appear, and their divine manifestation assures the dreamer of intervention, deliverance, or divine message.

Some of the reasons why aliens appear include bringing healing of incurable diseases, protection, and to provide assistance in an emergency. I have lots of personal experiences with aliens. While in prison, one came and used a towel to press hard against my ribs. He was healing me of a chest cold in my body that could have led to a serious ailment. I have also been visited by two angels who came and gave me an injection in the dream. It's a sign of a visitation for healing. A distinguishing feature of aliens is that they are all action and say little. I love aliens. They are friends to humans.

Alive: Whenever you see yourself alive in the dream, it means a revival, renewal, or exchange of death for life. Some people's death day, either by destiny or by occult manipulation, could have arrived, but God in His infinite mercy can exchange such awful incidents with life. There are people who the kingdom of darkness have judged and killed. They published their burial date in their coven, but when God intervenes, although that person may die in the spirit realm, they will still be alive on earth. There are things God does on our behalf that we will never know about unless it is revealed to us in a dream.

I have died many times and come back to life. These were so many times God intervened in my life and gave me more grace to live on. There are people destined to die at a certain age, but by God's mercy, that death could be exchanged with extra life. It means that such a person is living on by the grace of God.

Allocate: Receiving an allocation in a dream signifies good things. I once dreamt about my mum bequeathing some of my late father's inheritance to me in the dream. It meant something belonging to me has been officially given to me. My mum represents my guardian angel, so each time she manifests, something good happens. So allocating me my rights was good. However, the allocation may not be exactly what is displayed in the dream; it could signify anointing, progress, or grace.

Almanac or calendar: Almanacs or calendars are time- and event-keeping tools in dreams. An almanac is a time director that helps mark or foretell events. When dreaming about almanacs, the dreamer ought to pay attention to its contents and the timeline of events. Almanacs are a straight line revelation of future events.

Alone: Being alone in your dreams signifies sorrow or troubles. It's a very bad sign of evil or a temptation that may overcome you. If someone is alone under rain, that soul may die, or something terrible will happen to that person. Rain or nature signifies natural disasters that are beyond our control. When they befall us and we are all alone, it means death or circumstances beyond our control.

Altar: An altar is a symbol of divine oracle. It's a strong sign that you are called to serve God. This case is applicable to church-related altars. Seeing or standing on an altar reminds you of a service promised to God.

However, if you see an evil altar in your house, on your business premises, or anyplace connected to you, it means that an evil altar has been raised there, and deliverance is required. Anyone who sees an evil altar personally is connected to that oracle, and the altar is demanding to be served.

Ambulance: The sign of an ambulance in a dream reveals ill health, sickness, death, or anything associated to mourning and sorrow.

Ambush: This is a serious attack and strong setup by associates or friends you hardly expect to harm you.

America: Visiting America in a dream is a sign of good fortune or new experiences (e.g., fulfilled promises, new job, business, promotion, or discovery). The spirits that guard the entrance to America are the reigning powerful spirits of our time. America is the new world, and if you find yourself in person or in spirit, it has been clearly shown to you that new opportunities lie in store for you. However, you must carefully discern what activities in your life will attract favor to you—for instance, a new business venture, a pilgrimage, or an actual trip to the US in reality.

Amnesty: If you are granted amnesty or forgiveness in a dream, it is a sign of deliverance, liberation, freedom from bondage, and change of fate and destiny.

Amputate: The amputation of body parts does not hold a good connotation. It means the person's progress or destiny has been cut short. A person in this situation will find it difficult to get a good job or travel or change professions. In fact, it means to be stagnant and look morosely while others progress.

In one instance, I dreamt of my elder brother's leg being cut in pieces along with his shoes. At that time, I had created a vacancy for him to join our new joint-venture haulage business in Cross Rivers State, Nigeria. It was his responsibility to manage the trailers we hired to do our jobs. Shortly after he left the venture, the entire business collapsed. On a certain day, he narrowly escaped being crushed by a truck, which later had an accident. That dream meant something evil was preventing him from enjoying a profitable career. He has been at home, unemployed for decades.

Employing persons who are under a curse or in bondage can adversely affect your business. When a child of God handles a business, the business will thrive. If these mysteries are revealed to you in a dream and you are about to travel or indulge in a new business venture, expect only failure.

Amulet: Wearing an amulet in the dream shows signs of protection or signs of initiation, but this depends on the appearance of the amulets. Amulets could also represent family treasures, secrets, or the key holding a family together. Additionally, it could distinguish someone who has been chosen for priesthood.

Ancestors: Seeing your ancestors in the dream is a sign of divine visitation. In Africa, ancestors are departed souls of our forefathers. The Bible often traced the genealogy of great men. "So David slept with his fathers and was buried in the city of David" (1 Kings 2:10–12). When they visit us in the dream in a calm way, they have a strong message to pass on.

God uses their image to show how sacred and important that message is. It also serves as a sign to the dreamer that the message is from the spirits. Many pagans or traditionalists who do not believe in God believe there is a spirit of the land. The truth is that the spirit of God guards every land or family, and when His spirit visits us in dreams, they manifest with the faces of our ancestors. Ancestors manifesting to a dreamer means they have been selected to take up the mantle of leadership and authority in that family.

Anchor: Anchors are related to the marine world. Dreams about anchors are associated with business. Anchors could also symbolize self-control, a solution to a problem, or a weight holding one back. This depends on the circumstances in the dreamer's physical life and the details of the dream.

Ancient: Anything ancient is spiritual and divine. When your dreams take you into the ancient world, it usually means that God is revealing a reversal or change of things in the past mysteries or familial issues. The ancient world could also represent the underworld where dead people live. In dreams, things associated with ancient people are considered a foreboding of death. Visiting the ancient world is reserved for special people.

Angel: What a glorious thing it is to see angels in their original form or being. Whenever you encounter them in dreams, it means something dramatic will surely happen in your life. When Jacob saw an angel in his dreams, he wrestled with him and refused to let him go until he received a blessing. However, that boldness cost him a dislocation of his hip and a permanent limp (Genesis 32:22–31 KJV).

Angels are God's messengers and servants, and when they choose to appear to you in their celestial nature, God has something special in store for you. Whenever an angel visits you, their presence represents the divine presence of God with you. In most cases, they usually come for emergency response, deliverance, or healing. Angels always wear white apparel or garments, and they look glorious and supernatural without stains or blemish.

Anger: Feeling or showing anger in the dream is good. It's a way of charging the soul for action. It's also a strong turning point for a soul. When the astral body is angry, it creates a strong resistant force to repel attacks and resist evil or temptation. If someone prays with aggression in the dream, it's a way of *back to sender* or spoiling the enemy plan. Whenever a soul is angry, heaven is also alerted. The Bible says God does not despise a heavy heart (Psalm 51:17 KJV).

Whenever you pray with a heavy heart or in anger in the spiritual realm or physically, your prayers will be heard.

Animal: Some people can shape-shift in dreams or take on the form of an animal to accomplish some activities. However, the object for interpretation is the type of animal you transformed into and what activities you engaged in while in that form. Transforming into any particular animal shows your ancient kinship and affinity for that animal. You can't manifest with any and every animal; there are chosen ones for that purpose.

Animals like snakes, owls, cats, snails, and many creeping animals are affiliated with the occult, and such creatures are symbols of witchcraft. For ages, some animals have been synonymous with satanic influences. If you see yourself in animals affiliated with evil, please note that demonic spirits or spirits of witchcraft are attempting to or have already possessed you.

The animal symbol you turn into is your image, name, and code in the realm of the spirit, and it reveals the symbol of the demon that is manifesting in you. Additionally, you can't eat such animals physically on earth. That animal is the symbol of your deity. In some African societies, there are particular animals that they do not kill or eat. An excerpt from Chief Nengi James of the Nembe community in Bayelsa State, Nigeria, says, "In Nembe, the python is a totem. Our people believe that it is a transformation of the spiritual being." In Anambra State, the people refrain from calling the python a snake; they simply call it Eke Idemili. They do not eat its meat or kill it. However, no one alive can give a full story on the genesis of the practice because they only met their forefathers revering it as their deity.[32]

And so when someone appears in certain animal forms in dreams, it speaks volumes of the person's cultural heritage and belief system and reveals a lot about their religious life. However, God can turn you into some chosen creatures in the dream to perform certain spiritual assignments or learn lessons. This was reflected in the case of King Nebuchadnezzar, who was forewarned of his transformation into an animal in a dream to teach him humility and obedience to God (Daniel 4:23 KJV). Appearing as a lion, tiger, bird, dove, pigeon, sheep, or other clean animals may not be associated with occultism or witchcraft.

Sometimes the transformation is necessary to enable the soul to travel and experience certain things peculiar to that world. If God wants to take you to a water kingdom below, your guardian angel may turn you into a powerful sea creature to have access to that world. There are places your astral body is limited to go in its natural state, and this is why this shape-shifting is necessary. It grants the astral body unrestricted access to various realms.

Animals are more ancient than humans or earth. In the kingdom of God called paradise, animals there, described by most prophets and John the revelator, do not exist on earth. And so if anybody wants to visit such a place, their astral being or soul must clone itself into the animals there and visit the place. Spirit beings can clone themselves or take up other bodies to travel to other worlds consciously. Any animal form that assists the soul could be used to travel to any world

---

[32] www.thenationonline.net/revealed-nigeriancommunities/amp/.

in the spirit realm. Physically, some people can clone their bodies into an animal and harm others. There are folklores of great hunters and people who could transform into various predators to give themselves an advantage while hunting and to terrorize their enemies at nighttime. There are others whose spiritual symbols are predatory animals. Whenever they fall into danger in their dream, they can shape-shift into that animal, or the animal will pursue their enemies. That manifestation is a good gift from God.

In Jude 1:5–6 (KJV), the Bible talks about angels who left their official assignments on earth and took up human form to live on earth with humans. They married daughters of men who birthed a race of very large children called Nephilim, forefathers of giants, and indulged in various depravities that offended God (Genesis 6:1–6 KJV).

Some of the scientists who experienced animal transformation in their dreams spearheaded the theory of evolution. It wasn't empirical knowledge based on verifiable evidence; rather, it was a theory inspired by mere human dreams. Changing into an animal in dreams doesn't explain our origin; rather, it details the interaction of man and animal in the journey of life, spanning thousands of years on earth transition. Animals are beings; they have life. They can communicate and embody souls like humans.

In fact, both animals and humans are classified as mammals because both species share similar characteristics. Solomon couldn't distinguish between an animal and human but concluded that humans are animals or higher animals. The truth is humans have similar characteristics of lower animals, but we were made in the image of God, and this makes the difference.

The soul of a sheep can be equated to the soul of a human, and God figuratively uses it to explain the replacement of the obstinate soul of a sinner. The Bible also refers to humans as sheep and goats on the Day of Judgment to be separated from one another—the sheep on the right to a place of honor and the goats on the left to a place of rejection (Matthew 25:34–46 KJV).

In the past, the children of Israel would sacrifice sheep yearly to God to atone for their sins (Leviticus 4:32). However, the birth, death, and resurrection of Jesus put an end to this futile practice that needed to be repeated often. This is why Jesus is often described as the Lamb of God (John 1:36 KJV), because His death served as the perfect and ultimate sacrifice for sin (Romans 8:3 KJV, Hebrews 10:1–18 KJV).

Animals have a direct relationship with humans, but humans did not evolve from animals (Genesis 1:26 KJV). Animals are responsible for maintaining a healthy balance in the ecosystem. In the Garden of Eden, they served as our neighbors, friends, and subjects to Adam and Eve. God gave Adam and Eve a responsibility to care for all the animals He created by granting them certain authority when He said to them, "Be fruitful, multiply and fill the earth and subjugate it, rule over the fish of the sea, the birds of the air and every living thing that moves upon the earth" (Genesis 1:26 KJV).

Animals are very powerful spiritual agents and can be used for certain activities by both humans and spirits. In the Garden of Eden, Satan spoke to Eve through a snake and set in motion the activities that led to the fall of man (Genesis

3:1–24). Physically, animals can be trained to help humans accomplish good things, especially in the aspect of security and police work.

Whenever you see yourself in the form of one animal, please take note of that animal and the place you visited with it. Such dreams tells you so much about your personality. Always study the animal you see in your dreams because the type of animals you dream about have different meanings or warnings. It's difficult for demons to manifest in the form of a dove or pigeon to harm somebody because these birds have clean souls or pure souls and have a strong affiliation with the divine. For instance, if you see a snake in your dream, it means trouble, unhealthy temptation. Whenever it appears, Satan has announced his presence in your life. Genesis 3 verse 1 describes the serpent as more subtle, devious, and cunning than other animals and equates it to the devil. Wherever snakes appear, whether in prophecy, visions, or dreams, it means tribulation, strife, and troubled times, regardless of the size of the snake. Dreaming of creeping things reveals that underworld spirits are involved. Anything that lives in the ground represents the underworld, so take note of that particular animal, as it may be a sign of blessing or warning.

Creatures from the sea represent human souls. Any animal or fish you see in the water is a human soul. If you see many fish swimming, you have been destined to be a disciple or called to serve God and deliver souls. When you catch a fish, it's a sign of good luck. For a woman, it may mean early signs of pregnancy, but to see dead fish is not good at all. Seeing birds flying is a divine visitation, and to see yourself turning into a bird flying is also a good thing. It shows you are mature in spirit to overcome earthly problems, but if you are connected to witchcraft, it means you are mature enough to adventure in the witchcraft world.

Anointing: This signifies a call to serve. However, the dreamer should pay attention to what is used for the anointing. If it is oil, it must be sanctified (e.g., olive, palm oil—oil that is clean and not associated with evil rituals). Pure or purified water can also be used to anoint people in the dream. Experiencing anointing in the dream means various things. One of these is that heaven has commissioned the person to work for God.

It could also mean the person has been chosen to be a king (1 Samuel 9:15–16 KJV) or a leader of a community or organization. Anointing is a symbol of leadership, coronation, and spiritual completeness to lead or take ministerial responsibility. It's a sign of service to humanity. Please take note of the person doing the anointing; their appearance and utterances during the anointing are your mandate. The devil can also disguise himself to anoint people, and it is important to discern from the appearance whether it is a divine or satanic anointing.

Anthill: This is a sign of evil associated with land.

Applicant: Most things that happen in the dream world directly translate to some blessings or value in the physical world. It is not desirable to dream of being idle. The soul needs work (2 Thessalonians 3 KJV). Idleness can represent evil machinations against the dreamer. The person rendered as an applicant in the dream realm is most likely jobless in the physical realm. If an employed individual sees themselves as an applicant searching for a job in the dream, it means they could be sacked or lose their job under mysterious circumstances. If the person is in business, then they may become bankrupt or run into economic difficulties.

Archenemy: Dreaming of your enemy is a sign of an attack. The person who appears in your dream may not be the one who is attacking you in reality. Take note of the person you dream of, including their mannerisms, to determine the tactics your enemy might use on you. Additionally, your relationship with that person in the dream world will help you discern how close the attacker is to you in the physical world.

The enemy can appear in the faces of our loved ones to harm us in the dream. Seeing the person in your dream doesn't mean it's that exact person causing you harm, but it shows how close the enemy is to you.

Archive: An archive is a collection of historical documents or records providing information about a place, institution, or group of people. To encounter an archive or archive room in your dream means your file in the spiritual realm has been remembered, and your future is revealed to you. Seeing it is indeed a privilege.

Through the prophet Isaiah, God revealed to King Hezekiah that he was going to die due to his deathly illness. Immediately, King Hezekiah turned to the wall and pleaded with God in prayer for an extension of life, citing his devotion and faithfulness to God and His precepts. God hearkened to his prayer and extended his lifeline by fifteen years. Shortly after his recovery, the king of Babylon came to console him in his illness. King Hezekiah foolishly showed him the entire contents of his storehouse—gold, silver, spices, precious oil, armory, and everything that was found in his treasuries. This made God curse him, promising that everything that they had seen would be carried off to Babylon, and his descendants would be taken away as slaves to serve as eunuchs in the palace of Babylon (1 Kings 20:1–16 KJV). If King Hezekiah had died at the time appointed, the eventual enslavement of the Israelites would have been averted. This story just illustrates that God's time is the best for us.

Arena: Arenas or squares are places establishing events in a dreamer's life. An arena signifies and connotes the importance of a market square in the dream; any event that takes place there is established. Whenever you are in a public place in the dream realm, it is a good idea to comport yourself because events that take place there are difficult to reverse. If someone goes to a marketplace or a village square to summon you or instigate some ritual against you, your guardian angel may lead you to that same place in the realm to observe the evil work in order to cancel it.

Argue: To argue in the dream is an art of defense against a judgment established by an enemy. In a way, it's pulling resistance or cancelling an already established assignment, action, or evil plan against an individual. When the spirit of a person rises in their defense in the spirit realm, then arguments will ensue. To argue in the dream means expressing the spirit of persistence that helps people achieve something. Jacob argued and wrestled with an angel to receive a blessing (Genesis 32:22–31 KJV

Arm: Having a weapon in the dream is an act of defense. Whenever the spirit of a person no longer runs away from danger but rather picks up weapon or arms themselves to fight back, that person is now spiritually mature to defend themselves. Whenever you pick up any weapon in the dream, please unleash it on that enemy, evil, or animal without mercy.

If you kill the enemy or the source of danger, then you will never encounter that issue again, but if the attacker escapes with an injury or deadly blow, they will live to fight you another day. If the attacker manages to escape, that problem has only been alleviated temporarily.

I once dreamt of a big green snake with many horns. I quickly rushed to get kerosene to douse the snake. However, the snake escaped before I could spray it properly. On waking up, I knew that dream was concerning a police case I was having with my boss at the time. I needed to use the kerosene to kill it properly; the chemical components of kerosene kill reptiles slowly and painfully.

Army: The presence of an army of angels in dreams represents a time of war in your life. They usually come for war, not for peace, and their mission is to destroy without mercy. If an army of angels manifests in your dream, it is a good idea to connect them to your problems. Consider your enemies defeated and all your problems solved. No demons or principalities can withstand their authority.

When in trials, David prayed, "Let their way be dark and slippery, with the angel of the Lord pursuing and harassing them" (Psalm 35:6 KJV). Those angels are called warring angels; they pursue and harass workers of iniquity until they confess and die.

On the other hand, the presence of warring angels reveals conflict within a particular state or area. Their presence could mean public disturbance of great magnitude in the physical or spiritual world.

Arrest: If you are arrested in the dream, you will get into trouble shortly after, unless God intervenes. It is better for a person to be arrested in the physical realm than for their soul to be arrested or caged in the spirit. An individual could be a free person here on earth, but in the spiritual realm, they are a prisoner.

When you are in bondage, you could encounter tribulations and be denied ease, peace, and good things. If an arrest is revealed to you in a dream, please pray for God's grace to overcome the trial or intervene and avert it.

Being arrested by police is a clear indication of evil forces at work. Encountering police in dreams symbolizes trouble, temptation, or trials. If they detain you in the dream, the impending problem must come to pass, but if they arrest you for only a short while and let you go, that means the grace of God has liberated you. It is in that individual's best interest to consult a prophet or pastor to conduct prayers to release their soul from prison. Some people are locked up in the kingdom of darkness, suffering spiritual and physical stagnation. Whatever the kingdom of darkness decides is what happens in their life.

There are many people of God who have locked up the anointing and souls of many of their members in their inner prison yard to be serving them. He will gather all their anointing and use it to grow his church and perform miracles. Those members will never go away from that church or be able to break that cycle of spiritual abuse. Those types of people either remain stagnated with little progress or are successful and give their wealth to the church without remembering their families.

Any church whose members can't grow in spirit or become as rich as the founder or general overseer is not profitable to its members. When Christ was on earth, He desired His disciples to be more like Him and share in the glory bestowed on Him by His Father. "I have given to them the glory and honor which You have given Me, that they may be one just as We are one. I in them and You in Me, that they may be perfected and completed into one so that the world may know that You sent Me and have loved them, just as You have Loved Me. Father I desire that they also whom You have given to Me, may be with Me where I am so that they may see My glory which you have given Me" (John 17:22–24 KJV). Any circle or church where the members remain stagnated—the ladies can't marry or have children, and the men don't grow spiritually or physically—is suspicious.

Ascension: The ascension represents the uplifting of the soul to celestial cities. Without divine invitation, the natural human spirit cannot ascend to heaven in the manner of Christ's ascension. "So then, when the Lord Jesus had spoken to them, He was taken up into Heaven and sat down at the right hand of God" (Mark 16:9 KJV). "And after He said these things, He was caught up as they looked on, and a cloud took Him up out of their sight (Acts 1:9 KJV). Experiencing ascension in dreams reveals the position of the dreamer's soul before God. It means that soul has not been found wanting before God and is working in line with God's will. Our spiritual growth is geared to grooming our spirits to merge with God. Any soul that ascends into heaven is unlikely to remain alive physically on earth, but if the experience is resurrection or rapture through ascension, you are a heavenly candidate. Keep holding onto God and living right.

I once found myself ascending up into the clouds to meet our Lord Jesus Christ. He and two young men were ascending into the cloud, but no matter what I did, I couldn't get close to them. The more I struggled to catch up, the faster they moved, until I lost sight of them. When I descended, people around told me that was the apostle Paul. I was surprised but felt at ease, as it wasn't Jesus. While traveling with my boss the following day to Bayelsa, Nigeria, we were involved in a ghastly accident; it was then I realized that I had met the angel of death, who prevented my death. I gave glory to God because if I had been able to meet up with them in the clouds, I wouldn't have survived the accident. Therefore, if you dream of yourself ascending, the message is important.

Assassination: Dreaming of an assassination implies a serious direct attack on an individual. Only God's grace can make a dreamer survive an assassination attempt in the dream. Most people sleep, and they can't wake up.

Assembly: Belonging to a professional club, church gathering, or an assembly of leaders is a positive sign that you have received official recognition. It is a good omen when the gathering is harmonious and peaceful.

If your dreams lead you into an assembly of evil men, it is a bad omen and means your soul has been summoned for judgment before a particular deity or shrine. When you are able to recognize the faces around, there's a possibility you know where the deity is located.

Some dreamers have been craftily initiated into secret cults and evil associations and even attend their meetings. Their astral bodies are used to perpetuate so many evil assignments unknown to their physical body. It is in that believer's interest to meet men of God to intercede for them in prayer and untangle them from every evil association.

ATM card: An ATM card symbolizes a source of income or the key to your treasure. When you get an ATM card in the dream, it means you are about to experience huge success. In a short while, you will receive a windfall or experience monetary favor in your business or work life.

However, there are always evil forces and attacks that surround ATM card dreams; they are obstacles that hinder your success and rob you of your joy.

Atrocity: To dream of an atrocity signifies that God or other divine entities are drawing attention to an abominable thing has taken place in your life or family history that requires cleansing or sanctification.

Attack: Dreaming of an attack is a bad omen; it connotes trials, tribulations, and struggles ahead of the dreamer. The dreamer must take note of the mode of the attack and the mannerisms of the attacker to know how temptation will come about and where it will take place.

Attraction: Some men fall prey to the wiles of attractive women. Whenever a dreamer finds himself in an unholy attraction in his dreams, it signifies an entrapment. This unnatural attraction can also happen to things we have a desire for, like food, family, friends, or worldly possessions. Anything you are strongly attached to on earth has built a magnetic field like gravity that binds your astral body to it and makes it impossible for your soul to resist those things.

When someone close to you dies, it takes a while for your affinity and love to diminish. People with evil intentions take advantage of this law of attraction to trace or poison family members of the deceased. They use the faces of people or things you are attracted to harm you. They could poison food, beer, or anything you are attracted to. They could charm you or deceive your astral body to consume it. Demons use the law of attraction to seduce people.

Every woman has a gravitational pull of attraction around them; it looks like an aura or cloud around them. If a woman doesn't have a strong magnetic field of attraction around her, she won't command men or people around her. A woman could be pretty but not pull attraction. Attention is different from attraction. A beautiful woman may command attention but may not command attraction. A woman needs the force of attraction to hold onto a man. A man may explore a woman's garden once and lose attraction for that moment, but by the following day, he may be trapped by the same woman as if he hasn't gone there before. Attraction is natural. In fact, it is a gift like beauty, easily misused by evildoers or occult powers to command attraction around them.

Audible: If you lose the ability to speak or be heard in your dreams, you have been charmed not to speak. You shouldn't struggle to speak in dreams because it indicates you are under a serious spell or charm or bondage designed to cage you to submission.

Audience: See *assembly*.

Audit: If you are an employee or in a position of responsibility and you dream of auditors performing their duties, it is a clear message that you must be held accountable for your deeds. It's a warning to be careful in handling work and other responsibilities.

Audition: It is similar to an interview; if you are an applicant or a contractor and you see such a dream, it means you will soon be given employment or get a contract or whatever you are looking for in that period, whether promotion, employment, or admission.

Audiotape/videos: These represent prophetic records, either written or recorded. I dreamed I was in a studio that housed countless video players hanging on a wall, with frames demarcating the TVs or satellite stations that were playing different motion pictures simultaneously. Those motion pictures were details of prophetic ministrations of the lives and destinies of different people.

Author: Dreaming of the author of a certain book signifies that your lives are intertwined. The dreamer is meant to study the life or books of the author to emulate their lifestyle or receive a message contained in the book. If the author is already deceased and appears in your dreams, then you have some calling with them. Authors, by their lives or within the pages of their books, have a lot to teach you.

Autopsy: Related to *corpse*.

Avenge: Avenging means to punish or repay a bad deed done to you. When you dream of avenging a wrong done to you, God is revealing that He has delivered judgment in your favor. He has given you the power to deal with your enemies like David did to Goliath (1 Samuel 17:26–51 KJV). In the physical world, children of God are not allowed to harm others regardless of wrongs done to them. "Never take your own revenge, beloved, but leave room for the wrath of God, for it is written; VENGEANCE IS MINE, I WILL REPAY, says the Lord" (Romans 12:19 NASB).

However, in the spirit realm, you are at liberty to avenge yourself when God reveals that He has intervened on your behalf.

Awake: This is a state of physical consciousness or self-awareness. Being awake in the dream means a state of spiritual awareness or spiritual awakening.

In instances where you wake up from a dream but are unable to move your body or regain consciousness, it means your spirit person is out of sync with your physical body. This could be a result of nightmares that can cause a strong shock or vibration. This shock can swell the dreamer's head or cause goose pimples on the dreamer's skin. Sometimes the dreamer is awake physically on earth but totally unconscious.

Aware: (See *consciousness*.) This is the state of spiritual consciousness of the inner spirit in an individual. The spirit in many people can be likened to a baby unable to do much for itself. While in this state, many people are unaware of the mysteries occurring in the spirit realm. To them, there is no difference between the dream space and reality.

However, there are dreamers who are aware when dreaming; they can wake themselves up from nightmares. Pay extra attention of the dream state to practice in reality. It is a great spiritual maturity to be aware of yourself whether on earth or in the dream.

Ax: The type of weapon accessible to a dreamer indicates the level of force required to address that issue or enemy. For instance, a gun means a complete obliteration of the enemy. Using a knife to chase a snake means you have to get rid of that enemy in your life. But where it is a light weapon, the dreamer must proceed with caution; the dream is only serving as a warning.

PART B

Bag: Dreaming of a bag symbolizes certain contents or a possession of the dreamer. A bag is symbolic of a savings box, a house containing our treasured blessings and belongings. It should be personalized and guarded from jealously of intruders. The contents of our bag hold a lot of information about our financial and personal status.

Our bag should not be stolen, be in another person's possession, or be hidden away from us. If our bag is intact and in our possession, it means more blessings are imminent. When it is empty, we need to save and be cautious of expenditure. When the bag is filled with money or treasures, God has rained blessings upon the dreamer, who will notice a harvest of success and prosperity soon after. However, when our bag is on a journey with us, then it's a sign of relocation; we need to move away from our physical location or out of our comfort zone to get success. As a dreamer, you should pay attention to the actions of your bag. Your bag directs you to areas of prosperity.

When your bag gets lost in a dream, there is a great chance of losing money or treasure or having a business misfortune in the physical world. Guard your bag diligently against thieves and robbers in your dreams.

Car: Losing your car in the dream connotes losing your job, contract, or career. Losing your car in the dream has serious implications in the physical world. Your car signifies your power, anointing, or stronghold in the dream realm. In fact, losing your car in the dream can be likened to losing your significance as an individual. You must protect your car or bag in the dream; it's a direct message.

Phone: When you lose your phone in the dream, it means you might lose an important contact. You must pay close attention to the circumstances in the dream surrounding the loss. If your friend or someone familiar to you steals your phone in the dream, it means you will lose your business contact or a close person. This could also mean that someone is covertly destroying your relationship with one of your very important contacts.

Bank: This represents a treasury in the realm of the spirit. It is always guarded by powerful spirits of God. There is a difference between the spirit of God and angels of God. All of God's creations are guided by the spirit of God. Angels and humans are beings created by God and sustained by the spirit of God. The words of God are spirit, and they are life.[33] The words of God are living spirits. Whenever God utters a word, such a word becomes a living spirit that accomplishes the purpose for which it was created, without questioning.[34]

Everything on earth is a shadow of things in the realm of the spirit. Banks are a treasury storehouse in the invisible world. The invisible world is the mother of the physical world we live in; everything on earth is traceable to the invisible world. Every soul has an account in the bank in the invisible

---

[33] John 6:63.
[34] Isaiah 55:11.

world. Before we are born, our wealth in the invisible world has already been established.

Christ instructed His followers to store their money in the heavenly bank.[35] The heavenly bank He was referring to is the next generation bank, where each soul's wealth will be used in their favor. When you see yourself in a bank in your dreams, it simply refers to this spiritual treasure house. However, your activity in the bank determines the subject matter of communication.

a. *Working.* If you aren't a banker and you find yourself working in the bank, it means you have been chosen by God to create and share wealth with the children of men.

b. *As a customer,* if you see yourself in the bank to withdraw money, it means God is about releasing good money to you. Your time has come to be blessed.

c. *Being around the premises* means you have already walked into your prosperity. What you are about to do or are presently doing will earn you success.

d. *Watching the bank from afar.* If you find yourself watching the bank from afar, it means that a business will visit you soon.

One point to note is that most bank scenes in the dream world exude an aura of danger. You might encounter armed robbers, thugs, or uniformed officers chasing you, waiting for you, or guarding you. There always exist pockets of challenges; money in the dream world cannot be withdrawn

[35] Matthew 6:19–20.

with ease. In this scenario, the bank may represent your wealth, your business empire, or any opportunity currently enriching you.

Visiting a bank in the dream is not easy, especially when it involves taking value. That place is heavily guarded by police, armies, robbers, and thugs. If you are attacked in the process or the money is stolen, it means you will not succeed in that venture. This could also imply that you would be robbed in the physical realm.

Witches and people with evil intent have stolen a lot of people's money in the spirit. The devil can't go into the spiritual bank to take your money, value, or wealth without your consent. However, he cunningly devises means to defraud individuals by laying an ambush of tribulation, sin, drugs, or any other weakness to destroy the money.

In addition, after the fall of man, God cursed men to till and suffer to get money.[36] As such, the spirits of God on duty will continually fulfill that command until God instructs otherwise. Whoever tries to take money in the spirit realm must contend with God, His monitoring spirits, and the devil's agents as well. When God blesses you with money, He will also protect you from those trying to retrieve it from you. The blessings of the Lord bring wealth without painful toil (Proverbs 10:22 KJV).

By natural law, you cannot give what you do not have. The devil uses trickery to plunge people into perpetual poverty. Anyone who uses satanic or diabolical means to acquire riches finds that the money cannot last. What happens is that Satan withdraws all the money meant for the individual's lifetime

---

[36] Genesis 3:17–19.

at once and gives it to the person to enjoy for a little time. In fact, when you give the devil a blank check to withdraw from your heavenly storehouse, he will withdraw in excess to make you and generations unborn perpetually indebted. There are people who have taken their money beyond the next generations to come. When they die and are born again in the next world to come, they become very poor. They will labor and labor without anything to show for it. The spirit of God will hold that person's soul accountable until they pay their debt. Sometimes such a soul can live in poverty for generations. Most souls can't return to God after death because of a prior agreement with the diabolical. When they lose their physical body on earth, their soul body will be chained in the devil's hell, where they will suffer immensely until their debt is paid. Some of these individuals may have lived their physical lives in stupendous wealth for a few years and spend the rest of eternity in hell.

In conclusion, all wealth belongs to God alone, and when He gifts the children of men, He demands accountability. When you dine with the devil, you put yourself and your family in deep financial trouble that can extend to unborn children in that family. Most parents have mortgaged their family inheritance for a few years of illicit enjoyment.

It takes the grace of God to come out of the spiritual bank unscathed. Going to the bank or seeing it in the spirit realm is not easy, but it signifies good things. If you are a banker, then it represents your career or present work situation. If you see yourself in your usual office, pay close attention to every activity; there is a message for you. If you see yourself in another office, it means transfer of duty or promotion, especially if it's a higher office. It is not good to see yourself outside the gate of your place of work. Dream to be inside places.

Bar. Visiting a place where alcohol is sold and served means the spirit of drunkenness has possessed the person. If you have such dreams when you don't visit bars physically on earth, then you are possessed by the spirit of lust. Spirit of lust manifests in different forms, like drug indulgence, alcohol abuse, womanizing, and so on.

When you have such a dream, please change the people you associate with, especially those with an affinity for the fast lifestyle. Many things that manifest in the dream realm have the tendency to become formed habits of that individual unless broken by rebuke and rejected with prayers. The spirit of lust is a communicable spirit (i.e., it can pass from one person to the other like an infectious disease). If you become unequally yoked with a person of questionable character, before long, you will also exhibit such unwelcome behaviors.

However, if you are regular bar visitor, please pay attention, for there is a message for you. The events in the dream that take place in a bar are communication to you personally. If you are drinking your usual brand of alcohol, it is not an unusual experience but could imply you have been poisoned in the dream. Diabolic men usually use our weakness to poison us physically or spiritually. It's not good to see yourself drinking or eating in dreams. Drinking could also mean initiation. If you are drinking and possibly eating with people of questionable character or unknown faces, you could have been initiated into their circle.

Bat: The bat is a cursed bird. However, in some cultures, it may represent a good thing. Predominantly in the oriental world and Africa, bats are regarded as a sign of voodoo, witchcraft, or evil. Yet it is good to see a bat in the dream if you're under spiritual attack because it indicates that enemies are in your close vicinity, and the enemies are evil men or witches or wizards.

Bats are associated with witches and wizards, which they use to travel or manifest for meetings. Bats are night crawlers; thus. no well-meaning spirit or angel of God will manifest in that body except dark forces that are associated with evil operations.

Bath: A bath is a sign of renewal or cleansing of the soul. It means spiritual rejuvenation, washing away of the old and transformation into a new person (Ephesians 4:22–24 KJV). Another important meaning of bath is the upgrade to a new stage of life. It's a good spiritual exercise to bathe in the dream. Bathing could also connote a change of bad character traits, conduct, or lifestyle. When you dream of yourself bathing in the open, it means a public renouncement, which would be difficult to rescind. On the other hand, bathing privately means a personal turning point or self-cleansing for a higher spiritual growth.

A bath could signify an initiation to attain a higher spiritual consciousness. Whenever you dream of yourself bathing, please do it in the open or in an open place. The effects in the spiritual realm are long lasting and acceptable by all spiritual entities. Bathing in a river is powerful because the inhabitants of the sea, earth, and heavens will bear witness to the reason for the cleansing.

Dreaming of bathing in a public place with spectators is not a desirable dream. This connotes an exposure that will bring the dreamer shame or disgrace. The best spiritual baths are done in private, whether open or inside or in the river. A bath is different from baptism.

Bed: A bed shows the state of things. A bed could mean a transit or journey to a higher world. It could be used to depict sickness or death. A bed is huge information desktop in the realm of the spirit. It may communicate sickness, death, or a deeper spiritual journey beyond the ethereal world. The bed reflects the natural state. In reality, a person in bed is either sleeping, resting, dead, having sex, or lying down with someone.

- *Sleeping.* Sleeping on a bed in the dream signifies a deep spiritual journey of the soul. Our first sleep dream is a switchover of the physical body in the dream world. There are places our first sleep stage cannot take us to unless the soul sleeps in the dream to go further.

  When we sleep, the physical body rests while the soul body takes over to exist in the invisible world, which is our origin. The astral body needs to enter third-level stage dreaming to travel to that realm; when this happens, the dreamer may see themselves in a dream sleeping. It is risky for the soul to sleep without its guardian angel being on guard. Without spiritual protection, the soul may be lost, and by extension, the physical body may experience death. Some souls journeyed to heaven, found the place appealing, and refused to return to earth. When they make the decision to stay, with the consent of their guardian angel, the physical body is cut off and dies in reality. Our guardian angel is in charge of journey management for the soul, and we must be in tune with our guardian angel to direct us properly. Additionally, the extra infusion of the Holy Spirit of God assists our guardian angel to execute this job. There are many evil spirits in the invisible world ready to harm and judge people.

- *Sick.* If you dream of yourself on a sickbed, the dream is a direct message to be cautious because you can easily fall sick. Sickness in a dream could also mean a deposit of grace or remission of sins via forgiveness. There are several terrible situations that God intervened without our knowledge, but we may experience it as an ailment in the dream world, after which the situation is settled. God uses dreams to ameliorate a situation that may cause us great pain or loss of life, which is part of our destiny.

  There are events you can't prevent from occurring, and God doesn't intervene because it is written into your destiny. However, God can use His veto power to remove, prevent, or lessen the effects by His grace. In some instances, after falling sick in the dream, the illness also manifests in the physical realm. Your survival indicates God's divine intervention.

- *Death.* When a dreamer sees themselves on a deathbed, it doesn't always mean outright death. The message is simple; some evil forces want you dead, or divine forces have proclaimed judgment on you or are sending warnings to change a bad lifestyle. It might also mean a renewal of the soul; the spirit of God is changing the condition of your heart in favor of a new one. The psalmist David said, "Create in me, a clean heart, O God and renew a right and steadfast spirit within me" (Psalm 51:10 KJV). Dying in a dream means your destiny has been changed, especially when you die and wake up safely in the physical realm. Your case has been settled, and you wake up as a new creature. "Therefore, if anyone is in Christ, he is a new creation; the old has gone, the new has come! That God was reconciling the world to himself in Christ, not counting men's sins against them. And he has committed to us the message of reconciliation" (2 Corinthians 5:17 KJV).

- *Sex.* Sex is a powerful medium that can be used to transfer one's anointing or luck. It's an easy means to poison or transfer incurable diseases to people. Nothing good can come out of having sex in the dream. Sex in dreams can also be used to afflict a person with the spirit of lust, vanity, or promiscuity, and it brings bad luck. Doing it on your bed means a total defilement of your soul.

- *Lying.* When a dreamer is lying on a bed with someone in the dream, pay close attention to the circumstances in the dream. If you are lying with your wife and she turns her back on you, then she is not happy with you. If the dream scenario shows your wife with a strange man in bed, it means she is having an affair with someone. If a strange woman is lying there in addition to your wife, then someone is eyeing your matrimonial home. If you are lying there as a bachelor and you see a woman lying with you closely, it means that a lady loves you and could be your wife.

Begging: Begging is normal when you need something from someone or when you are in trouble. In the spirit realm, you get your desires by imagining or fighting for them. However, when you resort to begging, it is a bad omen. The dreamer must consult their pastor to pray for deliverance.

Begging could suggest pleading for forgiveness in order to obtain favor from a higher authority. It is a bad omen to be begging from someone whose physical appearance and status are beneath yours. Whenever you find yourself begging in a dream, take note of the circumstances to enable you to adequately address the issue in prayers.

Bell: This is a sacred object used to monitor and control emotions and the flow of invisible entities. The ringing of the bell draws the attention of human and spirit beings. The activities surrounding the bell are worthy of note.

If you possess a bell in the dream, it means you have been appointed to serve as an overlord or emperor in the community. The location you find yourself while possession of the bell tells you where you have been called to serve. Holding a bell is a sign of leadership—an elder, statesman, or priest. It signifies a high call to serve in a sacred office.

However, whenever you see a strange person holding a bell or you hear it ringing, it is a warning sign to the dreamer. Pay close attention to the events that unfold.

Bird: Birds are divine messengers. Spiritual entities can take on the appearance of a bird to manifest physically or in dreams. Birds don't appear for fun in the dream; they are symbolic and representatives of spiritual hierarchies or institutions. Different spiritual orders have an affinity with distinct species of birds. God and other divine entities would not manifest in unclean birds. This affinity develops from the characteristics, geographical nativity, and human perception of the bird. God classified birds into clean and unclean birds. An unclean bird was not fit for human consumption, according to the Torah handed down to the Israelites by Moses. After the human race was evicted from the Garden of Eden, they were driven into a world infested with microbes and disease-causing vectors. To keep the Israelites safe during their sojourn through the wilderness, God instructed Moses not to allow them to eat certain animals. Some birds classified as clean were created with natural defenses against infections. "And these are they which ye shall have in abomination among the fowls; they shall not be eaten, they are an abomination: the eagle, the ossifrage, and the ospray, the vulture, and the kite after his kind; Every raven after his kind; the owl, the night hawk, the cuckow, the hawk after his kind, the little owl, the cormorant, the great owl, the swan, the pelican, the gier eagle, the stork, the heron after her kind, the lapwing and the bat" (Leviticus 11:13–19 KJV).

Furthermore, every animal has a soul, and like humans, they have their life histories and records. Some birds in times past were cursed or used by the devil to disobey God. All the birds in the above category are classified unclean for human consumption. God can't appear to anyone using the vessel of an owl because the bird is considered unclean. The devil deceived the owl from ancient times, and he has been a willing tool in the hand of Satan. The kind of bird you see in the dream tells you the spiritual organization that has visited you.

Doves, pigeons, and similar species are sacred birds used by divine entities to manifest to humans. In this dispensation, the dove has been specially chosen to represent the Holy Spirit of God made manifest to humanity. "After Jesus was baptized, He came up immediately out of the water; and behold, the heavens were opened, and he (John) saw the Spirit of God descending as a dove and lighting on Him (Jesus)" (Matthew 3:16 AMP).

When you catch a dove by yourself, you have been initiated into the circle kingdom of heaven, and when they play with you, it indicates the Holy Spirit is your friend. The number of doves you can see or catch connotes the measure of anointing or spiritual gifts bestowed upon you. There are people who have several angels of God ministering to them.

When vultures manifest in the dream, they are a sign of witchcraft, voodoo, or familiar spirits in the land or community. They are great messengers of unclean ancient spirits, and their original function is to help rid the world of waste products.

In Africa, vultures are seen as cursed, ruled by ancestral spirits and malevolent spirits. To traditionalists and idol worshippers, vultures may represent a blessing or visitation by the deity or entities that they worship. However, to a believer in Christ, the appearance of a vulture is a sign of a serious satanic attack that requires urgent prayers.

Owls are associated with wizardry, enchanters, magicians, and every evil thing. The owl is doubly dangerous because she is intelligent, an accomplice to the kingdom of darkness. She aids them in hindering the progress of humans. Their physical presence at nighttime suggests evildoers at work.

In the spiritual realm, the primary assignment of a bird is to convey messages. They work with the heavenly bodies to foretell signs, seasons, and impending events. The elders and wise men of old can interpret their signs and manifestations. They can tell which birds represent evil and which ones bring good tidings to the community. The presence of different species could foretell the death of a significant personality or a great calamity impending. This will cause the elders to intervene.

The cultural perception of different animals help a dreamer understand the message that the animal is conveying. A divine entity may tailor communication to a dreamer's cultural beliefs and perception for better understanding. For instance, cows are revered in India but are eaten as meat in Argentina. A cow speaking in a dream to an Indian would convey a weightier message than if it were to happen to an Argentinian.

Birth: Every good thing given and every perfect gift is from above, coming down from the Father, who does not change like shifting shadows (James 1:17 KJV). In addition, God is a spirit (John 4:24a KJV), and He resides in the spiritual realm. A dreamer should not experience the blessings of God only in dreams; His goodness ought to manifest in their physical life. If an unmarried dreamer sees herself giving birth to a child, it is not a good dream. It is preferable to give birth with our physical body as God ordained and not our soul body. The human consciousness is made up of two entities: physical body and soul body. The existence of these two entities shows that they perform different functions. Previously, we acknowledged that the physical body operates in the physical world and can grow old and eventually die, while the soul of every person operates in the dream world and cannot die off. It lives forever. The things that happen in the dream realm have deep spiritual significance.

Giving birth in the realm of the spirit shows an ungodly attachment to spiritual entities. For example, a woman tormented by a spiritual husband could get pregnant in the spiritual realm. During this time, she will exhibit all the negative signs of a pregnant woman in the physical realm, like tiredness and change in complexion, and after birth, her looks will recover. Women like this, their beauty fluctuates between attractive and unattractive. This is a clear sign of a woman tormented by a spiritual husband; their physical body reflects the effects of soul body activities in the realm of the spirit. The downside of giving birth in the dream is that it narrows their chances of giving birth physically on earth.

On the other hand, giving birth in the dream could be prophetic. If a physically pregnant woman dreams of giving birth prematurely, she is likely to lose the baby she is carrying in her womb. It can also mean the baby will survive but she will die. The interpretation of these types of dreams can only be determined on a case by case analysis; one size does not fit all in the spiritual and prophetic realm. Dreams are puzzle images that require ancient wisdom to understand. It is better for others to dream of a woman giving birth. God can prevent evil plans from manifesting by revealing it in a dream. Other prophetic meanings for giving birth in a dream include deliverance, answered prayers, successful completion of a project, and the birth of a great idea.

Our guardian angels know the best way to reveal divine messages to us, to prevent misunderstanding and misinterpretation. For instance, in Africa, messages of the death of a family member are told to older family members with tact. The message is not blurted out harshly but may be cushioned with adages to control the effect. This is one of the ways our guardian angels look after our well-being. They bring divine messages in subtle ways that require wisdom or experience to understand, depending on the level of the dreamer's understanding. Additionally, some persons are endowed with the special gift of foresight. In Amos 3:7; the Bible says that God does nothing without revealing His secret plan to His servants, the prophets.

Finally, once a thing is revealed in a dream, that information can be easily accessed and manipulated by other forces. It is preferable to dream of an event, and it becomes reality in a short while. When prophetic utterances take a long time to manifest, they can be tampered with by evil entities. When a dreamer receives a revelation of a future event, it means the person should prepare for it with prayer and guard against anything that could scuttle the fulfillment of God's plan in their life.

In Genesis 37, Joseph, the son of Jacob, had multiple dreams of himself in a position of authority and exaltation. By sharing those dreams with jealous people, he went through much tribulation before he got to his destiny (Genesis 37–41

KJV). Although this could have been the will of God all the while, it holds an important message for every believer. "The one who guards his mouth [thinking before speaking] protects his life; the one who opens his lips wide [and chatters without thinking] comes to ruin" (Proverbs 13:3 AMP).

Block: Represents mysteries, secrets, closed not open, death, mourning, sadness, and so on.

Blood: "For the life of the flesh is in the blood and I have given it to you on the altar to make atonement for your souls, for it is the blood that makes atonement, by reason of the life [which it represents]. Therefore I have said to the sons of Israel, 'No person among you may eat blood nor may any stranger living temporarily among you eat blood'" (Leviticus 17:11–12 AMP). Blood signifies life, energy, power, and current. It could also mean a settlement or be used to seal a covenant. When you kill someone in a dream and the blood gushes out from their veins, it means the life force and energy of that attack has been totally defeated.

Activities in the dream that involve blood could mean various things:

- *Drinking of blood.* This could mean initiation into a spiritual organization or the occult. It is not desirable for a Christian to consume blood in their dreams. If you find yourself drinking blood in your dreams, you have been initiated already and need an emergency deliverance. Please consult your pastor immediately.
- *Seeing blood.* When you dream of blood flowing from your body without fatal harm, it means a settlement

has been made. The dreamer has paid the price for the settlement of a fatal situation that could have led to their death. When you sustain injuries in the dream, the effect settles a predestined situation that might have cost your life or serious bodily injury. Occasionally, the dreamer may still experience a physical manifestation of that injury, but a lesser degree of injury will occur. The dream revelation is an expression of God's intervention. If the dream is about the blood of another person, it signifies danger or a life-threatening event will happen to that person.

• *The sprinkling of blood.* This signifies the making of a blood covenant. "Then he took the Book of the Covenant and read it aloud to the people; and they said, 'Everything that the Lord has said we will do, and we will be obedient.' So Moses took the blood and sprinkled it on the people and said 'Behold the blood of the covenant, which the Lord has made with you in accordance with all these words'" (Exodus 24:7–8 KJV). A Christian should never be involved in blood covenants. This rule does not apply to pagans. If you visit a sacred place or perform any act of initiation or covenant and you see blood, it means that spiritual exercise is done or perfected.

Book: A book in a dream can refer to a scroll, microchip, or storage device of any kind in which the history of the world or universe has been written. These archives, which are reserved God's custody, contain a comprehensive record of the rise and fall of the civilizations of the world.

The knowledge contained in these books are not revealed to the general public. When a dreamer encounters a book in a dream, because they bought it, read it, or were given it, it indicates that they have been given special insight into a subject matter. If the dreamer remembers the title or content of the book, it gives a hint as to what knowledge is being revealed to the dreamer. "And I saw in the right hand of him that sat on the throne a book written within and on the backside, sealed with seven seals. And I saw a strong angel proclaiming with a loud voice, 'Who is worthy to open the book, and to loose the seals thereof?' And no man in heaven, nor in earth, neither under the earth was able to open the book, neither look thereon" (Revelation 5:1–3 KJV). This verse illustrates that books are ancient records that contain deep mysteries that cannot be viewed by anyone but the Creator and whoever He ordains to look upon the book.

Bus: A bus, vehicle, or car of any kind indicates the authority a dreamer wields in the realm of the spirit. The soul body derives strength, power, or anointing to accomplish things on earth from the invisible world. Having a bus or motor in the dream represents right, privilege, power, and authority of a dreamer to transit between worlds or to achieve anything.

When a dreamer finds themselves driving a vehicle in a dream, it shows that they are in a position of authority. The crux of the dream is the manner in which the car is being driven and the position of the dreamer; the interpretation of the dream could be prophetic or direct.

A prophetic vehicle could mean the dreamer will soon own their dream car physically on earth. When the dreamer is simply a passenger, it means transit or traveling. If you miss your bus in the dream, it means you will be disappointed in a particular endeavor or miss an opportunity. If the bus is snatched or stolen, it means an opportunity, project, or position has been taken away from you. If it is seized, that dream indicates that a circumstance beyond the dreamer's control will disrupt the dreamer's schedule and progress.

In a dream scenario where the dreamer is being driven around in their vehicle, the driver is the steward of the property of the dreamer. A crash or accident indicates that the dreamer will experience failure or difficulty in a current project. Traveling safely in a dream means the dreamer will get to their destination safely or an expected visitor will arrive safely.

Building: A building signifies a temple. When a symbol manifests as a building in the realm, it is a place for human or spirit occupation or an event center. The presence of buildings in dreams does not have a definite interpretation. Some buildings could represent a church, a court, a hotel, or a native building. So building is a general symbol representing many things to the dreamer.

Native building. Native buildings are outdated-looking houses that represent the existence of an ancient oracle. If the dreamer lives in an urban area with modern structures and sees a mud house among them, it looks very strange. While dreaming, if one encounters a native building, it is important to pay attention to the circumstances and events happening in or around the building. It could be a revelation of bewitchment, a family secret, or a curse hovering over a person. Native homes are often associated with evil machinations of familiar enemies.

Urban building. An urban building is a direct reflection of the present and current events or the state of a dreamer's life. Many modern structures have names or are easily identifiable. When a dreamer is in an unknown modern building or foreign location, that dream tells the dreamer they may travel soon. However, if the location of the building is in their current city, the dreamer will move houses within the same city.

Buy: To buy means having a means to purchase anything. This purchasing power can be used in the spirit realm to rescue one's self from situations or settle curses.

To purchase things in the dream, a dreamer must have currency in their spiritual storehouse or heavenly treasury. The means of exchange in the spiritual realm are commodities, favors, or value rather than paper currency. When a dreamer buys something, it is legally acquired property that will physically manifest at the appointed time. It is preferable to buy things in public rather than in private because things done in the public eye in the spiritual realm are confirmed by witnesses and established.

This property or thing bought in the spiritual realm cannot be taken from you, except dream robbers steal or snatch what was bought while dreaming.

Baptism: This is a sign of repentance, renewal, and the rebirth of a soul. Experiencing baptism in the dream is an indication of repentance of past wrongs and a rebirth of the dreamer's identity. John the Baptist felt the call of God to baptize the children of Israel by water unto repentance (Matthew 3:11 KJV).

Baptism could also represent an initiation into a spiritual organization. Water represents life and sustenance to the nations of the earth. Baptism in water is generally recognized as a method of initiation or recognition into one's chosen kingdom. Baptism in an ocean is of a higher hierarchy than baptism in a mere stream. The magnitude of a water body determines the quality of the baptism.

Banish: Banishment in the spiritual realm signifies separation, deliverance, or disconnection. If a person is banished from among his brethren, kinsmen, colleagues, or an association, the banishment could be foretelling death or an impending separation.

In the case of a church or any spiritual organization, it represents dissociation or excommunication of that member. Experiencing banishment in the dream is a warning sign not to engage in any act capable of exposing the organization to public mockery. But if someone is banished from an organization that is contrary to their beliefs, it indicates deliverance from spiritual cell, prison, or bondage.

Bankrupt: To be bankrupt in the dream signifies emptiness and lack. Bankruptcy in the spiritual realm reveals reduced grace, favor, or the spiritual oil of an individual. For instance, if a musician finds themselves bankrupt in the dream, the inspiration to compose songs or perform may be waning. That artist may also lose the favor and admiration of their fans and contemporaries in a short while.

In the spirit realm, currency is a medium of value exchange. If you do not give out value, you cannot receive value. Spiritual lack signifies a bad situation for the dreamer because it means they have nothing to tender in order to receive blessings.

The solution is any dreamer who experiences bankruptcy in their dreams should not take it lightly. Please contact your pastor or spiritual head to pray with you so that the source of all good things will replenish your treasury. If you are in business, a banker, or a broker, a situation leading to a great loss of trade or profit is looming. It's a stern warning. Please don't joke with it.

Banner: This is a sign board in the spirit world. It's a notice board used to issue a spiritual memo or predict or display an established decision. The content of any banner in the dream realm matters the most. Whenever you see a banner in the dream, please read what is written on it. Before a banner is issued or shown to someone in the dream realm, the subject matter has been decided already. The banner must be placed in a public place; a banner kept in privacy is shrouded in secrecy, a plan hidden and not yet established. A banner in the public is a spiritual way of establishing the matter so that its purpose cannot be challenged or truncated. For example, if witches judge any soul in their secret sanctum and condemn that soul to death. they will kill them there and place their burial arrangement with a date on a banner in an open place in their realm so that their act will physically manifest without objection. If anyone is caught in such a situation, it is necessary to intercede in prayers on their behalf for the grace of God to reverse the situation.

Banquet: (See *hall*.) This is a meeting place for events. Whenever you see a banquet, it means an event of celebration.

Banquet halls or event centers in the dream aren't intended for burials or solemn assemblies. Burial ceremonies are always outside under canopies in the open. In any case, a banquet reveals a burial ceremony; it means that such a burial ceremony will lead to celebration and not mourning.

Barefoot: Being barefooted in the dream is a symbol of authority. The manner of our attire in the dream realm is symbolic; however, many dreamers do not pay attention to their clothing when dreaming. When a dreamer is barefooted in a dream, it signifies divine authority to engage in a particular activity. "Then God said, 'do not come near, take your sandals off your feet because the place on which you are standing is holy ground'" (Exodus 3:5 KJV). Being barefoot indicates that the place is a sacred or holy place. If you physically recognize any place you visited barefooted in the dream, that place is worthy of note. When you go there physically, please remove your shoes.

Physical shoes protect our feet, but they also carry a lot of bacteria. Shoes should not be worn into the inner temple or church during worship. "You shall put it outside the Tent of Meeting and the altar and you shall put water in it. Aaron and his sons shall wash their hands and their feet. When they enter the Tent of Meeting, they shall wash with water, so that they will not die" (Exodus 30:16–19 AMP). Walking barefooted into a place shows respect and loyalty. In the case of Moses, the shoes he removed before God were those amulets or talisman he brought from Egyptian mysteries. But pulling of shoes means respect, obedient, and allegiance before God. If you are stepping into a holy place or sacred place, please remove your shoes before performing your spiritual exercise or prayers. Most people who do their spiritual exercise in the bathroom are postured to do it better because of their access to water. Whenever we are praying, we ought to be naked before God, physically and in our souls.

Bargain: Bargaining in the dream means negotiation. A bargainer must have a vested interest or stake in the object. Bargaining in dreams is a symbolic of a business transaction or activity. It's a good dream for people who are traders. This demonstrates that your soul is actively working in the spiritual realm to make you succeed in your business. Whenever you bargain for something in the dream, claim it in prayers when you wake up from sleep because it's all yours. Whatever you are doing that period should be handled with prayers and care so that you aren't shortchanged.

Bald head: This is a symbol of intellectualism and a mark of an elder statesman. Bald head in the dream signifies a man of intellect, a noble man or a great person. If you dream of yourself with a bald head, it is a sign that you will grow old.

It could also mean a person carrying the soul of an elderly person. Some individuals who have a bald head don't manifest it physically, but their soul is carrying it. The physical bald heads we see do not always have a spiritual connotation. Some are biological abnormalities like alopecia[37] or other hereditary conditions. Generally, spirit beings don't have hair on their head. Many of them are baldheaded.

---

[37] Alopecia is sudden hair loss that starts with one or more circular bald spots. It occurs when the immune system attacks the hair follicles and may be brought on by severe stress.

Barracks: A barrack is a spiritual enclave, frontier, or stronghold where some spiritual beings live on earth. The word *earth* here means this metaphysical world where humans reside. Wherever the location of this enclave on the natural earth is, the conditions of that location are horrible. Spirit entities who are fighters, members of a spiritual military or force, reside there. These barracks exist in the three elements of water, air, and land space.

There are also transit barracks for angels of God on heavenly assignment. Transit barracks are guarded by special military angels. All the armies of God are under the command of Angel Michael. The armies of God are stationed at strategic locations on earth for battle with evil forces. If you experience any of the following circumstances in a dream and you don't live in the barrack, you ought to pay close attention.

1. *Being arrested and locked up in the barracks.* This means the dreamer will experience a legal battle or a court case that may result in an arrest or legal judgment. If you stand before a commanding officer, surely the dreamer will be invited in a matter soon. The presence of barrack in your dream represents impending trouble.

2. *What type of military force.* It is also important to note what military force is involved in the dream. The army represents normal earthly trouble leading to courts and other legal arbitration. The police are used by dark forces or witches to harass their victims. When the police are involved, it may be a spiritual arrest of your soul in other realms to punish you or possibly kill you. When it is a police

case involving a barrack, it is a sign that the dreamer has been summoned before a spiritual deity for judgment. Having police trouble in your dreams is a sign of great tribulation. However, some of these dreams may not manifest physically because it's an undercover witchcraft operation.

3. *Barracks and your business.* When the barracks are surrounding your business premises, it shows that the problem might manifest in that direction. The presence of barracks suggests trials and trouble, and the source of the problems or the persons behind the issue can be found in the barrack premises. If they are members of the army or the police force, the dreamer will be summoned to court or the police station. However, if the people in the barracks are fellow businessmen, that dream signifies that you will have some trouble with the people you are transacting with. It could also mean that those people have the backing of diabolic forces.

Barrister: A barrister is a lawyer who specializes in advocacy and litigation. The presence of a barrister in the dream signifies the defense of someone not in the profession. It suggests a possibility of trial, controversy, or cases or events leading to legal matters. The activity of the barrister in the dream is the subject of interpretation. Dreaming of a barrister could be a sign that someone is judging you or has summoned you before a deity.

Battle: A battle symbolizes controversy. It is a direct message of violence, threats, or trouble of higher dimension. Battle scenes in the dream are usually prophetic, revealing the probability of an outbreak of violence or war in a community, state, group, or country. If you dream of being directly engaged in a battle against a person or group of people, but it doesn't manifest in the physical realm, it is a revelation of imminent violence. Some of the battles we fight in the dream are a reflection of our past, present, or future.

The forces of darkness and principalities wrestle with us on daily basis. "For we wrestle not against flesh and blood, but against principalities, against powers, against the rulers of the darkness of this world, against spiritual wickedness in high places" (Ephesians 6:12 KJV). They do not manifest in the physical realm, but they harass and torment in the dream realm. These forces may wear the faces of loved ones or may manifest in unfamiliar faces. When the manifestation is with known faces, it is likely in the present and is concerning family members, friends, or people you are linked to. However, if the faces are unfamiliar, it refers to unsettled problems in the past or your future battles. The manner of dressing, the size and numbers or your opponent, the venue, any weapons used, and all other circumstances surrounding the battle should be penned and critically analyzed.

Everything except dead people or past events has a physical representation on earth. Every human being on earth is a physical representation of soul living in the spirit. A lot of souls in the spirit realm don't have human representation on earth. This is because after death, they lose their physical body on earth. "For out of dust thou was taken, for dust thou art and unto dust shalt thou return" (Genesis 3:19 KJV). However, these entities can possess a living person or command existing matter to do their bidding. The souls of dead people in the dream realm are ghosts. When we lose our physical body on earth, we go back to dust, which signifies the underworld; that is the place for the dead. If your soul body ever visits the underworld, you may come across dead people you know and some you don't know. When you encounter dead people in your dreams, it could mean a variety of things. The first is that it signifies a case instigated against the dreamer by a dead person, or a bewitchment to cause harm or death, or it could be a revelation from a guardian angel. For this to happen, the dreamer must be linked by circumstances or have a score to settle with that person.

Another instance of battle is discussed in Revelation 12:4 (KJV), where John reveals that the kingdom of darkness tried to use Herod to kill Christ. "The dragon stood before the woman who was ready to give birth, to devour her Child as soon as it was born" (Revelation 12:4 KJV). This was a reference to King Herod's efforts to destroy Jesus shortly after His birth by ordering the murders of all male children two years and under who lived in and around Bethlehem (Matthew 2:13–18). But an angel had warned Joseph to flee to Egypt with his wife and Jesus to keep the child from being destroyed (note particularly verse 13).

In our current reality, the dispensation of the dragon has been taken over by events of God's intervention. The dragon now exists only in the spiritual realm, with no physical representation like Herod to kill Christ, except the devil chooses it for another mission. In this same manner, human bodies are direct representations of human souls in the realm of the spirit. Every human body is created to execute various activities; this mandate is called a destiny.

Whenever you fight a battle in the spiritual realm, you must fight to win because those battles manifest in the physical realm as tribulations. If you lose or become overpowered in a battle in the dream, please consult your pastor for fasting and prayer for God's intervention, because it is an ill omen. Committing sins acts as sowing a seed of trouble for the future, which is the principle of sowing and reaping (Galatians 6:7 KJV). Many battles people experience in their lives are harvests of evildoing that they sowed in the past. Anyone who always does battle in their dreams has a lot of scores to settle on earth. That person should repent and give their life to Christ for grace to survive.

Bereaved: This is a direct message of loss; it could mean the passing of a loved one or any pathetic circumstances leading to sorrow. Bereavement is a premonition of death, sorrow, and loss.

Besiege: This is a sign of demonic attacks. The kind of people, appearance, and method of attack determines the source of the attack. If the appearance of the attackers are the police, it's a good indication that an individual person has sponsored the attacks. Most unclean spirits manifest in police uniforms. If they are civilians who are strange to you, then it means a particular foreign deity.

Bewildered: Same as *confusion*. Whenever a dreamer finds themselves confused in a dream, it is an indication that the personality or purpose of that soul is lost. The harmony that exists between the physical body and the soul gives an individual a sense of direction and purpose.

One major illustration of bewilderment in dreams is dreaming of narrow paths river side or a forest without knowing the way out. This dream experience can lead to death or symbolizes death of the soul. It is good to remain your authentic self wherever you find yourself. Many people who lack a sense of direction in their physical lives are in the state of confusion. Some souls are lost in the spiritual realm and require prayers of intercession to lead them back to their true purpose.

Bite: This can signify an attack or a forceful means of infusing poisonous or venomous substances to a soul body in the dream realm. If a dreamer is bitten by an animal or human, it reveals that individual has been attacked in the spiritual realm or placed under a spell that could cause ill health or death.

Many evil people use animals like snakes, dogs, or other dangerous animals whose bites are venomous to attack. Snake means foes, enemies, and temptation, and their bites leads to ill health or defeat of the dreamer. However, if the dreamer spots the snake and is able to escape, it means the temptation or enemy will come, but surely the dreamer will overcome. In either case, it is good for a dreamer to be spiritually prepared with heavenly ammunitions to enable them to overcome. If a snake doesn't run away at your sight, it means, although enemies will come, they will be unable to prevail against you.

It is important in the dream to spot your enemies before they attack, which a dreamer can do by praying for a spirit of discernment and guidance. Even Jesus encouraged believers to "be always on the watch and pray that you may be able to escape all that is about to happen" (Luke 21:36 NIV). Whenever your enemy or an evil situation is exposed or revealed to you in the open or public in the dream, it means that problem will not overcome you.

Black: Black means a hidden or secret activity and darkness. Whenever you find yourself in the time of the night called the black of the night, it means sudden hidden agents will suddenly attack you. No good agenda is carried out in the dark. This is why we become apprehensive or fearful in the night, whether in the dream realm or physically.

"The human eye and brain together translate light into color, Newton observed that color is not inherent in objects, rather the surface of an object reflects some colors and absorbs all other colors."[38] Black is a light that absorbs all other wavelengths of light; however, we translate this color with our human eyes as the color black.

God doesn't operate in black light. He does His things in a bright light. His first command on earth was "Let there be light," and after He saw that it was good, this light illuminated a dark earth, after which He began the work of creation (Genesis 1 KJV). Satan does things that are an anathema to God, which is why he can only operate in the darkness, which is black light. Black light hides things from people, so evil people like it. Witches and members of the occult conduct their meetings in black light. This is why it's not advisable for a believer to conduct meetings in black light or do things in a hidden or secretive way.

---

[38] www.pantone.com/articles/color-fundamentals/how-do-we-see-color.

In a dreamer's lifetime, there might be many incidents of black times. They are difficult to predict and overcome. (Scripture says He didn't say bad times won't come.) Even Christ faced black moments during His sojourn on earth, the night before his arrest. Even after He prayed for hours, He could only see darkness ahead of Him. His power left Him. He became 100 percent human to face His divine role as Savior of the universe. When Christ cried out, "Eli, Eli," He was approaching a black hour (i.e., a black journey to the underworld or hell). In a few hours, He exited the black hours and gained light again and began His ministry in hell. When we are going to earth through a reproduction system called conception, we experience black hours for nine months before we see light again. It's proper for a baby to open their eyes to see light a few moments after the baby is born. Whenever you see yourself in a black hour in the dream, please pray hard. It's difficult to overcome whatever happens at night in the dream.

Blessing: Blessings can manifest in different forms, which can reveal prophetic or symbolic meanings to the dreamer. The following dream scenarios can serve as a sign of future blessings for the dreamer. The most common dream signaling blessings is a dream of harvest.

1. Harvesting farm produce, mushrooms, or fruits from a tree or gathering from the ground
2. Catching birds, fetching birds' eggs, or finding bird nests around your house or tree above you or around you
3. Hunting a good game or making an unusually successful catch while fishing

4. Encountering a tree with a lot of fruit on it

Whenever a dreamer chances upon unusually good things manifesting in their dreams, it is a sure sign that they have been blessed. When the dreamer is a woman, it may reveal she is pregnant. For a man, it means successful endeavor in business or career. It is important to mark the signs of your blessings in the dream. Before you are blessed on earth, it usually manifests in the dream. Some people may meet children or babies. This also depicts blessings.

However, not every kind of dream should be shared with people. Whenever you see your blessing in the dream, please start praising God and thank God first. Afterward, take a token and go to any living church to sow a seed of thanksgiving unto the Lord, who is the source of all good things for showing you kindness and mercy. It should be a private affair between you and your God; a dreamer must learn to be discreet. Then continue praying until you receive your blessings in the physical realm. When you receive the blessings of God, endeavor to follow the divine principle of increase to sustain it. If God gives you a child blessing, follow the biblical principles to celebrate God and dedicate the child to God. Do this with all other blessings of God. If it's money, give God His own portion by paying your tithe to the church.

Blue: This is the color of the sea. In the spiritual realm, the color blue represents the marine world. Blue is a color chosen by the higher-world astral water kingdom.

Board: (See *calendar*.) It's a public notice used to display things to be revealed in the public.

Boat: (See *transport*.) If you dream of yourself aboard a boat on a journey, the dream is talking about the course of life—the trajectory, conditions, and quality of the dreamer's life. Turbulent seas connote difficulties and tribulations, while calm seas indicate a smooth and successful journey. Boat travel is a rare experience for people who don't use usually use boats to sail on the sea.

Dreams of boats could also relate to a particular project or activity a dreamer is involved in. If you dream of losing your boat at sea, it's a forewarning that your project will suddenly stop for reasons beyond your control. A boat could also serve as a rescue ship operated by the spirits of God. Its presence in your dreams could mean foreign entities. The foreign entities are heavenly beings who have come to rescue you from any immediate or potential danger.

Whatever you observe or experience with a boat in the dream is directly related to you and your life journey on earth.

Body: It's the physical appearance of the human soul on earth. The physical manifestation of the invisible things or the invisible world is called body. The bodies we perceive in the dream are only a reflection of the physical realm. When Jesus, who was risen from the dead, invited Thomas to reach into the holes left by the nails driven into His hands as He was crucified, it was so that Thomas would believe Christ had indeed risen from the dead. This has helped illustrate the qualities of a physical body (John 20:27 KJV).

The bodies we see in our dreams are intangible; they can't be touched or perceived in the manner of the human body in reality. Bodies in the dream realm are motion picture images depicted in shadow forms. What this means is that bodies in the dream world are like pictures that can't be touched or felt. An easy illustration is how the television works. If you open the television to catch the people, places, or events you see on the screen, you won't find anything.

The bodies you see in the dream are only a reflection or stored projection of images from the real world. Without a body in the dream, there is no substance to entities. Invisible entities such as spirits are bodies too, although we can't see them with our physical eyes. A dreamer could duplicate themselves in the dream (e.g., you could watch yourself being buried or killed). The one watching the event is your real soul body, while the one being killed and buried is your imaginary body. Your soul body can assume or duplicate a body to reveal something. These dream world entities can't be killed or die.

The dream world can be likened to a drama where imaginary characters or images are used to play out scenes in order to illustrate, teach, or reveal things to a dreamer. Those imaginary bodies we see in the dream are imaginary shadows of people, places, or things used as symbols or characters to communicate with us.

PART C

Calabash: This could be a sign of initiation or voodoo depending on the manner in which it is shown to the dreamer. Calabashes are affiliated with ancient practices and communicate the existence of oracles, deities, and spiritual covenants.

Whenever a dreamer sees a calabash, they should interpret it according to whatever it represents in their culture and tradition. It's a direct language of the ancients relating to deities, ancient practices, voodoo, and covenants.

Calendar: Calendar is a time table for events already fixed within the solar timeline. When you see a calendar in the dream, please take note of the date and the events surrounding the calendar. Seeing a calendar in the realm of the spirit is a great privileged revelation. It is where all human future and past events are registered.

Calf: A calf could be a baby sheep or cow. The ancestral history of calves is that clean and pure entities like angels prefer to manifest through them. Their usage suggests sacrifice, prayers, or worship.

The appearance of a calf in a dream could mean salvation to a believer, while it may connote spiritual rebirth or covenant renewal to a pan or idol worshipper. When a dream reveals a calf to a child of God, it illustrates acceptance to God's kingdom or a sign that you have been forgiven and welcomed. It's a sign that you are chosen and your prayers and assignment have been answered or accepted. It's also a sign of divine visitation for a purpose. Calf or ram could also mean God's intervention or wrath.

Call: This is a high-level revelation that demands one's attention. A call in the spiritual realm is an order or command that must be obeyed. It's a vocal symbol used to pin down a human soul. If the voice symbol is coming from a higher authority in the spirit, that person's astral soul will be mandated to get information or carry out what is said. Voice symbols are a magnetic current attracting attention, and when that symbol is released, it gets to its target or attracts attention. In the physical world, if you want to get the attention of physical beings living anywhere, you can release a call symbol and speak. We call this technological advancement phone calls.

Camera: The camera is a powerful spiritual tool that records events and encapsulates events. It's in the family of calendar, television, or other forms of media broadcast in the spirit realm. Anything that is captured with a camera in the spiritual realm is established. Camera images are deciding events on earth. If you have it, please snap good pictures and go back to the world. Whatever you capture, the camera is sealed (i.e., is all yours).

If you capture a man and a woman with a camera, it is a revelation of a future relationship. Camera gossips, reveals, and preserves images. It's very difficult to erase when an image has been created or drawn. Whenever you are in possession of a camera, please pay attention to what you capture or the pictures already contained in it. It's a great tool of communication of the past, present, and future.

Campaign: Campaigning in the dream simply means drawing up support for a person. The person would be recognized as a public figure or occupy public office. The person or product being campaigned for would be a huge public acceptance. Whatever you campaign in the dream would be accepted by people, and it would be successful. Campaigning is a spiritual art of winning public acceptance for a person or product. When you have such a dream, whatever you are embarking on during that period will win people's approval.

Camp: This is an inner caucus meeting of people who have the power to decide various things. Camping with familiar faces is good, but if you find yourself camping with unfamiliar or dubious faces, you might be sleeping in the camp of the enemy. Whatever you are doing in that camp suggests collective events or personal events in your life that will be established. Anything done or decided upon in any camp is established.

Canoe: A canoe is a means of transportation in the realm of the spirit. It acts as a sense of direction or compass in a journey in the dream world. Canoes can be a symbol of future travel or an incoming visitor. The circumstances surrounding the canoe trip also reveal your present relationship with people and events in a particular community. If you sail on turbulent water or in a storm, it clearly reveals troubles or crises with people. But if the sea is calm, it shows peace and happiness.

A canoe trip is representative of one's journey through life. It is important to take note of the scenery, the people in that geographical location, and your eventual destination.

These pointers are key to understanding the direction your life ought to take.

Cancellation: See *reversal*.

Canon: Gun.

Candlestick: This is a source of light that reveals or attracts divine energies. When seen in the dream, it means there is a convergence of divinity or other divine forces requiring attention to reverent spiritual exercises and illumination of the mind.

Canopy: Also known as tent. A canopy is a geographical space in the spiritual realm that serves as a covering to allow people to conduct different activities.

Whenever a canopy is installed in the dream realm, all events that take place eventually occur in reality. The faces of people you see in the canopy are key to knowing whether the events is relating to you or close or distant friends. However, take note of the timing of the event to know if it is a present or future one, because if you are shown a future event, most faces will be strange, as there might be people you haven't yet met or children who are still growing up. But if you see past events, it's likely you will recognize most faces because their imaginary images still exist in your mind.

Captive: Imprisoned. Imprisonment or captivity in the dream realm is an undesirable situation. On the surface, it could simply mean an arrest or trouble with earthly police.

A deeper meaning is a revelation of diabolical influences to prevent physical progress or spiritual growth.

Every individual has a body and a living soul. The soul is the spiritual part of that person that hustles for them in the spiritual realm. The activities of the soul in the spiritual realm result in the physical manifestation of our lives on earth. If the powerhouse of an individual is caged in the realm of the spirit, then that person's success and progress become limited.

Some people are captive to their religious circle. Some have unwittingly surrendered their freedom by the activities they engage in. When writing to the Romans, Paul said, "Don't you know that you are slaves of anyone you obey? You can be slaves of sin and die, or you can be obedient slaves of God and be acceptable to Him" (Romans 6:16 CEV). Every individual ought to have a personal relationship with God through Jesus Christ and not through an organization or institution. As Jesus said to the Samaritan woman at the well, "Woman, believe me, the hour cometh, when ye shall neither in this mountain nor yet at Jerusalem, worship the Father. Ye worship ye know not what; we know what we worship: for salvation is of the Jews. But the hour cometh and now is when the true worshippers shall worship the Father in spirit and in truth; for the Father seeketh such to worship Him" (John 4:21–23 KJV).

Now the risk in yielding to the church or organization rather than directly to God is God does not want us to elevate anyone but Him in our lives. Additionally, if the church is built on a shaky foundation, such a foundation will affect the person's progress in life. Before the coming of Jesus, the

Pharisees used teachings to cage God's people for a long time. However, Jesus said, "The Spirit of the Lord is upon me, because he hath anointed me to preach the gospel to the poor; He hath sent me to heal the brokenhearted, to preach deliverance to the captives and recovering of sight to the blind, to set at liberty them that are bruised. To preach the acceptable year of the Lord" (Luke 4:18–19 KJV). There are some people whose gifts of anointing have been caged in their various churches. They can't make progress there. They look up to one man every day; we should look up only to God as the author and finisher of our faith.

An example of spiritual captivity is illustrated in the story of Jacob, son of Isaac, when he spent twenty years of his life in servitude to his uncle Laban. Although the blessings of God were strong in his life, he was not able to enjoy the full benefits of his wealth because he lived as a servant (Genesis 31 KJV). At a point, his uncle tricked him into marrying the wrong sister, Leah, after which he bound him to an additional seven years of servitude in order to marry Rachel. After those long years, Jacob had to force himself out of his uncle's house by inspiration and the wisdom of God.

In reality, this is how the world works. There are so many Jacobs not living life to their full potential or toiling for others because they have unwittingly bound themselves to service. Always be aware of yourself if you are in captivity. By virtue of salvation, every child of God has been set free! "If the son of man sets you free, ye shall be free indeed" (John 8:36 KJV).

Caravan: This is a sign of royalty. Anyone who is seen riding in a caravan is a blue blood. The person's original soul lineage is traceable to a royal blood. Caravan is likened to a *chariot*.

It's an ancient means of transport, but it symbolizes power and authority. It's a good thing to see it in the dream. The person riding in it is a subject matter of interpretation.

Carcass: The carcass of an animal is a sign of wealth and fruitfulness. Carcasses of big animals hold fortune. In Judges, on his way to pick his wife in Timnah, he killed a young lion that tried attacking him. The next time he passed the lion, bees had swarmed inside and made lots of honey, which he and his parents enjoyed (Judges 14:5–9 KJV).

Card: This means authority, permission, access, acceptance, or membership enlisted. Whenever you carry a card in the dream, you have been granted access or entry. A card also serves as a form of identification, showing that the card bearer belongs to a spiritual circle or place. There are places in the realm of the spirit you can't enter without a card. It serves the same purpose as the badge and identity cards serve on earth. Places you go with a card are not your domain. In the dream world, you do not require a card to enter a space you belong to.

Caretaker: This is a position of trust.

Cash: Cash in the dream is a means of exchange just like the earthly value exchange system. Seeing or handling cash in the dream is an indication of wealth and good fortune. Cash in the realm of the spirit is a value chain of goodwill that is embedded in each person's soul or abstract body. When a person's soul is rich in goodwill, he/she can command anything he/she wants without labor. Whatever he/she imagines or wishes comes to pass immediately. Such a person doesn't require cash or money to transact things in the spirit world. When a person is handling or using cash or coins to transact in the realm of spirit, that person is rich in goodwill. Cash coins represent a value chain on earth and in spirit. Any person possessing it on earth or in a dream is gifted to have it. Money is a spirit of God that controls it, and it's not easy to possess it in the dream if you are not rich by birth. If you are in possession of cash in the dream that is not protected by God, thieves, policemen, or bandits will try to rob it. It's a powerful force that is cherished by every entity. But someone's goodwill or a good name is bigger than money both on earth and in spirit. Someone with stars on their shoulders can enter many places in the spirit world and command cash.

But someone with cash alone can't enter all the places or cities in heaven. With goodwill value, you can command cash to transact on earth. When Christ was on earth, He lacked nothing. His goodwill and personality were worth more than money. At a time, He could command funds to be made available if needed. For example, at a time His disciples needed to pay their taxes, he commanded them to open the mouth of the first fish they caught, and they would find the requisite amount of coins inside to pay Caesar (Matthew 17:27 KJV).

Castrate: Castration in a dream is a sign of the influence of witchcraft. Men who have been castrated do not enjoy sex or become unable to impregnate their wives. Weak erection, sterility, and barrenness in women are the result of diabolic castration. Our inner soul body is the active body or powerhouse of the physical body on earth. When any member of this body is cut off or damaged, it adversely affects the physical body. I had an experience in the dream where a group of demons came and took my entire manhood. I resisted them, retook my manhood, and fixed it back to my soul body, after which I woke up.

Spiritual husbands are also a cause of spiritual castration. It causes the earthly wife and husband not to enjoy their marriage. The spiritual husband will paralyze their earthly husband's manhood or inflict the women with pain or disease to scare men away from them. It's a grave battle, and any man without God will lose.

Cell phone: Mobile phones are new technology introduced into the dream world. Prior to now, men communicated via letters, scrolls, or messages carried by birds. The use of trumpets, especially in Revelation, was intended to draw people's attention for communication.

In the computer age, cell phones represent connectivity. It is nearly impossible to be a part of the digital age without this modern means of communication. So when our cell phone is stolen in the dream, it simply means someone is plotting to take our personal link or a business contact very important to us. If the cell phone falls off from you unknowingly or accidentally, or someone smashes your cell phone, you will lose one or many of your contacts on earth. If you make a successful call to someone in the dream, it means you will be connected to someone who will assist you, but if the call is unsuccessful, you have some challenges in reaching out to your destiny helper.

Most people we meet on earth on different occasions are in our spiritual realm cell phone. They manifest to us through some circumstances beyond our comprehension. There are people who you are predestined to meet in the course of life; at the appointed time, they appear to help you fulfill your divine mandate. These people are called destiny helpers, and as soon as you meet them, your life will change for the better.

Because your spiritual cell phone is where all the contacts of your life are stored, it should be guarded jealously. Whatever happens to it has spiritual and physical consequences. When your phone is stolen, it is impossible to meet your destiny helpers and change your life. If your contacts have been hijacked and manipulated, the person will meet people who will endanger them. It is good to be watchful and pray for opportunities for connectivity.

Chaos: Controversy. This is a sign of trouble involving more than one person. Chaos in any form is very dangerous and should be avoided. Whenever you see it in the dream, please endeavor to note the location, the people involved, their faces, and, most importantly, the bone of contention between them. The locations and faces you see will tell you whether it is an indoor trouble or outside trouble. Season and weather observed in the dream during the chaos will help you reveal the time that such an event may occur.

In 2015, I saw chaos in a strange land of Christian extraction. Women and children were driven out of their homes by violence, and they were camped in public schools. Most people were killed and their homes ransacked by what seemed like ethnic cleansing or genocide. Although I was different from them, I found myself running for safety amid the chaos. I woke up and prayed. Although I knew genocide would take place somewhere in Nigeria due to that dream, I did not know the exact location. In the year 2018, homes in Benue state were attacked by Fulani Herdsmen. The same scenario I dreamt about played out, and I saw it on the TV. I had never physically been to Benue state. Dreams can reveal future events.

Charm: A charm is an evil spell projected against the soul of a person. Evil spells are the manipulation of elements, energies, or powers to attack someone in the dream, leading to physical harm. This harm can result in serious illness, paralysis, or total loss of life. When charms are projected onto a person, it depletes their strength or power from the realm of the spirit.

Diabolical people can harness the earthly elements to attack a person. In this instance, the ground could prevent the person from walking or open up and swallow them whole. When these charms succeed without any divine intervention, that person has a big problem. Charms can be used to remotely control the soul of an individual to eat, have sex, or do anything they want to achieve. The moment a charm or evil spell is projected or cast at someone, it takes God's divine intervention to escape it. When a person becomes spiritually mature, it is impossible to cast charms or spells to control them.

Children: Children symbolize angels or divine creatures. The soul of a child depicts purity and lacks guile and cunning. "Verily I say unto you, except ye be converted and become as little children, ye shall not enter into the kingdom of heaven. Whosoever therefore shall humble himself as this little child, the same is the greatest in the kingdom of heaven" (Matthew 18:3–4 KJV).

Angels choose to appear in that image because children are naïve, innocent, and harmless. Baby angels are very powerful. They wear white and look clean and friendly. On the other hand, demonic spirits come in a perverted childlike form. They look like dwarves with unattractive faces, tattered clothing, and horns.

Chorister: When you see choristers singing in your dreams, it is a call to worship God. It may be a reminder to sing for god if you are gifted. Choristers are angels of God who perpetually praise and worship Him in heaven. When they manifest to you, it means you have something to do with that office. They reveal new songs of worship and adoration of God to the world, and they inspire ministers to create new songs of worship to move heaven.

When you hear them singing an unfamiliar song, always try to copy or remember the words of the song. If you dream of choristers singing a known song, that particular song holds the answers to your prayers. If you use that song while praying, it will work like a cheat code and bring divine answers speedily. Any Christian song you hear or listen to in the dream is a key weapon to destroy the devil or to overcome temptation. In every song you hear, there is a message, a solution embedded for you. If you find yourself singing among the choristers, it shows harmony with God. However, singing with the angels in heaven can be a sign of impending death of the dreamer.

Career: When you see yourself doing what you are in the dream, it means you will succeed in that thing. However, if you dream of yourself in a different career path than you are currently in, it might be an indication for you to change your profession. It is good to receive a sense of direction from the divine. Lots of people live their entire lives without receiving spiritual direction.

The deceptive aspect of dreaming of a career is that a person's soul could be captive and perform jobs against their true purpose. When you work for other people in the spirit, you can't achieve success or result or money (i.e., value back from what you are presently doing). The results or value back will be channeled to other people to succeed (i.e., people who enslaved that soul). There are people who could see themselves doing odd jobs they never do on earth—using bare hands do dig or gather sand, cracking kernels with stones, working like slaves in a forced area, cutting grass. Such revelations simply suggest someone is using you to succeed in life. You are bewitched and enslaved to work for others to succeed.

Cat: Cats have several lives, so most witchcraft organizations use their image to perform voodoo. A cat has a soul that travels very fast and hardly gives into death. When you see a cat in Africa, it's a sign of spiritual attack or witchcraft. Cats have a life connected to witchcraft. Cats are private and secretive; they don't excrete in the open or leave their excrement for the public to see. Witches use the image of a cat to carry out their operations. If you expose witchcraft in an operation that is supposed to be done secretly, that operation is void. When a witch is exposed before the public, he or she loses his or her secret life of power and charm. We call them a smooth operator.

Celebrity: Meeting a celebrity in the dream is a good omen; it reveals one's personality and highlights possible important personalities you might encounter in the future. The people you encounter are not the exact people you may encounter physically on earth. Faces are symbolic of the characteristics of the person you will meet or may become like. We can understand that the people or faces we meet in the dream are illustrative, in that we can use those faces or people we see or encounter in the dream to interpret our dreams. This is called a dream bank.

Dream banks are archives of all the faces, people, and events your soul has been exposed to over the entire course of your soul's sojourn. God and other divine entities sometimes use information in your dream bank as symbols or images to communicate things to you.

Celestial: Celestial refers to heavenly bodies created by God to serve humans for the purpose of differentiating day from night, heralding new seasons, and revealing auspicious events. The sun, moon, clouds, sky, and stars are celestial bodies.

Celestial things are heavenly bodies and thus do not conform to earthly natural laws. These celestial bodies are controlled by God through His angels and spirits. Spirits are God's living breath, which exists in all His creations. Every creature that exists on earth or in heaven has the life of God resident in them and is guarded by God's angels. Every celestial body has a symbolic meaning distinct to it. For example, the moon represents ecclesiastical organizations (i.e., spiritual organizations like churches). It is also used to reveal events on earth. The moon signifies divinity and purity. Any events shown in the moon are already established and must come to pass.

We are given powers to control the earth and not celestial bodies. When we see them in the dream, something divine will take place in our life, but we must be careful to observe the celestial body used and the events surrounding it.

Centipede: These are earthbound souls. Earthbound souls are creatures that inhabit the underworld. The underworld souls or spirits that live on earth or in the underworld take on the image of animals that are corrupted to appear in the dream. God can also use the symbol of these earthly creatures, whether clean or unclean, to communicate to us. And the symbol of the animal used should be interpreted according to that person's cultural beliefs. If an Indian dreams about a cow, it is simply a divine visitation, but if a Nigerian dreams about cow, they will see it as an attack.

Centipedes belong to lower elemental spirits of the underworld. When you see them, someone has invoked your name before an evil altar. Just the way companies, churches, or organizations have a trademarked logo that represents them, shrines, evil altars, and temples have earthly creatures through which they manifest to humans. When God reveals their secret, please pray against it for yourself and your family.

When ugly and rare creatures appear physically in your home, it's a clear sign of evil. The land demons or gods are informing the dreamer of impending evil. It can also be a sign of demanding appeasement or a revelation that the spirits want to claim a dead person's body. Whenever a person dies, watch out for the earthly creature that visits to know if the person is evil or a clean soul. Always watch out for symbols or images of churches, organizations, or cults. It will be easy to recognize them whenever they manifest with their image.

Certificate: This means results or success gotten through hard work. When our concerted effort or energies in the form of education, career, apprenticeship, business, clergy, or political aspiration are successfully completed, we are awarded a certificate to prove that we have been through the process successfully.

When a dreamer receives a certificate in the dream, it means they have been favored to succeed. If the certificate is stolen or hidden away, it indicates that evil forces have locked up the dreamer's success. It is preferable to write exams in order to get a certificate.

Writing exams in the dream is a sign that the dreamer will succeed at the end of their endeavors. If the exam is difficult, it is a clear illustration that the project the dreamer is embarking on requires extra preparation and effort before the goal can be achieved. If you couldn't answer the question during the exam and there are other people in the exam who try to assist you, it is a clear revelation that you need other people to assist you to succeed in that task.

For anyone to upgrade to the next level in life, the powers that be must test their level of preparedness. These temptations, trials, and tests can come in the form of exams or tests, after which certificates are issued to the successful candidates. The certificate acts as a proof that the bearer is qualified for that position or upgrade. Receiving certificates, writing exams, and going to school are good signs of success.

Class: Class refers to the stages of progress in an individual's life in regard to academics, business achievement, accumulated wealth, and endeavors. For our easy comprehension, God communicates with us using familiar concepts, such as school classes, to explain life progression. For example, primary school would refer to early years of learning, while university would refer to mature or advanced learning. If a university graduate finds themselves learning in a secondary school class in the dream, it can communicate several things.

- The first scenario is that God is replaying a past event to help the dreamer repent, learn a lesson from that experience, or prevent history from repeating itself. It is a warning sign.
- This occurrence could also highlight backsliding into an old lifestyle.
- It could also be communicating the level of spiritual or physical growth of the dreamer. When we are growing slowly, we can't achieve things that should equal our current status.

The spirit world is the best place to upgrade our class because the spiritual must manifest in the physical. When you dream of yourself in a lower class than you ought to be, reject it wholeheartedly with your subconscious mind. Don't be complacent in low levels of progress. Whatever you are uncomfortable with is what you have the willpower to change. What is important in this dream is that being in a lower class is a reminder that events surrounding you or about to happen in your life are a test situation that can demote or promote you. When you see yourself in a higher class you have not attained before, it's simply a sign you have been promoted, initiated to the next level of life or in your calling. Situations in our lives are in a circle, like history that repeats itself from time to time. School class or any other classes of events in our lives are veritable images that can be used to communicate with us.

Chain: This is a symbol of slavery—someone who is under a powerful authority. To be in chains in the dream is a sign that a person has been enslaved and is restricted from progressing.

Chalkboard: This device is used to reveal deep, established secrets. Anything can serve as a chalkboard, including walls or digital boards. Please take note of whatever is written on it. Those writings hold important revelations and information for you.

"Suddenly the fingers of a man's hand appeared and began writing opposite the lampstand on [a well-lit area of] the plaster of the wall of the king's palace, and the king saw the part of the hand that did the writing" (Daniel 5:5 AMP).

In Daniel 5, the Bible chronicles the first divine chalkboard writing. The king of Babylon, Belshazzar, dishonored the golden and silver drinking vessels taken from God's temple in Jerusalem by using them to throw a party. No one but Daniel was able to decipher the meaning of the words written on the wall.

"This is the interpretation of the message; 'mene—God has numbered the days of your kingdom and put an end to it. 'tekel'—you have been weighed on the scales [of righteousness] and found deficient. 'peres'—your kingdom has been divided and given over to the Medes and Persians" (Daniel 5:26–28 AMP).

"In that night was Belshazzar the King of the Chaldeans slain. And Darius the Median took the kingdom, being about threescore and two years old" (Daniel 5:30–31 KJV).

God's judgment came upon him swiftly. When a chalkboard is used to write information, the foretold events are serious and close or imminent. They can't be altered.

Cherubim: Cherubim are angelic beings that serve in sacred offices in heaven and other worlds. They carry out special assignments delegated to them by God. Cherubs are presently guarding the gates to the Garden of Eden, lost by Adam (Genesis 3:24 KJV). They usually appear like innocent babies but are very powerful. If a dreamer encounters them in the dream, it is a sign of divine deliverance that is crucial for the dreamer.

There are also unclean cherubim who were deceived by Lucifer during his failed political campaign in heaven. "And the great dragon was cast out, that old serpent called the Devil and Satan, which deceiveth the whole world: he was cast out into the earth, and his angels were cast out with him" (Revelation 12:9 KJV). These unclean cherubim are still powerful but no longer operate under the commands of God. Unclean cherubs also look like babies but have lost their original form and beauty. Due to their uncleanness, they have become demons. When you encounter clean cherubim looking innocent and beautiful like babies, it's a sure sign that something divine will happen in your life.

Citizenship: If you become a citizen of another country in the dream, it is a clear indication that there's something there for you. It is also a sign that you will live there successfully. When God first spoke to Abram, He instructed him to leave his country and kindred unto a land that God would show Him, where God promised to make him a great nation and a blessing (Genesis 12:1–3 KJV). There are places that God has ordained for every person to live successfully. Because Abram obeyed God wholeheartedly, it was counted unto him for righteousness, and his lineage became great (Romans 4:3, Genesis 15:6 KJV). If you are living in a place not ordained by God for your life, you will encounter setbacks.

When Abraham's nephew Lot lived with Abraham, the blessings of God flowed freely to him. His and Abraham's servants began to quarrel over grazing rights of their numerous animals. At a point, Abraham and Lot parted ways. He was given the choice to live where he chose, but he never sought the will of God (Genesis 13 KJV). When God's judgment came upon Sodom, where Lot chose to live, Lot lost all his wealth and property, including his wife. Things became so terrible for him, and his daughters committed incest with him, raising the cursed tribe of the Moabites (Genesis 19 KJV). Another example of living in a place outside the will of God that attracts dire consequences is the story of the family of Elimelech, chronicled in Ruth in the Bible (Ruth 1:1–22 KJV).

Citizenship in the dream doesn't come with paper passports; you will find that there is a place in your dream that you can visit unhindered. Whenever you visit a particular country, things come to you with ease, and you are happy and comfortable. It is a clear message that you can live there and do well. If you apply for a visa to travel to such a country as seen in the dream, you will be accepted easily. I usually visit the US, UK, and China. It means I have a lot of things to do in those countries. It doesn't mean you must live there permanently. Sometimes citizenship may come by a sign of a foreign visitor, or possibly for a woman, it might mean a place of marriage. Citizenship in the dream is good because it tells you where you are coming from and where you will possibly go.

Clairvoyant: The first perfect man was clairvoyant in nature. The ability to see things from very far distance and interpret it was our very nature. Adam usually saw angels worshiping God in heaven from his garden home. But when the glory or the powers of God left him as a result of going contrary to God's command, that special nature was taken away. Every spirit, whether clean or unclean, is clairvoyant in nature. Every human retains a little of their clairvoyant nature. This quality of life can be developed over time as we grow in our spiritual lives. In our dream state, our soul is very clairvoyant in nature. Our soul body senses danger, hears information or signals from afar, and acts very fast. In the dream world, our true powers are made manifest. We can know how powerful and gifted we are from our dream life experience. A lot of people are great personalities that can perform extraordinary things in the dream that we can't do here on earth. Any soul that is not clairvoyant in the dream state is weak and needs a spiritual upgrade. When we are connected to God, we become more powerful, but if we are not connected to God, we sees death both in spirit and on earth.

Clear: Is related to clairvoyance but clarity relates to vision. Clear is the sight of the soul, which we use to see things in the realm of the spirit. You need clear sight to receive information and revelations in the dream realm. Sight disability is when people lack the ability to see clearly in the spiritual realm. Some people have a terrible dream life; they sleep and have dreams, but they don't see clearly or remember what is dreamt about.

Witchcraft operates with a dark color in the realm of the spirit so that other human souls that visit that area will not see them clearly. So whenever you see dark light in the dream, it means evil perpetrators are hiding something from you. Seeing clearly is a sign that you are spiritually alert and conscious of yourself.

Clergy: To be a clergyman or to find yourself amid of clergy clearly reveals your call and personality. If someone shows you a clergyman performing functions, please observe what he does. What he does in that dream is a divine message to you. For example, if he gives you an envelope or an offering box, it means God is demanding an offering from you. If he preaches a message of salvation, it means God wants you to repent. Dreaming of a man of the clergy is the same thing as being in a church. Whenever you find yourself in the church or spiritual circle, please observe what is happening there or what you are doing there. There is a very important message for you.

Cloth: This is a symbol of an individual's personality. It represents their glory, aura, and well-being. Whenever you see yourself in the dream, you always wear clothes. The original clothes created by God to cover Adam and Eve after the fall were very powerful, dispelling dirt and infection. They also detected danger and scared away dangerous animals.

In the realm of the spirit, I wonder if anyone has ever taken note of the clothes we wear while dreaming. If we are naked in the dream, it is a sure sign of disgrace, humiliation, or regression. Such dreams always come to pass if the incident occurs in the open or in a crowd. If the incident happens in your inner room or circle, then there is hope of reversal of the embarrassing situation.

My younger brother had such a dream of me in 2014. He saw me in a queue, and suddenly when it was close to my turn to be attended to, my trousers fell from my waist. After I left the line to adjust it, I lost my original position and went back to the beginning of the line to start over again. I prayed against it, but at last I became a millionaire even after I found myself driving taxis to survive.

Climate: This talks about seasons of a person's lifetime. "To everything there is a season and a time to every purpose under the heaven" (Ecclesiastes 3:1 KJV).

Clock: This is a symbol for the timeline of events in an individual's life. The normal time frame for every event in the world and everybody's life is tied to time and the clock. The clock is a symbol of time. Whenever you see a clock or any device regarding time in the dream, observe it well, for it has something to tell you about the time schedule for an event in your life.

Cook: Cooking in the dream is a symbol of ritual initiation, covenant, or spiritual assignment. What you prepare or see other people prepare in the dream is a putting together of sacred elements, charms, or esoteric materials to achieve a desired result. Whenever you see people cooking or you see yourself cooking in a manner that suggests you are part of the cooking activity, it means you have already partaken of the ritual. Cooking and eating are different activities. It's better or safer to cook than to eat with your mouth. When you cook or see people cooking, it means you are part of that assignment or initiation.

Cooking in the dream could also reveal a forthcoming ceremony or event to be celebrated by your family (e.g., burial, naming ceremony, etc.). When cooking is done in the open with people gathered, the event that would lead to such ceremony is already established in the spiritual realm. Things done in the open in the dream are hard to reverse.

Coronation: This is a symbol of anointing to a revered, respected, or sacred position. A crown is a sign of reward for righteousness bestowed by God. People who experience this in their dreams are born leaders or elite. Anyone who experiences coronation is a chosen leader by birth.

Some people have been chosen as leaders from birth but don't achieve or attain this greatness even when it's revealed to them in the dream. Joseph had two dreams about his brothers and his parents bowing down to him. In his naivety, he shared it with his brothers, who were very upset with him (Genesis 37 KJV). Their actions set in motion the turmoil and tribulation that eventually brought him to greatness and exaltation.

God uses many symbols to show us our greatness (e.g., riding in a king's chariot). Whenever you see yourself as a subject of coronation or been crowned, please believe it and thank God but don't share it with people unless the prophecy told you to do so.

Correspondence: These are scripted messages usually seen in the dream. The content of those papers are written information for the dreamer. Correspondence in the dream is very important because it's a direct message to the dreamer. Care should be taken to understand what is written in it.

Court: A courthouse is a place of judgment. It is normal for a lawyer or other judiciary personnel to be in the court. In this case, it's a symbol of revelation of events surrounding your workplace. See *career.*

For those who don't work in the judiciary, it's a symbol of legal battle or judgment. God doesn't accuse or judge people. "For sin shall no longer be your master because you are not under the law; but under grace" (Romans 6:14 NIV).

"Then I heard a loud voice in heaven say: Now have come the salvation and the power and the kingdom of our God, and the authority of his Messiah. For the accuser of the brethren who accuses them before our God day and night has been hurled down" (Revelations 12:10 NIV). If you have a dream of being summoned to court without any current court case in reality, it is a sign that diabolical people have set you up. Their judgment will stand without the intervention of God. It is important to pray about dreams like this.

This is why Paul advised the Roman church to strive to live at peace with all men (Romans 12:18 KJV). When evil men accuse you of a wrong you did to them before, your soul will manifest in their evil court unconsciously for judgment. After winning, they can easily project their evil spell onto their victim, who may not wake up from sleep.

Let us say this prayer together. "Any evil man accusing you rightly or wrongly unknown to you before any evil court, may God set you free and acquit you from their case because there is no condemnation of sin against those who believes in Christ. For one who God has set free is free indeed, and who the Lord has blessed no one can curse or judge. Amen!"

Criminals: These are demons or unclean spiritual beings who are vandals, thugs who operate in several lower worlds. They are only found in the lower world, (i.e., below first heaven). They are accused and witch-hunt men for their sins. They don't want men to receive blessings and answered prayers from God. Whenever you see criminals in the dream, it is a sign that your blessings are on the way. Wherever they manifest, they come to steal, kill, and destroy.

These criminal fallen angels are freelance demons. They don't give an account to anyone. Most evil men hire them to kill people and rob them of their spiritual wealth. There are people who were meant to be millionaires who are presently poor because of the activities of these criminals. All the demonic agencies in the lower world use them to execute their will. They can render a rich man poor and close businesses. Whenever God reveals them to you, please double your prayers and fasting; someone has placed you on their satellite without invitation to judge someone on the reason you should not be given anything good.

Cry: The soul weeping is a bad omen for an individual. When the soul cries, a grave or serious situation that will deeply affect the dreamer is imminent. The good news is that some of the events or situations that always lead to us crying or mourning in the dreams do not always come to pass physically. Whenever our soul cries out, it shows a strong objection to that incident. And it's a strong petition or prayer of the soul to God to change that incident or situation. Whatever makes us cry in the dream is real, but most times, God listens to the cry of the soul to stop such ugly occurrences that were to take place. Most people have witnessed their father's burial in the dream and cry bitterly and still wake up crying. It is good to cry out when we see things we don't want to happen on earth. By so doing, we change it by God's grace. Crying is a strong petition prayer we must use to change situations for the good. If we have such an experience in the dream, we must wake up in that mood and start praying to condemn that incident immediately.

Crown: It's a sign of power, authority, dominion given to a person by God to rule and lead people, organizations, and business of life.

Cultivate (farming): It's a good activity in the dream that symbolizes fruitfulness. The item you are farming or cultivating is the real subject of interpretation. Cultivation is good, but what you are cultivating is what justifies the goodness of the activity.

In married women, it symbolizes early pregnancy. To a man, it is a sign of fruitfulness in a current endeavor. However, when someone is cultivating or hunting fish, it means the person has been called to serve God as a fisher of men (Matthew 4:19 KJV). The reasons why Christ used fishes to symbolize men follow:

1. Water represents nations, tribes, dominion, kingdoms, and so on.
2. Fish represent the men and women who occupy those natural kingdoms and dominions.

Christ, in one time, describes eventually what happens to humans, like fish in the water that could be caught by a fisherman's net. Heaven speaks in symbols, codes, and parables.

If the fish you are cultivating are dead or dying, it means you have lost so many souls. Everybody called to serve God is assigned a defined number of people they are destined to preach to before their death. If you are cultivating reptiles or unclean animals, it means the evil deities symbolized by those animals are strongly attached to that person to serve them.

It is good to cultivate a crop that can be harvested quickly. Planting season is cyclical; there are annual, perennial, and biennial crops. Annual crops can only be harvested once a year, while biennial crops take two years. If you plant a biennial crop, it means the blessing will take a longer time to mature than an annual crop. A dreamer should carefully observe what they are planting because there is a time frame attached to that cultivation.

Cult: It is an act of initiation in the dream. If you dream of being in a different cult, different from your religion or circle, it means you have been secretly initiated into another one.

Cunt (vagina): It is represented by snails' and other animals' symbols that best describes the nature of the cunt. Witches use this symbol to charm and imprison carnal and primitive-minded men. It's a magnetic symbol that represents emotional attraction. Whenever the symbol of the cunt is presented to any carnal man, he will be trapped forever. Making love in the dream is an evil act.

PART D

Date: Date is a timeline tied to events. Date is a time sequence upon which events are linked. Dates in the dream correlate with our earthly time, but dream dates and time are not exact (i.e., June 10, 2018, in the dream could be June 10, 2019). It means most of the dates and times in the dream are future. Sometimes dates and time are moved backward to represent an event that has already taken place.

Dejected: This is an emotional experience where an individual is unhappy, disappointed, or feeling hopeless. When we experience any of these feelings in the dream, it portends something sinister. This feeling can be associated with the physical and spiritual realm. Sometimes our emotions can transfer to our astral body during our dream experience. Dejection is a symbol of unhappiness due to a current or impending circumstance. It is important to note the activities, places, and people surrounding you and leading to this state of dejection.

Demarcate: Demarcations are the limits or boundaries that define people, classes, or places of living. Everything in the world and heaven has demarcations or boundaries. If you dream of a demarcation between you and a deceased person, it symbolizes the difference between the land of the dead and the land of the living. If the person you are demarcated from is alive, it shows disunity, quarrel, or apathy between the dreamer and the person.

Demarcation in the dream could be about land boundaries or promotion and demotion. If you see yourself in the office demarcated from your former office and vice versa, it could mean a promotion or demotion. You could see yourself on the altar in the holy assembly; in this case, you are chosen among people of the same class for a special purpose.

Demarcation also speaks of division or separation. In the kingdom of Christ in heaven, there would be demarcation among the twelve tribes of Israel (i.e., separating God's children into various classes of people).

Deposit: If you see yourself deposit waste, money, or any valuable thing into a treasury, bank, refuse, or offering box, it is a sign of blessings. Whatever God blesses you with will be safe and secure. In fact, it's a symbol that represents security, savings, keeping for the rainy day, sowing for the future. If you are blessed in that season, don't spend that money or good thing, as it is a seed destined for harvest. Wherever you invest that money or value, it will be safe.

If you see yourself depositing money into the church offering box, sow seed or give an offering to the church. There is something God wants to use that deposit to do for you. If it is in the bank, then save that money or value. An investment requiring that money will come. Depositing money in the bank tells you that you are rich and blessed. You can't give what you don't have or what God has not entrusted into your hands.

Desire: Desires are triggered by our primitive nature (i.e., the old man). "That ye put off concerning the former conversation, the old man which is corrupt according to the deceitful lusts" (Ephesians 4:22 KJV).

When a person is nurtured according to some certain societal norms, that person borrows those behaviors and character as a second nature, or the person becomes civilized in the approach of things while suppressing his/her original nature.

Desires don't care about our second nature; they are free radical emotions triggered by our primitive nature as humans. Our desires in the dream are our real feelings inside that have not been destroyed by personal experiences about life. The desires to eat, have sex, fight, and swim reveal our true nature. It's a symbol of who we are and what our primitive body is susceptible to or capable of doing. Every person has an area of life that they struggle with. Some desires in us are dead, and some are alive. Whatever desire you encounter in the dream is a pointer to your area of weakness. We need to cut off those desires that influence us to do the wrong thing.

Primitive desires act as a break in the hedge of protection God has put over our lives. This is how evil men and the devil are able to deal with people. They use our primitive desires to enslave us and harm us both in the dream and on earth.

Detain: Detention implies imprisonment by forcefully preventing someone's freedom of movement. Such an experience in the dream communicates police arrest, trouble, and legal battle leading to detention. But in most cases, it reveals the true state of someone's soul. Most human souls are imprisoned spiritually or under someone's command.

As a prisoner, the person doesn't have any right or will of their own and lives at the whims and caprices of the person or organization that detained them. When a person is detained in the dream, they become a slave, a convict awaiting judgment. Detained souls manifest some slavery character trait physically on earth. For example, a womanizer's soul is detained in the spirit and is controlled by the spirit of fornication. At any time, those adulterous demons desire sex; they will use his body to execute their will without resistance. The physical body of such a person becomes a vessel in their hand to operate.

The most dangerous detention is when witches or evil men detain a soul in their coven for judgment. When this happens, that person's physical body is vulnerable to attacks. They may not even wake up from sleep. Evil forces can detain someone's soul in the spirit and cut off their connection with the physical body, leading to their death. Anyone who has such an experience should fast and pray fervently and consult their pastor, prophet, or priest for bailout. Our guardian angel does a lot of work to prevent us from being detained.

Detest (Hate): This is an expression of emotion that symbolizes dislike and disharmony. Hate is an emotional feeling that tells the soul to avoid someone or a thing. If you hate someone in the dream, it means your soul is not compatible with that person. Human souls in the spirit have a powerful emotional sensor that detects danger and other harmful signals from afar. So when the soul emits hate signals to the soul's consciousness, something is wrong with the figure or place they find themselves.

Dethrone: Dethronement is a direct communication of demotion, dismissal, bad luck, and loss of position. Any leader or person in authority who dreams of being dethroned is losing authority, command, dismissal, demotion. Sometimes wise guardian angels can use opposite meaning to reveal a secret to someone they consider a security risk. If the angel gives the person the direct information, the person may not handle the secret, which will jeopardize its fulfillment.

Devil: Seeing the devil in the dream is a sign of an evil presence. The devil has many appearances and symbols.

1. The snake represents the deceptive nature of the devil. "Now the serpent was more crafty (subtle, skilled in deceit) than any living creature of the field which the Lord God had made. And the serpent (Satan) said to the woman, 'Can it really be that God has said, 'You shall not eat from any tree of the garden?" (Genesis 3:1 AMP).
2. The dragon reveals his fighting nature. "And there was war in heaven: Michael and his angels fought against the dragon; and the dragon fought and his angels, and prevailed not; neither was their place found any more in heaven" (Revelation 12:7–8 KJV).

The devil has many symbols attributed to his various natures. Its presence communicates temptation, sickness, trouble, and controversy. No one has ever seen the real devil. The appearances he inhabits are his agents. Your ability to recognize the devil symbol you see tells you that evil men, organizations, or devil agents are in operation.

Diamond: To see a diamond or be in possession of any valuable ornaments, jewelries, or things is a sign of good luck, good fortune. It's a gold mine of opportunity before you. A diamond could represent a nice woman, husband, position of authority, carrier opportunities, business opportunities, and things that can promote someone's personality and progress.

Die: To die in the dream signifies a renewal of someone's soul in the spirit realm. It doesn't mean the person is dead or will die in that season. It's a very good thing to experience death in the dream and still wake up.

We are living in two different worlds simultaneously. Our physical body lives in the physical world, while our soul body lives in the invisible world (i.e., realms of the spirit). These two worlds coexist and function simultaneously with different timelines and laws. An event that shapes our destiny occurs in these two worlds. It means that events that happen to us in the spirit realm are part of us in the physical realm.

Our spirit realm experiences override our physical experiences on earth. Someone may be destined to die physically on earth or have a terrible sickness, but with God's intervention, that person's soul absorbs the illness in a dream. By His intervention, God passes events and temptations that may overwhelm our physical body to be experienced with our soul personality.

There are experiences destined to happen to us in our life's journey. "According as He hath chosen us in Him before the foundations of the world, that we should be holy and without blame before Him in love. Having predestined us into the adoption of children by Jesus Christ to Himself according to the good pleasure of His will" (Ephesians 1:4–5 KJV).

From the foundations of the world, Jesus Christ was destined to be born, live, and die for the sins of the world. "Therefore the Lord himself will give you a sign. The virgin will conceive and give birth to a son, and call him Immanuel" (Isaiah 7:14 KJV).

He became the perfect sacrifice. "Sacrifice and offering you did not desire but my ears you have opened, burnt offerings and sin offerings you did not require. Then I said, Here I am, I have come it is written about me in the scroll, I desire to do your will, my God; your law is within my heart" (Psalm 40:6–8 KJV).

At the last minute, He prayed for the cup of suffering to be taken away from Him but ultimately surrendered to God's will and His destiny. "And he went a little farther and fell on His face and prayed saying O My Father, if it be possible, let this cup pass from Me, nevertheless, not as I will but as Thou wilt" (Matthew 26:39 KJV).

Without the spirit realm experience Christ had in three earthly days (earthly counting), salvation would not have been completed. "I am He that liveth and was dead and behold I am alive forever more, amen I and have the keys of hell and of death" (Revelation 1:18 KJV).

The death experience in our dreams is divine intervention. It doesn't necessarily mean such an event will happen exactly as it has been revealed to you. Having bad experiences in the dream is good because "the secret things belong to the Lord our God but the things revealed belong to us and to our children forever" (Deuteronomy 29:29 KJV). This means we have been given the power to do something about it.

Most bad dreams are prophetic pointers to a future event. When you see someone die, whether you know the person or not, it means something sinister is about happening to that person, and that person needs prayer for divine intervention to avert it. However, God uses other people's faces to show us what may happen to us. So when you see someone die in the dream, it may be referring to you. If you can't handle the information safely, God will use another person's face to show you the experience. For the purpose of intervening for that supposed person, you are actually intervening for yourself. It's advisable to always intercede for other people in prayers because sometimes that person is what is required to deliver you from such a problem.

Dial: To dial a phone number or make a phone call in the dream means connecting to contacts who can assist you. Whenever you make a phone call in the dream, you will surely get a contact for something good. Your phone symbolizes the World Wide Web in the realm of the spirit. It's your link of contact or connecting to people known and unknown. Whenever you place a call, please note and remember the communication. Sometimes the communication is direct, and sometimes it's prophetic (i.e., future events). You can use a phone call to tap into or read someone's mind or secrets. A call in the dream calls our attention to something of great importance in our life. Please don't break your phone or allow it to be stolen in the dream.

Disabled: To be disabled in the dream symbolizes someone's lack of willpower to travel. If someone plans to travel and later sees themselves disabled in the dream, it means the person will encounter difficulty along the line or needs to end the journey.

Being disabled could be an act of deliverance in the sense that slowing down a soul may protect them from a trap on a speed lane. If you ever find yourself disabled in the dream, it's a warning to be careful in your approach to the subject matter of the interpretation.

Being disabled in the dream could also be a reflection of part of someone's appearance in a former life. Every soul can appear in different forms, depending on the environment, time, and place. Someone can appear to be a lion in the dream in order to overcome the situation in that realm. So disability is a form of appearance someone can take in the dream as part of that person's personality.

Discover: (See *consciousness*.) It's the process of growing in self-awareness and self-discovery. It's the process of ascertaining your true identity and hidden self. At birth, every soul loses their true identity and personality. We need to go through the rigors of self-discovery to realize who we are in God's plan for us.

Discuss: It's a channel of information or communication. The details of the information discussed, whether by self or with others, are the subject matter for interpretation.

Dive: It's a type of movement in the dream realm. There are places in the dream where diving is the only mode of travel. Most people who can dive in the dream are linked to heavenly bodies or worlds. If your soul travels to astral worlds or dream worlds in heaven, the soul will probably dive or fly. A deep dive can transport a soul to another world in a split second, using the method of keeping time in the physical world.

Divorce: Divorce in the dream is a sign of separation between a soul and another soul or a soul and other spiritual deities and personalities. Every soul has links to the past. When you divorce in the dream, it implies you are disconnected from that past. For example, people who have spiritual spouses need a divorce in the spiritual realm. So when you experience a divorce or separation between you with some women or men, it means you are delivered from that network. When you notice women or men in the dream don't have access to you like before, then know you have been set free.

Sometimes it's a direct message of controversy with your wife or husband when the dream scenario incident happens with your direct wife or husband.

Dream: Dreams connect your past life experience to your present. When God gives your soul another body in the life civilization, you can still be dreaming of your past life in your present reality. It won't look real, just the way your dream seems like movies. Thought of the past will always crop up. But God will do something about it because it's disturbing. He said He will erase it so that it doesn't come to mind. It's indeed a great privilege for God to know your past and future.

Drink: It is a doing word that symbolizes consuming something. In most cases, drinking symbolizes initiation, covenants, oath, poisoning, oral treatment, inhibition, occupation, or possession. What you drink in the dream matters. For example, drinking blood means initiation or covenant with an entity. What appears to be water or a mere soft drink can actually be the blood of living things concocted to initiate someone. Some drinks in the dream are actually poison, evil, spells, or charms configured in liquid substance to defile the soul body.

Drown: When you are drowning in the dream, it means your life has been changed for good. It's a spiritual exercise where one's old self is buried, and a new one replaces it. Drowning in the dream is a change of personality and character.

Drowning to a fisherman or someone who sails or travels through the seas or waterways is a sign of mishap.

Drowning also means that a problem or situation you find yourself in among people or a person may overcome you. If you are struggling to float or swim out, it means going out of difficulty or struggle.

Dump: This is a sign of rejection.

PART E

Eagle: Seeing an eagle or being in the form of eagle is a very good sign of a strong personality. An eagle is a huge information desk. The image of animals could be used to give information to the dreamer considering their unique features and characteristics. The eagle is the symbol of power, authority, height, royalty, specialty, peculiarity, and defined uniqueness. Anything relating to the eagle has to do with ego, determination, and accuracy. The soul of an eagle gives off the aura of dignity, royalty, strength, and fear, so when you see it, interact with it, for it just shows you are a strong personality or you will be among dignitaries as colleagues or meet one. It shows divine intervention in the case of attack. The circumstances of your encounter with this special bird are the subject of interpretation.

Eat: Eating in the dream opens a gateway between your physical body and the soul. Eating is a metaphysical or seamless process through which the soul body ingests materials. Most foods served in the dream are not real food but are spiritual waves in disguise. Without spiritual maturity, our soul is naïve and can be easily deceived without the spirit of discernment to guide it. Some ailments we suffer in our physical bodies are manifestations of things we pass into the soul body through eating in the dream. Those ailments cannot be cured with physical medication but only by God's intervention.

Eating is not always a bad experience in the dream. If you eat in your church, temple, holy gathering, worshipping ground, congregation, coven altar, or meeting place you are familiar with, it's a sign of union, covenant, spiritual rebirth, oath of allegiance, and protection. Partaking of a meal at these events brings healing, life, spiritual powers, strength, and prosperity. When you personally buy your food or prepare it for yourself, it's an act of putting the soul together, mostly in the process of healing and strength. It's extremely dangerous to eat food you didn't cook or buy with your money. Don't accept free food from unfamiliar or strange faces. Whenever you dream of yourself eating, please consult your pastor or prophet immediately.

Educate: It's the process of receiving new information. There are parts of the brain connected to our mind that cannot be seen with the natural eyes. These are the seat houses of our intelligence. The mind and invisible brain emit waves of ideas, knowledge, thoughts, and visions. The aspect of the brain that creates motion images in the dream is not known by humans, but it lives inside us. Whatever our inner brain gets from the dream world, it emits it to the physical brain to think about it. Education in the dream can be discovery of hidden information already residing in someone's mind.

Egg: Symbolizes wealth, prosperity, richness, success in life, and life-changing opportunities. Whenever you see a lot of eggs in your possession, it reveals your greatness. The amount of eggs in the dream shows how big your success may be. One egg alone is a good fortune.

Possession of eggs in the dream may also represent the number of children a woman will have in her marriage.

Eggs can also represent the fragility of life and should be handled carefully when given to you in the dream. It could be used to appease certain deities or perform spiritual rituals.

Employ: To be hired in the dream is a sign of future employment. To someone who is already employed, it may mean promotion or a new contract. However, if we use reverse meaning to interpret it, it means termination of employment. An individual who already has a job shouldn't see themselves as employed again unless they're dissatisfied with their present job and hoping to get another one.

Endorse: Public contract, advertisement, or any business endorsement is good. Whenever you approve of anything publicly, it must come to pass. It's a straight meaning. Endorsement in the dream is a two-way interpretation. It's either of the sides. It could be a literal interpretation or the opposite, especially in good things. Reverse meaning is used to reveal something to someone to check if they can handle the situation.

Engagement: (See *employment*). In terms of engagement, it is simply an act of demonic possession unless it's prophetic (i.e., revealing a future event). Good events in our lives should have physical manifestations instead of dreams unless it's for prophetic revelations.

Entertain: You are a public person. It shows your typical nature, the real person inside you. Sometimes it reveals happy moments, a good mood, and good things to come. Entertaining people in the dream shows a sign of celebration too. The caliber of people you are entertaining is the subject of interpretation. If they are dignitaries or celebrities, then you are one of them.

Escort: If you are being escorted by military or other uniformed men, it is a sign that you are a big personality. If the person is a dignitary already, it means the person needs security around them in that particular time.

It could also be a sign of impending danger requiring security. If the person is escorted into a prison, police station, or courtroom, then the person has been arrested, and it will become difficult to overcome if it manifests in the physical realm.

It is better for the dreamer to be escorted during a journey or movement. Sometimes the escort team symbolizes angels guarding an individual. It tells how many angels are in charge of the person and their present rank in spiritual hierarchy.

Exam: Exams reveal a test to measure the dreamer's readiness for advancement. At every stage in the business of life, there will be exams for every soul to take before moving forward into the next level of achievement. If you see yourself writing exams in the dream, it's a revelation that your elevation is coming.

Some people are in nursery, primary, secondary, and university stages of progress. If your present stage of education is university and you see yourself writing an exam in secondary school, there is a message for you. If the exam is simple, it means you have crossed over that stage in life maturity. If you have difficulty with the exam, it means there are some character traits you need to change that are not letting you progress. What makes some of us poor today is our character and attitude toward life. We need to overcome certain character traits before success can come our way.

Exams are assessments of our character to ensure our readiness to proceed to the next level. It can also be a wake-up call for one to desist from unwanted behaviors that are hindering their progress. Excelling in exams is good news to the dreamer. When faced with an exam, try to pass it, whether in the dream or physical. Don't be caught unprepared.

Exile: To be in exile in the dream means someone's soul is in captivity. Captivity means having your freedom restricted or being lost without a means of escape. When our soul has been held captive, we can't get the power, energy, and inspiration needed to navigate the physical world. A captive soul lacks vision, inspiration, and a sense of direction in their physical life. A captive person will never achieve full potentials and will always have challenges.

The good interpretation of exile is freedom from diabolical association. If a person who was formerly part of a cult dreams of exile, it means that their soul has been set free. On the other hand, if a good person who belongs to a good organization is exiled, it means that person has been initiated into another evil organization knowingly or unknowingly. It also means the person is involved in abominable things that God doesn't tolerate.

Expose: Exposure in a dream can mean a thing has been established or a bad outcome has been cancelled. If something desirable is exposed in your dreams, it means that thing is established and cannot be changed.

However, when any evil thing done in secret without your consent or knowledge is exposed in the dream, it has been reversed and cancelled. If you're planning something on earth and it is exposed in the dream realm, it means there will be opposition and obstacles that will strive to stop it from happening.

Eye: Eye in the dream represents our vision and ability in the realm of the spirit. Some people are presently blind in spirit; they have dreamless sleep. There are some people who are also physically blind but who still have dreams. We need to have spiritual insight to see ahead, to visualize events hidden in the spiritual realm.

PART F

Faith: Now faith is the assurance (title deed, confirmation) of things hoped for (divinely guaranteed), and the evidence of things not seen [the conviction of their reality—faith comprehends as fact what cannot be experienced by the physical senses] (Hebrews 11:1 AMP). From this definition, it means we can't exercise this faith in a vacuum (i.e., without basis).

In the beginning, when God created the heavens and the earth, He had a clear imagination of what He wanted to achieve. When He spoke out, "Let there be light," there was light (Genesis 1:3 KJV). His power fulfilled His words. The power to manifest our imagination lies in the secret of creation. "By faith we understand that the universe was formed at God's command so that what is seen was made out of what cannot be seen" (Hebrews 11:3 NIV). The only way you can attract God's attention or please Him is to practice faith. "But without faith it is impossible to please Him; for him that cometh to God must believe that he is, and that he is a rewarder of them that diligently seek him" (Hebrews 11:6 KJV). The first step is creating the mental image of what you want to achieve. Next, you must believe that God has the power to accomplish it and it shall come to pass.

In Mark 5, from verse 25 (AMP), the woman with the issue of blood for twelve years believed that if only she could touch the hem of Jesus's garments, she would be made whole. Her faith was so powerful that Jesus felt the virtue had left Him even as they were in a crowd of people. "And he said unto her, Daughter, thy faith had made thee whole; go in peace and be whole of thy plague" (Mark 5:34 KJV).

"But I can promise you this, if you had faith no larger than a mustard see, you could tell this mountain to move from here to there and it would. Everything would be possible for you" (Matthew 17:21 CEV).

It means that even a little faith and belief in His power has the ability to move great things out of their natural places.

Faith is an art acquired by continuous spiritual exercise. "So faith comes from hearing what is told] and what is heard comes by the [preaching of the] message concerning Christ" (Romans 10:17 KJV). If you don't know or hear what God is capable of doing by listening to His words, you will not have faith or trust what He can do. When you abide in Christ, then you understand the secrets of the kingdom, and you start exercising faith with maturity. Faith is not a gift of the Holy Spirit but is a secret of the kingdom that you must practice for it to grow. You can't create a mental image without a timeline. Time is tied to events and creation itself. Anything that doesn't follow a time rule is miracle or magic. So create things that are achievable within a timeline you desire. We must separate miracles or magic from faith. Faith and prayer are interconnected; if you practice one without the other, it becomes an academic exercise or rote recitation. "Do I hear you professing to believe in the one and only God but then observe you complacently sitting back as if you had done something wonderful? Demons do that but what good does it do to them? Use your heads! Do you assume that you can cut faith and works in two and not end up with a corpse on your hands? Wasn't our ancestor Abraham made right with God by works when he placed his son Isaac on the sacrificial altar? Isn't it obvious that faith and works are yoked partners, that faith expresses itself in works?" (James 2:19–21 AMP).

When we practice faith, we must be careful not to alter the divine order in our life because we have the right to choose. We must seek God's divine revelation first before exercising faith. When Jesus was teaching His disciples how to pray, the first line of His prayer read, "Thy Kingdom come. Thy will be on earth as it is in heaven" (Matthew 6:10 KJV). This shows that we should exercise faith in harmony with God's will. And so we must not abuse faith as a practice for self-aggrandizement. Our physical senses must be put to use to exercise faith. You shouldn't pray from vain words from your head or intelligence, but you must pray from your mindset (i.e., from the substance you have created already through meditation).

While you are praising God and meditating inside you, you are creating substance of chains of events, images, and motions of what you want from the Father. When you begin praying, you are pouring out the words of God on your desires to come to pass.

"It is the spirit that gives life; the flesh conveys no benefit [it is of no account]. The words I have spoken to you are spirit and life [providing eternal life]" (John 6:63 AMP).

It means there is a spirit God put in every word spoken by God. The Word of God is sufficient to address every situation in our lives. It is so important to study the Word of God. In the exercise of faith, you hold God to His promises by knowing those promises for yourself. Knowing what His Word says concerning you comes from your study of the Word of God. Meditating on the Word of God is another important exercise in the process of faith. "This book of the law shall not depart out of thy mouth; but thou shall meditate therein day and night, that thou may observe to do according to all that is written therein; for then thou shalt make thy way prosperous and then thou shalt have good success" (Joshua 1:8 KJV).

The best way to imbibe a new skill is with consistent practice, like exercising a muscle; the more you exercise, the stronger your body gets. This natural law applies to our faith walk. When we exercise our faith in God, it becomes our second nature in Christ. We can practice faith to the point that our body can unconsciously tap into God's authority and bring instantaneous results.

If you want to do anything in your life, first develop it in a picture or image and keep it on your altar. If you are exercising faith, you must always purge yourself of movies, music, and other distracting things. You can also fast to give your mind clarity of purpose. Watching TV and even unnecessary conversations tend to alter your own creations in your mind. Whenever the mental body has downloaded so many images, it purges it by creating dreams or other methods not well understood to remove it. You must clear your body of distortion.

Now regarding physical objects, you must connect to something with the Word of God or an image object or mental motion to build your faith on it and water it with the Word of God every day until it manifests. In the case of Abraham, God connected him to the heavenly bodies (i.e., stars) to visualize the greatness of his future generations (Genesis 5:15 KJV). Each time Abraham sees the stars of heaven, he remembers the promises of God concerning his future generations. Images and desires are all seeds of creation. You can sow it in your mind, water it with prayers, and nurture it to maturity. The words we speak are fertile seeds that can germinate. "Death and life are in the power of the tongue. And those who love it and indulge it will eat its fruit and bear the consequences of their words" (Proverbs 18:21 AMPC). Continue to confess the good words of God over your life even in times of trouble.

Fail: Failing is a direct indication of failure.

Fall: Falling means returning to your original point. Falling is a means of movement in the dream realm. When you fall in the dream, you usually wake up. There are places or heights you will climb to in the dream, and only falling will allow your journey back to your original point of departure.

Farming: Farming represents the process of sowing and reaping success. When a man who is not a farmer is farming in the dream, it means the man will get a job, contract, or project that will soon be successful. For a woman who is married, it could be a sign of pregnancy or a sign of success in what she is presently doing.

Feeding: If you see yourself in the dream feeding people, it means the following:

- You are a great person who people will benefit from (i.e., you are a destiny helper).
- You need to organize a get-together to do freewill, giving to a particular set of people. If you are feeding

children, then it should be children only. Always check the set of people you are feeding.

- It shows you have been called to be a humanitarian or philanthropist. You need to do humanitarian services for God to do something for you.

In fact, it's a good thing to feed people in the dream. When that happens, replicate it physically to attract the blessing of God in your life.

Feel (emotional): These are signals transmitted from our soul to the physical body and vice versa. The physical body can send sexual urges, hunger pangs, and other signals to the soul body to generate mental motion images, imaginary motion images, or characters to help the physical body ease itself from such an urge. When such things take place, feelings or emotion will take place to create an effect. If feelings or emotions are not felt when dreaming, then the cord connecting the body and soul is not synchronized.

Fighting: This is a method of self-defense programmed by the soul to defend itself from external attack. Fighting in the dream reveals external attack or controversy coming through a person or a medium. Whenever you stand and fight a thing, person, animal, or monster, those things are not able to overpower you.

Take careful note of the thing or person you are fighting with because it is a clear revelation of where the attack is coming from. If you fight with an angel like Jacob did, it means you are struggling with heavenly agencies to take your destiny. Fighting is very good in the dream because it is a way of overcoming troubles. If you always run from things, it means you are spiritually weak. Little problems can overwhelm you, so you need a lot of prayers for intervention. When you withstand a thing in a fight and defeat it, it may not come again.

Flood: Means a group of people and an event or tribulation caused by events or people. It shows trouble of a great magnitude that will affect a lot of people. If you are swept away by a flood, it means the trouble will overcome you. But if you walk on it or in it, you will go through the people or trouble successfully. A flood that comes with a heavy current is a critical controversy or trouble that will sweep across the land. When it overruns buildings, then such an event will lead to devastation of human properties and life. It's better to see a calm flood you can walk on or through.

Find: When you find something in the dream, it means you have located your destiny, your star, your luck. Whenever you find anything you were looking for, it means you have located your blessing and rediscovered your lost glory. You will surely receive a surprise and good luck in a short while.

Evil forces are always against the progress of individuals, which is why dreaming of finding something hidden is good.

Forget: There exists a passage between the physical body and the soul. This passage is separated by darkness (i.e., sleep or a state of inactivity). While in the dream realm, every event will be recorded unconsciously by our mental brain, but while returning through the dark passage to earth, we forget some things. Our physical body records everything happening to us consciously and unconsciously, even when we feel we have forgotten. To forget dreams is common, but later an event may trigger you to remember the dream. Nothing is totally lost in our memory, but the information is hanging in some passages of the dream realm.

Whenever any soul is reborn on earth, the soul passes through the dark light, which wipes out the memories of their former lives. After a certain age, some of these memories will start flashing back. It was at the age of twelve that Jesus Christ recognized His divine sonship. "The next day they found him in the Temple seated among the teachers, listening to them and asking questions. The teachers were all taken with him, impressed with the sharpness of his answers ... He said, why were you looking for me? Didn't you know I had to be here, dealing with the things of my Father?' But they had no idea what he was talking about" (Luke 2:46–49 MSG).

Forgive: To be forgiven in the dream is a very good experience because it's a sign that you have been forgiven. If you forgive someone in the dream, it means God wants you to reconcile with that person. There are difficulties we are encountering today because we lack a forgiving spirit. Withholding forgiveness hinders prayers and success. "In the same way, you husbands, live with your wives in an understanding way [with great gentleness and tact, and with an intelligent regard for the marriage relationship] as with someone physically weaker, since she is a woman. Show her honor and respect as a fellow heir of the grace of life so that your prayers will not be hindered or ineffective" (1 Peter 3:7 AMP).

To be God's friend, we must forgive people who offend us. "But if you do not forgive others their trespasses, neither will your Father forgive your trespasses" (Matthew 6:15). We must not wait until we dream about it before we obey. It's a command to forgive because God forgave us and sent Christ to die for us while we are yet sinners. "But God clearly shows and proves His own love for us by the fact that while were still sinners, Christ died for us" (Romans 5:8 KJV).

"If anyone says 'I love God' and hates his own brother, he is a liar; for who does not love his brother who he has seen cannot love God whom he has not seen" (1 John 4:20 ESV).

"Lord how often will my brother sin against me, and I forgive him? As many as seven times? Jesus said to him, 'I do not say to you seven times but seventy times seven'" (Matthew 18:21–22 ESV).

Forgiveness is integral to our walk as children of God.

Freedom: This means liberation or liberty. When you are freed from a cage or prison or trouble, you are free indeed. "If the son therefore shall make you free, ye shall be free indeed" (John 8:36 KJV). It's a good experience that helps the soul move forward in life. Any day you see yourself freed, you have been liberated from a chain or from bondage. From that time henceforth, new things will start happening in your life, but don't go back to the old ways.

Freeze: Freezing is a mysterious current used by demons to hold someone's soul. They usually send it like an electric cold current wave through the ground space to prevent the soul's movement. Whenever you are frozen in the dream, it means you have been charmed by evil forces. In most cases, your foot will feel glued to the ground, and as a result, you cannot move your foot or body. Such a current can paralyze some parts of the body. When you wake up from such an attack, you may not be able to move as usual. The earth surface has a current that can drain life from humans or anything that has energy or force. When a human body receives or absorbs the freezing effect, it will cause shock leading to paralysis.

Fire: It's a strong symbol of warfare. Fire symbolizes gunpowder, and any object that is propelled by powder, fossil fuels, heat, or a current appears as fire. When moving or flying objects fall and explode into fire, it means someone has willfully caused a disaster.

Fire also symbolizes the divine power of God. When God appears with the symbol of fire, He is aggrieved or angry. "Now the people became like those who complain and whine about their hardships, and the Lord heard it. When the Lord heard it, His anger was kindled and the fire of the Lord burned among them and devoured those in the outlying parts of the camp" (Numbers 11:1 AMP). It is a sign of war and not peace. Fire is not a peaceful sign.

Fire is also a sign of deliverance, renewal, action, and revival. "John answered them all, 'I baptize you with water. But one who is more powerful than I will come, the straps of whose sandals I am not worthy to untie. He will baptize you with the Holy Spirit and fire'" (Luke 3:16 AMP).

"They saw what seemed to be tongues of fire that separated and came to rest on each of them. All of them were filled with the Holy Spirit and began to speak in other tongues as the Spirit enabled them" (Acts 2:3–4 KJV).

Demons are always afraid of fire because it's a powerful manifestation of God's divine power. "What communion hath light with darkness" (2 Corinthians 6:14b KJV).

Fly: (See *airplane*.) Flying above the earth in the dream means you possess the powers to beat the earth's magnetic force. It is an indication of great spiritual authority; no terrestrial powers can harm such a person.

Anyone person who flies in the air is related to heavenly kingdoms, and their domain in the realm covers heaven and earth. Some demons don't operate in the air but on land only. So when they launch an attack from earth, God may intervene by giving you wings to fly above them. Flying can also be a defense system to run away from danger.

Some diabolical people initiated in the kingdom of witchcraft can also fly, although their powers are limited.

PART G

Gambling: Gambling in the dream, for someone who doesn't gamble in real life, means the activity they are currently engaged in is a game of chance. There is a high probability of success or failure depending on the circumstances interpreted in the dream. The interpretation of the dream will aid the dreamer in knowing what actions to take that would help them succeed.

For someone who gambles in reality, it is a revelation that the person has been possessed by the spirit of gambling. Gambling can be very addictive, and it takes the power of God to deliver someone possessed from its power over their mental body.

Garden: A garden is a place where beautiful things reside. A garden is a symbol of good fortune and fruitfulness. When the garden has fruits, it's a good sign of things to come. When the fruits are ripe, harvested, and eaten, it means there is good fortune coming your way. For most married women who experience harvesting fruits in a garden, it usually means pregnancy.

Gather: Gathering things in the dream is synonymous with harvesting. It's a sign of claiming what belongs to you. Something meant for you is due to come to you. There are symbols of things someone may gather that symbolize problems, slavery, or bondage, depending on the representation of such symbol or image. For example, the gathering of snakes is a sign of big trouble or temptation; the gathering of snails may mean limited progress. When you gather fruit or mostly edible things or good animals, it's a sign of good things.

Gift: Giving or receiving gifts is a sign of good fortune in the dream communication. When you give a gift, it means you should give a gift to someone. Mark the symbol of the gift(s) you gives and the nature of the receiver. That will tell you what to use and who to physically present the gift to.

Giving gifts sows a seed for you. "A man's gift maketh room for him and bringeth him before great men" (Proverbs 8:16 KJV).

When you accept gifts from someone, it means someone will bless you. If the gifts you accept are divine images or sacred symbols, it's a sign of a spiritual call (for example, receiving a Bible as a gift).

There are gifts we should vehemently refuse in the dream, like eggs in a calabash or native pot. Receiving such gifts is a summons from an occult organization.

Giggle (laughter): Laughing is an expression of happiness. Its occurrence in a dream calls a dreamer to pay attention to a sudden surprise.

Glad (happiness): Gladness is an emotional feeling of true happiness flowing from the soul. Happiness was humanity's original nature that was lost after the fall of man. When a dreamer is divinely happy, nothing should disrupt that state, even when the dreamer wakes up from sleep. Strive to be happy and avoid sin and unrighteousness because in that state of happiness, the body and soul will attract good things to you. "Thou hast loved righteousness and hated iniquity; therefore God, even thy God hath anointed thee with the oil of gladness above thy fellows" (Hebrews 1:9 KJV).

God: God is a spirit. He does not reside in a natural body. He appears with symbols. "The [presence of the] Lord was going before them by day in a pillar of cloud to lead them along the way and in a pillar of fire by night to give them light, so that they could travel by day or night" (Exodus 13:21 KJV).

"And behold the Lord passed by and a great and strong wind rent the mountains and brake in pieces the rocks before the Lord, but the Lord was not in the wind, and after the wind, an earthquake but the Lord was not in the earthquake: and after the earthquake a fire, but the Lord was not in the fire: and after the fire a still small voice" (1 Kings 19:11–12 KJV).

Sometimes we're expecting the presence of God to be a mighty thunder with plenty of fanfare. "But God has chosen the foolish things of the world to confound the wise; and God has chosen the weak things of the Lord to confound the strong" (1 Corinthians 1:27 KJV).

We can feel Him, perceive His presence, and hear His voice, but we can't see Him. "But He said; you cannot see My face, for no man shall see Me and live!" (Exodus 33:20 KJV).

When God appears to you in any symbol, He is magnificent and glorious. "When Moses came down from Mount Sinai with the two tablets of the Testimony in his hand, he did not know that the skin of his face was shining [with a unique radiance] because He had been speaking with God" (Exodus 34:29 KJV). His presence takes away every evil disease, curse, and bad thing. It is a glorious experience to see God's symbol. In the history of humanity, people who have seen God in the dream are usually transformed after their experience.

Gold: Treasure that is lasting and permanent. When you see or wear gold, the event it is associated with will stand the taste of time. Gold trinkets are for strong personalities, and if seen by a dreamer, it means dignity has been bestowed on the person likened to a royal person. When gold is given to you as a gift, it means you will soon be promoted or elevated. If the gift is a crown, it is a sign of coronation as a ruler, leader, or king.

Grief: See *groan* or *cry*.

Gun: It's a symbol of weaponry in the dream. Whenever you see it held by people or see yourself in possession of it, it communicates an imminent attack, fight. Guns can kill the soul as well as the physical body.

If an enemy shoots at you with a gun lesser than your soul strength, you won't die (i.e., you soul can't disconnect from your body). But if it's a big gun that your soul can't withstand, the person may not wake up from sleep. Gun sends vibration and shock waves to the soul that can disconnect it from the physical body. Some people never wake up from sleep because they were shot in the dream.

When you are in possession of it in the dream, it shows the level of your spiritual rank or maturity in the spirit. When you shoot at your opponent with a gun in the dream, that enemy is gone. It is a big defense when you possess it. There are people who gunshots cannot kill because the spirit of God is their defense. "Because thou hast made the Lord which is my refuge, Even the most High, thy habitation; there shall no evil befall thee, neither shall any plague come nigh thy dwelling" (Psalm 91:10–11 KJV).

A knife symbolizes the total killing of a thing.

Gorilla: A gorilla is an animal with a lot of physical power and strength. Although many animals represent kingdoms, dominions, and circles of beings in a particular location, monkeys and gorillas represent the plant kingdom.

Plants have souls like other living things. Most times, the soul of a plant appears in the forms of different animals. Plants that can invigorate the strength of a person appear in the form of monkeys, chimpanzees, and gorillas.

When this sort of plant is formulated into voodoo magic or recipe, it can give supernatural strength to fight and conquer. The symbol of the gorilla is an aphrodisiac. They are stronger than a human's soul in the realm of the spirit. If you possess the soul of a gorilla, you will be nearly impossible to defeat. They are not peaceful but rather ready for a fight with humans. When you fight with a gorilla or encounter them in the dream, it's a sign of strength and vigor in you. Your spiritual energies attract gorillas in the dream to test you in a fight. There are herbs and magical liqueur and charm recipes that add power and strength to an individual. When they take it, the gorilla or any of their family species will appear to test that person in a show of power.

Gospel: This is the message of the coming of the Messiah and salvation that ought to be preached to the whole world. "This good news of the kingdom [the gospel] shall be preached throughout the whole world as a testimony to all the nations, and then the end [of the age] will come" (Matthew 24:14 KJV).

Whenever you dream of hearing the Gospel, the message is intended to change your life and then be shared to others. Adhering to the words of the Gospel will bring life and liberty. "The Spirit of the Lord is upon me, because he hath anointed me to preach the gospel to the poor; he hath sent me to heal the brokenhearted, to preach deliverance to the captives, and recovering of sight to the blind. To set at liberty them that are bruised and to preach the acceptable year of the Lord" (Luke 4:18–19 KJV).

Gossip: It's a dream symbol that reveals what has been spoken in secret concerning an individual. Gossip is abhorrent to God. "These six things doth the Lord hate; Yea seven are an abomination unto him; a proud look, a lying tongue and hands that shed innocent blood, a heart that deviseth wicked imaginations, feet that are swift to mischief, a false witness that speaketh lies and he that soweth discord among brethren" (Proverbs 6:16–19 KJV).

The content and people engaged in the gossip are important because it's the subject of attention and interpretation by the dreamer. Although people gossip all the time, sometimes those things said can become fiery darts of evil that manifest in a dreamer's life. We use our sensory organs to perceive the gossip. We see the people involved with our eyes and hear the words they have spoken with our ears.

When secret things are revealed to us in a dream, it is for our private consumption. It is intended to make us cautious around the people concerned in the dream and for the saving of our souls. It is not advisable to confront the parties involved, or your guardian angels will refrain from revealing things to you.

Government: Represents the rulers and leaders of the geographical location you reside. Seeing the governor or government of the place where you live and do business means you are welcome and will prosper.

Governor: If you attend the same event with the governor, it is desirable because it indicates that elevation and success are around the corner.

When a governor or ruler visits you at home, it is a sign of permanent favor from God to your family. In reality, if a governor visits your home, it improves your status, and the perception that the community has of you will be upgraded.

A governor represents the commander in chief of spiritual forces and the physical government of your town. When they visit you or you find yourself with them in the dream, it means you have been initiated into the circle of great people on earth and in the realm of the spirit.

Grade: See *class*.

Graduate: This is a sign of success on the path that you are currently on. Being a graduate is a symbol of success. Whatever you graduate from in your dreams is a clear message from the Lord that your troubles, temptations, hardships, and training are over. The next thing is to be rewarded and start experiencing divine favor.

Gramophone/microphone: These are symbols of communication in the dream realm. When a gramophone is used to play a message in the dream, or a microphone is used to announce a message, that message is for public consumption. Such messages are established, and there is a strong warning to obey because it attracts witnesses. The content of the message from such symbols is the object of interpretation.

Grandparent: These are the symbols chosen by guardian angels to reveal a secret or give advice or instruction, especially concerning a family matter. These symbols are used to give the message an air of importance and gravity.

There is a popular saying, "What the elders see while sitting, the young ones climbing to the top of an Iroko tree will not see."

This saying highlights the wisdom, judgment, and importance of an elderly person in society. Messages regarding family matters, family issues, and personal matters always come through these parental figures. Their love for their good children, selfless attitude, and life experience make their messages important to adhere to.

Sometimes evil men try to deceive dreamers by wearing the faces of their loved ones in the dream. This is why the content of message and the spirit of discernment are important qualities for a dreamer to possess. The attitude of your grandparents' image in the dream will quickly reveal their intention. When God uses the image of your grandparents to reveal something to you, it will be an informative experience.

Graven image: This is a sign of idols or pagan religion. If you dream of a graven image, try to remember it when you wake up. You can use the graven image to determine what pagan or occult organization visited you. It is a serious issue you must pray against. Graven images can't appear in your dream unless you have ties with it or someone is trying to make you associate with it. What you don't know will not know you. "A curse you don't deserve will take wings and fly away like a sparrow or swallow" (Proverbs 26:2 CEV). Amen!

Gravity: Gravity is a natural phenomenon by which all things with mass or energy are attracted to one another. On earth, gravity gives weight to physical objects. This is why humans do not fall off the earth even though it is continuously in motion.[39] In the realm of the spirit, there is a force separating the earth and heaven. "And God said; Let there be a firmament in the midst of the waters and let it divide the waters from the waters. And God made the firmament and divided the waters which were under the firmament from the waters which were above the firmament and it was so. And God called the firmament Heaven" (Genesis 1:6–8 KJV).

The law of gravitational force operates in the spirit. Water, earth, and air are different plains or kingdoms with different laws. There are forces like gravity that hold them apart, and whenever you want to enter, you must be permitted to have access by your guardian angel or by your level of spiritual maturity. When Christ lived on earth, He defied the laws of the earth. "And in the fourth watch of the night Jesus went unto them, walking on the sea. And when the disciples

---

[39] www.wikipedia.com.

saw him walking on the sea, they were troubled saying; "'t is a spirit; and they cried out in fear" (Matthew 14:25–26 KJV).

In the dream realm, our soul is a spirit, and its level of consciousness and spiritual maturity can enable it to beat the gravitational force. The ability to fly, walk on water, and travel to other kingdoms is reserved for special souls.

It's easy to travel on earth and to underground kingdoms because it's our ancestral place, but sea, air, and heaven are for special souls. When you have access to these plains without any gravitational force restricting your movement, then you are a recognized soul before God.

Grazing: If you are leading sheep or animals to graze when you are not a shepherd, it means you are called to be a leader or person of God.

Ground: Represents the earth. The ground has life. From the ground, the plants grow, which gives animals and humans sustenance. Ground symbolizes dust, but the ground is not life. "By the sweat of your face you will eat bread until you return to the ground, for from it you were taken. For dust you are and to dust you shall return" (Genesis 3:19 KJV). The ground is humanity's origin. It also symbolizes earthly, humanity, and terrestrial things.

In the spiritual realm, the ground is a network that connects to so many worlds. It stores energies, and elements originate from it. The ground is just a covering of the earth. In pagan countries, the ground symbolizes the gods that are there. For instance, in Nigeria, libation is poured out as an offering on the ground.

Guardian angel: As soon as we are born, God assigns us a guardian angel to guard us and report our activities on daily basis. "Are not all the angels ministering spirits sent out [by God] to serve (accompany, protect) those who will inherit salvation?" (Hebrews 1:14 AMP).

When we sleep, they guard and watch over our souls. They defend us against prowling demons. At death, they return to heaven and close our files or records. As we grow up in the knowledge of God, having a lot to accomplish on earth, God usually sends other guardian angels to an individual at every stage of life with different work to do. "Do not forget to show hospitality to strangers, for by so doing, some people have shown hospitality to angels without knowing it" (Hebrews 13:2 KJV).

Our guardian angels partner with the Holy Spirit to minister to us. We wrestle not against flesh and blood but principalities and powers and the rulers of this world (Ephesians 6:12 KJV). Our guardian angels are always there to minister, defend, and look out for us. Review Daniel 10 (KJV). In this scripture, the angel of the Lord revealed that although Daniel's prayers had been answered from day one, the prince of Persia had resisted him for twenty-one days.

It is important to be in tune with our guardian angels; we should not do things they don't like. A lot of people have done bad things that have made their guardian angels angry and less effective. "And do not bring sorrow to God's Holy Spirit by the way you live. Remember He has identified you as his own, guaranteeing that you will be saved on the day of redemption" (Ephesians 4:13 NLT).

PART H

Harm: To be harmed in the dream is a message of caution. There are predestined incidents, but by God's grace and intervention, we only experience the harm in the dream. When we suffer such an incident in the dream, it may be diverted entirely or experienced to a lesser degree.

The interpretation of the dream depends on what part of our body was injured. A wound on your leg indicates the harm is associated with movement like a journey. If the injury is on your arm, it means the work of your hands might be unsuccessful or bring mishap. A head injury is associated with plans, while an injury to your sexual organs is a serious warning against a sexual adventure.

Harvest: Harvest is generally a sign of good luck and success in your endeavors. It is good to harvest fruits, vegetables, or mushrooms—anything that involves sowing and reaping. Harvest is a personal revelation that should not be revealed to everyone. Anyone who dreams of harvest should give glory and thanks to God while they wait expectantly.

Heal: Healing is a symbol of divine good health. When you take medical treatment in the dream or get healed of a particular disease in the dream, it means God has healed you permanently. It is also a sign of sickness or a serious health challenge in your life that may occur in a short while. A lot of ill health we suffer from is from the pit of hell.

Hear: It means your sense of hearing is open spiritually. The human soul reads minds or understands things by reading the minds of other souls or entities. They also perceive things by intuition, and the human soul uses telepathy to communicate. These were human capacities to communicate in our first perfect nature. Most of these qualities are practiced by our soul but not the physical body without divine training. There are times your soul communicates in a language that is alien to the dreamer. In such cases, the dreamer will use other alternate senses of communication to know if there is danger to run away. If someone hears other people's language in the dream, that person has a high level of communication abilities (i.e., spiritual maturity).

Heaven: Heaven is a symbol of divinity. It is the dwelling place of God, His angels, and righteous men of old. There are many dimensions to heaven. Life starts from hell to heaven.

In our world, there are four worlds inhabited by beings. The first is hell or the underworld, and the next is the sea, the earth, and the first heaven. The sea and the earth reside on the same plane, and the inhabitants of these realms interact. Each of these worlds have their own laws, ways of living, and rulers. All the souls living in these worlds have sinned and fallen short of the glory of God.

All the souls and beings living in the universe of these four worlds have sinned due to the fall of Adam and have come short of the glory of God (Romans 3:23 KJV). After we die, our bodies go back to the earth, while our souls transcend to hell. Before the sacrifice of Christ (John 3:16 KJV), the king of hell held every person who was dead in their world. After Jesus was crucified, He went down to hell and defeated the devil. He took the keys of hell and death (Revelations 1:18 KJV) and liberated the trapped souls who believed in him.

Hell is real; it is total and absolute separation from God's blessings and favor. It's a place of suffering, pain, and anguish. No child of God lives in hell; they have all been liberated by the death and resurrection of Jesus Christ. The gates of hell can't prevail against any child of God (Matthew 16:17–19 KJV). So when we die now, our souls will be with God in a special world, awaiting the first resurrection.

Interpretation: whenever you dream of heaven, it is a test of discipleship. It's an appraisal for every child of God to know their status in the afterlife. As a child of God, heaven is our final home, a place of eternal hope where God resides. Heaven is associated with the wonders, rapture, resurrection, or coming of Christ. It is a reminder to check your preparation integrity.

Dreaming of heaven is also a sign of one's death. Be careful to note the circumstances occurring in the dream because it has to do with your life and future in heaven. Whatever you encounter in heaven is a general warning for the world, and you must disseminate it as a witness. Anyone who sees heaven is a heavenly candidate; heaven is interested in you. It is more desirable to dream of heaven than hell.

Hell: Hell is the world below our earth. It is also known as the underworld. It's a world like our world with spiritual entities. There are countless evil spirits who have been banished to hell. It's a home for every creature of God that commits evil, including animals, plants, and spirits. It's a cruel world for sinners and disobedient children of God. It's described as a lake of burning fire (Revelation 20:10 KJV). The description of "burning fire" is a symbolic representation of the desolation that exists there.

When Adam first stepped into our world from the Garden of Eden, the earth might as well have been hell to Adam until he got used to it. "And unto Adam he said, because thou hast hearkened unto the voice of thy wife … cursed is the ground for thy sake; in sorrow shalt thou eat of it all the days of thy life; thorns also and thistles shall it bring froth to thee; and thou shall eat the herb of the field; in the sweat of thy face shalt thou eat thy bread, till thou return unto the ground; for out of it wast thou taken; for dust thou art and unto dust shalt thou return" (Genesis 3:17–19 KJV).

In hell, there is no opportunity for repentance or mercy. Whatever you are is how you will be seen and treated without mercy. You have been warned. Hell is real!

A dreamer can't visit hell in a first sleep dream; one needs to go into a deeper level of unconsciousness. It is easier to visit heaven than to descend to hell. A clear indication that you are in hell is that you are surrounded by dead people. Make note of whatever you witness while you're there because you're on a mission directed by God. Dead souls in hell are not permitted to come out, but you can visit there and come back to earth.

I went to hell one day to see my late father who had offended me before he died. When I got there, I saw it was a terrible place, and I saw him crying, begging me for forgiveness; I cried with him and forgave him. That event is very important in my life. He released my blessings he was holding before he died. There are cases that require you to visit hell to get it done. If you visit hell or heaven by God's permission, no authority will harm or prevent your movement. Any person on this journey doesn't need to wake up quickly or be woken up suddenly, or else he/she will be disconnected from getting the complete message or revelation. Third-level dreaming is very dangerous for the soul of the dreamer. The person has to regain consciousness on two levels before returning to earth.

There are uninvited guests in hell. Anyone whose life was wrongfully terminated by evil forces or died prematurely may end up there. The soul's guardian angel might make a case for that soul to be returned to earth. Visiting hell or going to the land of the dead uninvited is a sure sign of death hanging over the dreamer's head. That person needs to reverse that decision or movement by special assignment and prayers.

If you dream of dead people coming to attack, talk, or show themselves to you, it is an indication that someone is invoking dead, evil spirits to kill or poison you. These evil spirits can wear the faces of the dead to execute their mission. Interacting with hell or dead, evil spirits is bad. When you wake up, please cleanse yourself with special prayers and a bath. That kind of bath should be like baptism, totally disconnecting yourself from dead, evil spirits; otherwise, the aura or the dead will be following you.

Hide: If you successfully hide in the dream from your enemies or your pursuers or from some people against you, it means the following:

- You have disappeared from their view.
- You are invisible.
- You are covered by God's protection and cannot be reached.

Summarily, when you hide successfully, you are saved and protected by God.

History: History reviews past, present, and future events that transcend our physical existence on earth. Without history, we are lost.

Holy: This is a sacred symbol of purity. "But just as he who called you is holy, so be holy in all you do; for it is written: 'Be holy because I am holy'" (1 Peter 1:15–16 KJV).

Home: When we dream of home, it is referring to historical events or symbols telling or giving us information about a situation. A home in the dream could be represented by trees, a bed, or a bus. When the information is about the past, the manner of home will look archaic, like a mud or thatch house. Good-looking homes could be used to describe the future events or situations. Home is also used to describe your privacy, your defensive walls of protection in the dream.

Honey: Honey is a symbol of wealth, blessing, and good fortune. Any form you see honey in, whether in the pot, beehives, or bottle, it's a sign of blessing to the dreamer's family. "Hence I have said to you, 'you are to possess their land and I Myself will give it to you to possess it, a land flowing with milk and honey.' I am the Lord your God, who has separated you from the peoples" (Leviticus 20:24 KJV).

Hospital: Dreaming of a hospital is a sign of ill health and visitors. To a sick person, a hospital is a symbol of recovery, while to the healthy, it is a sign of ill health or warning to desist from unhealthy habits. A hospital could be seen as a sign of accommodating people (i.e., visitors).

Human: These are the physical entities presently existing in the world.

PART I

Iceland: Communicates life.

Idea: An idea is a wave of knowledge from our mind or another mind. Most ideas are waves of thoughts or knowledge from other beings or worlds. The human mind is ancient, but our fallen nature may not allow us to explore it deeply. Our personal experiences through our life transitions across different worlds are stored in our subconscious minds. During dream states, stored thoughts, knowledge, and experiences manifest to the soul mind as ideas. Sometimes ideas manifest in the form of motion pictures, events, or dramatic art. A lot of things we dream about are actually ideas playing out from our innermost mind.

Identify: Identifying individuals or people is not static. Identifying people in the dream is sometimes difficult, especially when it involves unknown faces. The human memory, which the soul uses for recognition and storage, is very short and insufficient to trace a backlog of historical events stored in the soul's subconscious mind. If someone lost their father while they were young, accurately recalling the father's face as an adult would be difficult without the aid of pictures. It would be difficult for them to identify the father in the dream when God may decide to use the late father's symbol to communicate. Every person we usually meet in the dream realm is connected to us in one way or another. God uses personalities, images, symbols, events, and experiences we are familiar with to communicate with us. When strange symbols or images are used, we need wisdom to unravel the interpretation (Daniel 4:8 KJV).

The appearance of an image in the dream may have multiple interpretations or identification codes. Someone may manifest as a lion and later manifest as a rat. What is fundamental in identifying things in the dream is to know the characteristics of that thing to identify the interpretation code.

Idle: To be idle in the dream is bad. The only place people are idle is in hell. Human and other entities are busy in all spheres of their lives. So it is bad to see yourself idle in the dream. When someone is rendered idle in the dream, it means such a person is no longer productive.

Idol: The presence of an idol in any form in the dream is a manifestation of evil appearance in your life. The shape and appearance of the idol will tell the dreamer the kind of deity or evil appearance the idol represents.

Ill (sickness): This is a symbol of ill health. In a short while, the sickness will manifest physically. When we feel ill in the dream, it is a sign that we are sick already, but sometimes God is using the reverse meaning to restore our health. Ill health or sickness in the dream is actually divine intervention to prevent a worse outcome. It is a good sign of intervention for something very serious.

Immigrant: Dreaming of being an immigrant in another country or place means relocation. Seeing an immigrant suggests a visitor is going to visit. An immigrant is a direct communication of traveling or having a visitor. The scenes and the contest surrounding the dream are the object of interpretation.

Image: These are the characters and vowels of expression used to communicate with a dreamer. This entire dream language is a book of images.

Imagine: The imagination is the first step to our creative expression of our faith. These waves of thoughts are already stored in the mind or in the subconscious mind. These thoughts sometimes create fear, confidence, happiness, or unhappiness in the mind.

Imbecile: This refers to a low state of reasoning exhibited by an individual. When you see it in the dream or manifest such characteristics, please pray against it. This state of intelligence doesn't suggest anything good, except it's a weapon to fight your enemies or if God converts your attackers to imbeciles.

Impeach: Means to dethrone, demote someone from an exalted position, unless God reverses the interpretation or image to promote you in your place of authority because of your inability to handle good news. Impeachment to someone in a position of authority suggests controversy, leading to a vote of no confidence on the dreamer or possible removal.

Implicate: This indicates incrimination of a dreamer to indict the dreamer before spiritual entities. It is a fault-finding exercise to pass a judgment to a dreamer in order to nail them.

"For the accuser of the brethren is cast down, which accused them before God day and night" (Revelation 12:10 KJV). Watch out for sins used in implicating you; most of those sins are not confessed or forgiven. We must confess every sin and pray for forgiveness so that Satan will not use it to implicate us.

Import: This is a language of trade to receiving something valuable. It's a good symbol for a businessman. It is a good sign to import something foreign or a new contact for business.

Impotence: It's a symbol of weakness of a man's sex organ or weakness of his character. It's a sign that something is wrong with the dreamer's sex organ. It's also a sign that a man's strength is being tampered with by an evil spell.

A man can be rendered impotent due to an evil spell or charm given to him by his wife, lover, or an evil power. He will no longer have a strong personality to command authority over the woman. His guardian angel may reveal this incident by using impotence to show the man no longer has authority.

Women who have a spiritual husband may render their husband impotent. Impotence is a strong sign that something is fundamentally wrong with the man.

Impregnate: When a married woman is pregnant in the dream, the most direct interpretation is that she will be pregnant soon. At the earliest stages of pregnancy, because it is a well-kept secret, God can utilize other symbols to reveal the pregnancy.

However, direct dreams like these usually connote a reverse interpretation or negative meaning. This means that she might not be pregnant. If it is an old woman or a woman who has finished giving birth who finds herself pregnant, then the dream is indicating that her daughter or relative is pregnant. A man could be pregnant in the dream if someone is pregnant in his family (e.g., his wife, daughter, etc.).

Additionally, pregnancy stands for a blessing that will soon mature.

Inaugurate: This means to establish. Anything that is inaugurated in the dream is already established or decided in the spiritual realm. It is only matter of time before it is made manifest on earth, unless a reverse interpretation is used to reveal it to the dreamer.

Incarnate: This is a visual image that symbolizes the circle of life. When we experience incarnation in the dream, it means God has added more years to us. It could also mean we have outlived a particular life cycle and are ready to begin living in a new existence. In other words, it is a countdown to our death day.

The body refreshes itself within each cycle of its existence. "The years of our life are seventy, or even by reason of strength eighty; yet their span is but toil and trouble; they are soon gone and we fly away" (Psalm 90:10). By God's law, the human body cannot live beyond 120 years; "Then the Lord said, 'My Spirit shall not abide in man forever, for he is flesh: his days shall be 120 years'" (Genesis 6:3 KJV). The Spirit of God is what gives life to our mortal bodies. As the time for us to leave the earth grows closer, the body begins to weaken. It is more difficult for cells to refresh themselves, and old age really sets in.

Incarnation manifests in the form of death in the dream. Someone may see themself die in the dream, but they remain aware of everything happening in that dream. Such a death is a revelation on soul incarnation and not physical death. Sometimes incarnation can reveal the soul personalities God may bring into your family circle.

Incense: It's a symbol of God's aura surrounding a person or place. The scent of incense can attract or dispel the presence of divine beings and other entities. When we praise and pray to God from a pure heart, our prayers rise like sweet-smelling incense (Psalm 141:2). "For we are to God, the pleasing aroma of Christ among those who are being saved and those who are perishing" (2 Corinthians 2:15 NIV).

Incense also announces God's plans and interests. Whenever incense is involved, it could mean intervention or execution. Incense is a signal. It can attract good spirits or chase away evil spirits.

Incest: Incest is a symbol of abomination. It points to a primitive, incestuous nature. When such an act or symbol is shown to an individual in a dream, it is an indictment on them. If the act is committed in public or the participants are caught, it reveals that the sin or abomination has been settled and its effects reversed. But when an incestuous act is done behind closed doors and does not attract public attention, that abomination is still a stain against the dreamer's soul.

An indirect object or symbol can be used to reveal that a close relative has committed an incestuous act (e.g., a father can see himself making love with his own daughter in the dream). This doesn't mean he is directly involved in such, but his face is being used to reveal that an abomination has occurred within his family. Sometimes the act may have been committed by a previous generation, but its consequences are still affecting the family. Any dreamer who has this kind of dream should seek deliverance. The effects of abomination can plague a family for generations. Before God made a new covenant with humanity through the death of Jesus Christ, the law was that generations unborn paid for the sins of their forebears. "For I the Lord thy God am a jealous God, visiting the iniquity of the fathers upon the children unto the third and fourth generation of them that hate me" (Exodus 20:5 KJV).

A lot of families facing untold hardship may have a history of incest or other abominations occurring in their family, but this can be washed away by the blood of Jesus. "Behold, the days come saith the Lord, that I will make a new covenant with the house of Israel and with the house of Judah … and they shall teach no more every man his neighbor, and every man his brother saying; "Know the Lord: for they shall all know Me, from the least of them unto the greatest of them, saith the Lord: for I will forgive their iniquity and I will remember their sin no more" (Jeremiah 31:31, 34 KJV).

Incision: It is a language associated with medical treatment of the soul body or a kind of spiritual protection against evil spells. Since the physical body and the soul body are connected, whatever happens to the soul body affects the physical body with time. Any incision to the body symbolizes divine fortification, repair, or immunity.

Incident: When things happen in the dream, they are designed to inform or bring revelation to us. Every incident in the dream contains an encrypted message or information that affects us directly and otherwise.

Income: This is a sign of receiving value. We spend value more in the dream world than we receive value. Spending in the dream is a sign of acquisition of value, and when we spend in the dream, we are actually planting what we will reap on earth.

When we dream of receiving money, it's a symbol that money will soon visit us. Such money or value is specially meant for a special project and should not be spent on vanities. Every income or money that God releases to an individual has a purpose, and when it is channeled to that purpose, it will grow progressively. A lot of people have squandered special income meant for future investment or prosperity on vanities. It doesn't matter how little that income is; always ask for the will of God to prevail.

Incomplete: (Antonym is *complete*.) Every human being is made up of two entities; the physical body and soul make up a complete person. The soul is the true person that functions with the physical body on earth. When the physical body loses its existence on earth, the soul keeps on living in God or returns to God. At resurrection, it's the soul that will take up another body to live again. If you wake up from a dream feeling incomplete, it means your soul body is not completely connected back to the physical body on earth. In that case, you will not regain full consciousness. You may also wake up here on earth while your soul is still left in the dream world. Whenever you sleep again, you will continue dreaming from where you stopped. Anything incomplete in the dream is not good. We must strive to create harmony and completeness in whatever we are doing, except for evil things.

Incorporate: Establish—something that has been decided to happen in your life or someone else's.

Indebted: It's a language of liability, owing, and failed promises or failing to fulfill a divine covenant or promise. The symbol of indebtedness can manifest in the form of a treasure box, savings box, or tithe card. Whenever you see any of these symbols, it suggests indebtedness. Indebtedness manifests according to your culture or religion. The image will be anything used to collect treasure or money. When it manifests, it means you are owing or you need to fulfill a covenant or promise.

Indictment: This is a communication of conviction by divine foundation or an organization. When a dreamer experiences indictment in the dream, it means the dreamer is guilty or may have offended someone. If the dreamer is in court, they may possibly lose their case. The location of the dreamer is key to the interpretation of the dream. If it's before an oracle or a spiritual organization, the dreamer should seriously pray against it because someone may have summoned their soul before a deity. It's only a matter of time before consequences of the indictment manifest.

Independent: This is the opposite of imprisonment. Whenever we feel independent or become independent in a dream, it means liberty, freedom. It also means completion, graduation, mastery of an activity or profession. Independence means maturity, self-discipline, and self-control. When you dream of yourself standing alone, doing something without any assistance, it means you have mastered that thing. If you are set free from confinement, room, cage, camp, or out of restriction, you are free indeed.

Indigene: When you see indigenes from your place of origin visit you in a group, it is not always a good omen. It means someone has summoned you before a deity or enchanted your name before an evil oracle, or someone may have cast an evil spell on you. It also suggests a looming trouble in your place of residence concerning you.

On the other hand, the presence of indigenes of a place announces acceptance into that community. It can also announce good news concerning your family life or business, but in most cases, indigenes point out issues and controversies.

Industrial: This is a symbol of a contract, work, or employment on a large scale. Whenever you see an industry, depending on who you are, it suggests job employment or a contract. The location of the industry is the key to the message. Please see *company*.

Industry (company): It is a language of work or a contract engagement. Whenever you see yourself in an industry, working or participating in construction or production, it means you will soon get a contract or job. The location of the industry is very important because our geography here on earth is different from dream geography. For instance, you may dream of an industry located in a place you once lived, away from where you presently reside. Tracing the time and geography of an industry or event in the dream world is difficult. Each individual must use their personal perspective to interpret what place, location, and timing mean. There is no generally acceptable meaning to locations in the dream.

I have personally seen myself working with expatriates in an oil and gas-servicing company in Bonny Island of Rivers state while presently living in Port Harcourt's main town. But I worked in Bonny Island from 1996 to 2005 and left for the university. While residing in Port Harcourt, I saw myself working in Bonny Island. What it meant was that I was going to get a contract with a foreign company related to an oil and gas company in Port Harcourt, not necessarily Bonny Island as dreamt about. Bonny Island was just used to refer to the oil-servicing industry, and because I had been in that location previously, it helped me put things in perspective.

Location of a place is always used as a qualifying symbol to simplify interpretation of a major object of dream symbols (e.g., using Bonny Island as a qualifying symbol to simplify working with expatriates in Port Harcourt). Bonny Island was used as an old experience in my personal life experience to tell me what would happen to me now. When you see yourself in a company located in a place you don't have any personal life experience, it means you will be connected to someone from that place or a company not from your immediate environment for a job or contract. The type of industry is key to understanding the dream language.

Infant: (See *child*.) These are all symbols of guardian angels and angelic beings. There are adulterated versions of infants. On the surface, they look like children, but they are really ancient spirits. These categories of infants are earthly demons. They are very powerful and merciless.

Infection: Infections are evil concoctions, spells, voodoo, or evil powers created by witchcraft and evil kingdoms, used to inflict diseases on humanity. These infections are produced scientifically in the realm of the spirit and replicated in earth laboratories through ideas. Infections could be transmitted through the air, water, plants, or contaminated food.

We avoid sickness and disease by practicing healthy habits, but it is more difficult to avoid infections spread through our souls. When a supernatural infection manifests in our physical body, it defies medical solutions, even though the symptoms look treatable. Spiritual infections are the reason minor ailments kill people easily. It's very important to fast and pray. "Howbeit, this kind goeth not out but by fasting and prayers" (Matthew 17:21 KJV).

Interceding for the sick, even while ministering drugs, absolute reliance on medical treatment is not advisable. "For we wrestle not against flesh and blood, but against principalities, against powers, against the rulers of the darkness of this world, against spiritual wickedness in high places" (Ephesians 6:12 KJV). Our daily lives are a spiritual battle. We must arrest evil infections before they overwhelm us. Some ways to protect yourself from spiritual infections include not eating in the dream, avoiding dead people, and not sleeping with prostitutes or loose women. All these are access gates through which infections can gain entrance into your soul.

Infertile: Infertility is caused by evil spirits. Evil spirits can cause infertility by having sexual affairs with a man or woman. A woman could be physically pregnant on earth, but the moment an evil spirit has sex with her in the dream, that pregnancy will terminate. They usually cause situations or events that suddenly induce an abortion of the baby or sudden termination of the pregnancy.

Although there are genuine biological factors that affect fertility, the original plan of God was that man stays fruitful and multiplies. Children are a blessing to the family unit, and Satan fights hard to block blessings. It is easier to get pregnant when we are young and irresponsible. The moment we get married, issues and trouble start. We should seek deliverance when we have sex or extramarital affairs in the dream because it leads to infertility.

Infidelity: (See *unfaithfulness*.) It is a sign of low self-control or evil possession. Some people may be unfaithful to a wife or husband because of lack of self-discipline without being possessed by any demon.

It is also a sign that our primitive nature, the old man, is still alive. "That regarding your previous way of life, you put off your old self [completely discard your former nature] which is being corrupted through deceitful desires and be continually renewed in the spirit of your mind [having a fresh, untarnished mental and spiritual attitude]" (Ephesians 4:22–23 AMP).

More often than not, infidelity is caused by demonic possession. The dream symbol is multiple women or men in the dream having extramarital affairs with different women or men in the dream.

Inflict: To inflict means to cause pain or other unpleasant feelings to a third party. It is a sign of impending danger that has a high probability of occurring, although God can intervene to lessen the effects. For example, someone may have an accident in the dream but survive or cut him or herself with a knife accidentally, but in real life, the person may have not experience it at all. Whenever you are afflicted with anything in the dream, surely it's coming your way. Pray for mercy for God to intervene.

Informant: This is a symbol of leaked information, a gossip, or secret. If you see an informant in the dream, it means your secret has been exposed or God wants to use a source or person to reveal a guided secret for you. The role the informant plays in the dream is an object of interpretation.

Inherit: To inherit something in the dream is a sign of receiving your rightful possession. Some symbols that represent inheritance include riding horses, cars, houses, crowns, and keys. A dreamer could ride on a white horse, or a dreamer could be given a crown to wear. God has bestowed an inheritance on all. "House and wealth are the inheritance from fathers, but a wise, understanding and sensible wife is [a gift and blessing] from the Lord" (Proverbs 19:14 AMP).

"No weapon that is formed against you will prosper; every tongue that shall rise against thee in judgment thou shalt condemn. This is the heritage of the servants of the Lord, and their righteousness is of me, saith the Lord" (Isaiah 54:17 KJV).

The following images are symbols of inheritance and what they represent:

- *lion*—speaks of promotion, leadership, ruler, authority, and power
- *staff*—a sign of royal priesthood, kingship, spiritual mandate, and the mantle of leadership
- *crown*—ruler, head, authority, or commander
- *egg*—treasure, sign of prosperity, life, wealth
- *key*—solution mandate to take charge of your greatness, destiny, or family wealth; the solution to problems, a destiny helper
- *heavenly bodies*, including the sun, moon and stars—command over humanity or popularity
- *horse*—speaks of royalty and leadership
- *land or house*—ownership of landed properties, assets, or wealth
- *children*—fertility, productivity, blessings of the womb
- *throne*—represents the seat of power

Initiation: Initiation in the dream world can be conducted in diverse ways. There are diverse symbols that can be used to reveal to a dreamer that they have been initiated into a circle, group, or society.

An initiation can be conducted without a dreamer's knowledge or acceptance. The symbol of initiation tells the dreamer what kind of kingdom they have been welcomed into.

The most common means of getting initiated in the dream is eating. Attending and participating in a ceremony could be an act of initiation. If someone finds themselves in the inner courtroom of the church or at the altar, it means that person is initiated into the call to serve God. If someone is given raw meat or blood to drink, it can also be an act of initiation. If someone finds themselves in a circle of familiar or unfamiliar people, it shows a sign of initiation. Marriage covenants, oath taking, putting a ring on someone's finger, and being crowned are also signs of initiation. If you dream of yourself doing a degrading job in a secured place like a prison, it is a sign of initiation.

If a dreamer finds themselves in any of these situations, they should seek a man of God to cancel the dream. People initiate others to have absolute control over their destiny and life.

Inject: It's a way of channeling power waves into someone's soul body. Angels of God could inject healing powers into a dreamer's soul to heal the person physically. Receiving medical treatment by way of taking injection or taking drugs is a very good healing encounter with angels because it shows a sign of healing. There are incurable diseases planted by powers of darkness that need the quick intervention of angels to cancel or treat in the dream to rescue that person. Receiving an injection in the dream or taking drugs in the dream is a sign of divine healing. In fact, such dream experiences clear out diseases from a person's body.

Injunction: See *courtroom*.

Injustice: This is an act of vindication for a dreamer. When scenes of injustice appear to a dreamer, it means betrayal, breach of trust, and unfair treatment. The circumstances of the dream are the subject of interpretation.

In-law(s): It is information about people outside your immediate family. Dreaming of your in-laws is a sign that they will visit, or there might be family problems from the maternal side of the family.

Insanity: This is a total loss of human intelligence and knowledge about the past, present, and future. An insane person has knowledge about things but doesn't have self-consciousness. When that kind of situation happens in a dream, it means the soul's intelligence has been tampered by energy waves to cause a temporary or permanent blackout (i.e., loss of consciousness). During a surgery, medical doctors can sedate a patient to enable them to perform painful surgery.

When a dreamer loses consciousness in the dream, they become like an insane person due to a gap between their soul and physical body. If an individual's consciousness lifts suddenly, the person will not be in control of themselves due to losing the mind-body connection. The soul is the intelligent consciousness residing in a physical body. When there is a consciousness gap, that soul is like a beacon inviting evil spirits and demons to inhabit. "When a defiling spirit is expelled from someone, it drifts along through the desert looking for an oasis, some unsuspecting soul it can bedevil. When it doesn't find anyone, it says, I'll go back to my old haunt. On return it finds the person spotlessly clean but vacant. It then runs out and rounds up seven other spirits more evil than itself and they all move in, whooping it up. That person ends up far worse than if he had never gotten cleaned up in the first place" (Matthew 12:43–44 MSG).

Inscriptions: These are established facts or messages for the information of the dreamer. It is not subjective but a direct message or established truth.

Insignia: This is a seal of authority and logo of an object of interpretation. It reveals the hierarchy and known symbol of an organization. If you see an insignia in the dream, it reveals information about the source of an object of interpretation.

Inspect: It's a force that calls on the dreamer's attention to scrutinize or carefully study something. In the dream, we usually lose self-control. Our dreams are guided by forces or energies beyond our understanding. Our guardian angel plays a major role in guiding us in the dream realm, while our primitive mind and conscious mindset on earth also play their own roles. If a guardian angel is very active in a dreamer's life, they will control and direct the dreamer's activities in the dream world. When the influence of the Holy Spirit is weak in a dreamer's life, evil entities begin to influence them, with little interference from God's spirit.

Dreams are controlled by whatever spirits the dreamer is subject to. The kind of spirit ruling or possessing someone determines the kind of dreams or information the dreamer gets.

Intention: These are deliberate and purposeful emotions or actions with a defined aim, target, or objective. Intentions can guide the dreamer's soul body to achieve certain things in the spiritual realm.

Internet: Universal dream world. When you see the internet or are hooked to *www* in the dream, it means the information or message is generally acceptable and known or has universal acknowledgment. Such a message or information is already settled.

Interpol: The presence of international police indicates the magnitude of controversy or trouble an individual is involved in. This is a clear sign that high-ranking spiritual kingdoms are interested in your matter. Encountering international police in any disguise reveals a strong personality that is universally known in the spirit realm and in the natural world.

Interpret: The human soul is telepathic, meaning it has the ability to read minds. When a guarded secret from an unknown realm is revealed to the dreamer, interpretation might be required to aid the dreamer's understanding. When John the revelator received the visions about future events, there were countless symbolic scenarios that required a heavenly interpreter to interpret those things to him. To receive interpretation in the dream realm is to receive revelation of unknown symbols.

Interrogate: This is a language used to prove guilt or innocence. It's a communication of indictment of a dreamer. To interrogate a dreamer's soul is the sign of an attempt to justify a judgment against a dreamer. The ability of the dreamer to defend themselves against the charges brought against them in the dream is the subject of interpretation. An interrogation can end in a war, battle, or fight. An interrogation can also be a symbol of an attack rather than peace. The subject matter of the interrogation in the dream should be taken note of because it's a point your enemies are using against you.

Interruption: This is a disruption of flow of communication in the dream realm. It is also a sign of intervention to pull you out of a case or judgment or attack. An interruption can come in different forms in the dream. The state of the human body can interrupt a dream streaming. For example, if the physical body needs to use the restroom, the brain signals can trigger interruption stream scenarios, signals, or sequences to stop dream streaming.

In fact, the general condition of the physical body can cause disruptions in the dream world. The room temperature, either too hot or too cold, can disrupt sleep and dreaming. Ill health is another culprit of dream disruptions. Some illnesses can cause hallucinations and confusion, which can distort the dream. Whenever you notice disruption or interruption in the dream, something is wrong somewhere.

It is advisable to maintain good and healthy habits to sustain the body. Adhering to rules like not drinking too much water or eating heavily before bed can assist in preventing dream interruptions.

Intervention: These are acts of God's saving grace to humanity. Whenever you are miraculously saved from problems, it means you have been delivered and saved from evil.

I once had a dream where ceremony was ongoing and tables of food were served for the invited guests to eat. When the food got to my table, a sudden heavy storm started that destroyed the food table and canopies. Everybody began running helter-skelter, and I woke up. God used a storm, rain, and wind to intervene for me in that evil attack.

In the past, I used to experience wet dreams. When I fasted and prayed over the issue, I suddenly discovered that whenever the women manifested for the sexual encounter, I was unable to penetrate their vagina. In fact, their private parts were nowhere to be found, and I would search for them in vain. These are some of the many ways God intervenes for His people. Intervention can come in different forms, God can give you wings to fly away from danger. You can even be invisible or disappear in the face of evil. We can go on and on recounting the saving grace of God in our dream experiences.

Intimate: Intimacy in the dream is a sign of oneness, unity, friendship, relationship, acceptance, understanding, and cohesion. Whenever you are intimate with someone in the dream, it means the person has accepted you and has no quarrels with you. It is a sign of a clean heart that is bearing no grudges or grievances.

Intimacy: Intimacy in the dream reveals the level of harmony that exists between and among people. In dreams of intimacy, it's not unusual to see your parents, your children, or your wife. Intimacy is a sign of a happy coexistence. When intimacy exists between two people, they are usually one in spirit. When a husband and a wife become intimate in their marriage relationship, they become one body in spirit. When that happens, they begin exhibiting the same aura, sharing the same thoughts and dreams, and after a while, they will even begin to look alike in physical appearance.

Introduction: (See *initiation*). Introduction is the language of welcome and acceptance, a sign of new friendship, marriage, and meeting new people. It is also a symbol of spiritual exposure, knowledge upgrade, and authority to act. If you are introduced to someone in the dream, depending on your sex, it means you are about to meet a destiny helper.

In the dream realm, we can encounter people from the past, present, and future. The known faces you meet are the people you know, and the strange faces are people you don't know who are of the past or are yet to come to earth, or they are presently here, but you have not yet met them. Each person you meet in the dream realm may be your destiny helper, people you can learn from or teach, or people who sharpen your vision of your future and define you as a person. Some people we meet enter our lives to teach us lessons for good or evil.

Introduction in the dream is all about meeting people. God usually shows people who will play an important role in our life before they manifest physically. God uses our information database of people we know to explain the character or the kind of person we are meeting. The faces we see in the dream are symbolic; they might not be the exact person we know in reality.

I have a friend who always tries to cheat me whenever we have business dealings. Although he is still my friend, in my subconscious mind, he is a cheater and unreliable about money and business. Anytime I dream of his face and personality concerning any transaction, I immediately become cautious of the persons within that transaction. No friendship or contact is useless, but there is a need to approach people with wisdom and discretion.

Jacob had to reverse the cunning wisdom of his uncle Laban in order to deliver himself out of servitude. Subsequently, to Jacob, Laban becomes an important symbol of craftiness and cheating. If Jacob is to be reborn again as a person in this present civilization, his subconscious mind will still be using the symbol of Laban to give hints and warnings, but he won't remember the face anymore or discern the warning.

Every face you encounter in the dream has once played a role in your life before or will play a role in your life.

Investigate: This is a symbol of an evil summons. Sometimes it's a warning of impending trouble or a notice that you're already caught in the trap. Evil people usually take people's names to evil shrines or altars for the deities to attack people on their behalf. When an evil summons occurs, the human soul appears before the altar for judgment. Your guardian angel may accompany you to prove your soul's innocence or help defend you.

Dreaming of an investigation is a warning of an impending legal battle. In my personal experience, I once had two brothers agree to sell me a piece of land for fifteen million naira only. I paid them five million naira in advance and promised to pay the balance in a month's time. While sleeping one day, I dreamt of these two brothers in police custody. I decided to go in and plead their innocence, but the investigative officer in charge asked me not to leave and demanded that I make a statement, although he knew I was not directly involved. I told him explicitly that I was not involved in the matter. He told me to wait for him to confirm from the complainant. Knowing that the policeman was about to make fool of himself, I allowed him to make the call to ask if I was involved. I was furious but began laughing while he was calling, after which I was allowed out of the police station.

In the morning, I met the two men who sold the land to me and told them that this land sale would cause trouble that would only be settled in a native court or turn into a civil case. I advised them to involve their third brother in sharing the proceeds of the sale of the land. Otherwise, their brother would make case against them. They hesitated. The following day, their third brother came into my office to inform me that he was an interested party in the land in question and that he had already gone to summon his brothers to the native court for judgment. When I remembered what God had shown me in the dream, I welcomed him and promised not to pay the balance until the matter was settled amicably. The initial parties used so many tactics to try to intimidate their brother, but I refused to complete the payment until the coast was clear. At a point, I asked them to refund my initial payment of five million naira. They realized I wasn't going to be intimidated into defrauding their brother. They eventually settled and came together to tell me to pay the balance to everybody's account. Without God's dream revelation, I would have been caught in serious legal trouble.

Invigilate: This means you are under the guidance of a spirit being. If you dream of invigilating people, this means you will mentor or counsel others. Any face you can clearly identify or recognize needs your advice or instruction for direction. A lot of us have been sent to be destiny helpers to so many who are suffering. When we step into their lives, things change for good.

If you are the one being invigilated, you are under the watchful eyes of heaven in whatever you are doing. Especially for a person in places of authority and leadership, it's a warning to be cautious in your dealings.

Invisible: When a dreamer becomes invisible to other people in the dream, it means you have been cut off from those people. You are no longer on the same spiritual or substantial level with them. It is a sign of elevation. God usually hides human souls from enemies in the realm of the spirit by making us invisible to their senses.

There are people, trees, and herbs that can be physically invisible on earth. Invisibility in the dream is a powerful form of defense by the human soul. Disappearing from danger back to earth by waking up from a nightmare can be done by any dreamer, but the ability to become invisible is a sign of high-level spiritual protection by guardian angels. When a soul is invisible, it can't be harmed. If land demons come to harm you in a dream, but you are flying in the air, those evil spirits from land can't harm you up there. Invisibility can manifest as different forms of protection, but the best mode of invisibility is to be present without being seen.

Invitation: This means that you have been remembered. You may have been forgotten by some people or your friends, but when you dream of an invitation, it means you have been remembered. If you have quoted for a job or contract, or submitted a proposal or job application, or applied for anything physical on earth, and you are invited in the dream, then it's a sign you will be remembered. Some people may have applied for something ages ago and forgotten about it, but when you dream about being invited, you have been remembered. Invitation is associated with celebration of good things. Whenever you are invited in a dream, please intensify your prayers because your case has been remembered for good. I pray you won't be invited for evil.

For an individual in authority or in a top management position, it may mean investigation, query, or something leading to questioning.

Invocation: This act is a telepathic spiritual exercise. It is the ability to connect to various spiritual frequencies in the spirit realm. It can be likened to the World Wide Web where different websites and people are interconnected. When you have this ability, it is an indication that you are a conscious soul with the power and authority to affect things in the spiritual realm. Priests, pastors, prophets, and seers with spiritual authority can perform invocations.

If you witness an invocation being performed on you, your soul has been summoned before an evil deity. The witchcraft kingdom can spiritually invoke a human soul to appear in their coven. So when you see someone performing invocation on you, don't take it lightly; try to defend yourself because your soul is under judgment or threat.

Isolate: (See *desolate*). To be isolated in the dream is a sign of abandonment or the end of one's existence. An individual who dreams of isolation should be careful not to be abandoned to their fate in the midst of a serious problem.

It is also a state of idleness or inactivity. Someone in prison or jobless isn't doing anything. Anything that can place someone in a state of inactivity is not good.

Israelites: The Israelites were chosen by God to be a holy nation. They were set apart to serve God forever. In the dream world, they represent the true generation of heavenly citizens. The human race that will live in heaven after this civilization will be subdivided into twelve nations. So Israelites on earth are a foreshadowing of the structure of nations in heaven. And every tribe of Israel and other tribes that are now reunited in Christ in this world will form new nations in heaven. When you dream of being a part of this future kingdom of God and you are a priest by birth, it also depicts divinity and a call to serve God.

Irrevocable: An irrevocable thing is something that cannot be changed. The physical body uses the heart, while the soul body uses the mind. The mind plays an important role in interpreting scenarios and outcomes in our dreams. If a dream scenario is something that your mind agrees with, that thing becomes irrevocable. On the other hand, if you are confronted with an outcome you disagree with, you must reject it in your mind. When we accept things in the dream without objection, it becomes irrevocable, meaning it cannot be changed.

When we were created by God, He intended for us to have a freedom of choice without coercion. If we receive an unwelcome revelation, it means we have the authority to reject and rebuke that outcome.

However, there are certain predestined events that are part of one's life journey on earth that must be experienced to shape a dreamer's future. When those events are revealed to a dreamer, it is intended to enable them to prepare for it because it cannot be changed. When we force ourselves out of certain events or experiences in our life journey on earth, we won't achieve our destined greatness.

When He took up the mantle to lay His life down to save humankind, Jesus Christ knew He would eventually die. But when the hour came, He prayed for the cup of suffering to pass over Him. "Saying, Father, if thou be willing, remove this cup from me: nevertheless not my will, but thine, be done" (Luke 22:42 KJV). He went further by submitting Himself to the ultimate will of God because the course of events that followed was necessary for the salvation of humankind.

In multiple dreams, God revealed to Joseph that he would be a respected ruler. Joseph was sold into slavery to Egyptian merchants by his own brothers. He was falsely accused of raping his master, Potiphar's, wife and imprisoned. While in prison, his good behavior and ability to interpret dreams caught the attention of people there. At the appointed time, Joseph was rescued from prison. Pharaoh made him a governor and placed him in charge of storing food ahead of an impending famine (Genesis 37–50 KJV). There are things we must experience that prepare us for elevation to the next level. Gold and other precious metals are refined with fire to remove their impurities and bring forth their true beauty.

When you pray against things in the dream, ensure that you conclude your prayers by saying, "Father, let Your will be done. Amen!"

Island: Represents royalty. It is also characterized by distinct people. Take note of these people because it is a direct revelation of the people the dreamer will meet for special business. The aquatic or marine world represents people with their political, social, and economic lives. Your activity in the dream is the subject for interpretation.

PART J

Jaguar: Represents royalty, blue blood, leadership, dominion, or kingdom. Every family or species of the cat family represents royalty, a position of authority, or promotion.

Jail: To be in jail in the dream is a revelation of idleness and inactivity. When a soul is caged in jail, they become like a slave or a convict who has no rights. When a human soul doesn't have freedom, or it's not at liberty to exercise freedom, that soul is in a state of inactivity. Inactivity physically manifests in various forms—indecision, procrastination, lack of will power, and so on.

Some people lack a sense of direction for how their lives should go. Some others don't have the willpower or motivation to change the trajectory of their existence. They just accept their fate and move around in circles without much progress. The state of indecision in life, lack of willpower to resist temptation, lack of visionary idea to move forward, and the inability to accept responsibility are signs of imprisonment in the dream.

To make progress in reality, your soul must be as creative as your mind. You have to dream of yourself making moves and connections to move forward. The inspiration you receive from your soul directs you to execute ideas and flourish in business. You could even receive a new direction or learn a new trade because your soul is trying something new in the spirit realm.

Your physical body must be in harmony with your soul to make progress. But when your soul is jailed instead of working, it means you are restrained somewhere by powers stronger than you. If someone is thrown into jail physically, that person is no longer connected to the outside world. He is idle with restricted movement, achieving nothing. There are people on earth who never change, year in, year out. They are moving but not making progress. If someone works for years without making progress, that person is in jail. That is a good symbol to communicate to the dreamer that something is wrong!

Jail can also indicate impending legal trouble. It is a sign to be cautious and prepared. Caution would not prevent the trouble from happening but can prevent an accident or cushion injury.

A jail could also refer to possession by evil or occult associations. When a person is a slave to an occult, they become a slave and can be manipulated to do the wishes of the occult. The person becomes like a puppet, unconsciously carrying out evil assignments. That person doesn't know why they do wicked or evil things. Someone could be a blind witch. That means the person's soul is tied down in the kingdom of witchcraft, but the person is unaware. They may notice strange behavior but lack the understanding and the willpower to resist the manipulation. Any dreamer who finds themselves addicted to womanizing, prostituting, or taking hard substances is probably in jail.

A lot of human souls are presently in the jail and shackles of evil kingdoms, being manipulated into doing their biddings. Only the mercy and grace of God can deliver them.

When you see yourself in jail in the dream, please run for deliverance before it's too late.

Jewel: This is a sign of treasure or wealth. It is a good omen to see jewels in the dream realm. Wearing them means something good will become your personal possession. Jewels are sure signs of treasure and wealth coming to you.

Journalist: This is a symbol of a special message intended for the knowledge of the society at large. When you dream of a journalist, pay special attention to what they have to say.

When you have a career in journalism, it is a sign of what career you should be involved in. Any person you dream of with a career in journalism would do well in that profession. It could also mean that person has some information or a message for you.

Journey: Journey in the dream is a transition of the dreamer from one state to another. The soul uses different means to embark on its journey. The soul could travel with light speed by disappearing, traveling via land, water, air, or underground. The human soul is a spirit and can adopt any form to make its journeys.

In the spirit realm, time is meaningless; the soul can travel to the past and future. If the soul is permitted to journey to hell or heaven, there is an important message that is key to the dreamer's present journey on earth. There are some human souls that can fly, swim, drive, or disappear during their journey. The journey refers to the movement of the soul in the dream realm in order to retrieve information for the dreamer. This process advances our experience of earth and adds to the wealth of our life experiences.

Job: Being occupied with a job in the dream is a very good experience. When we are in harmony with our soul, we seem to do the same job we do on earth in the dream. What this experience means is that the dreamer will succeed in their current endeavor. If there is difficulty in the present job the dreamer is doing on earth, it may reflect in the dream for the dreamer to take caution.

Doing a job in the dream is a work in progress. It is a sign that you will be engaged in a job soon. Whatever you can do with ease in the dream is your talent. There are dreamers who see themselves doing different kinds of jobs any time they dream. It is a simple indication that the dreamer is multitalented. If someone is unemployed and sees themselves doing a job, it means they will soon be employed. Engaging in a different profession in the dream realm than reality is an indication that one needs to change jobs. If your soul is not in agreement with your current profession, it means your body and soul are not in sync.

Working under duress in the dream is a bad omen and an indication of bondage or imprisonment. There are people who have been caged and forced to labor while others reap the benefits. If a dreamer finds themselves working as an apprentice when they have their independence, it is a sign of bondage. Working in confined spaces or at a labor camp is a sign of serious bondage.

A lot of members in our churches are working for their pastors. Their souls have been confined in a circle to work for the success of the pastor. What it means is that whatever you yield yourself to, you are a servant of that thing. So if a pastor belongs to an occult to grow his church, every member who operates under his spiritual authority will serve him in the realm of the spirit. And when that happens, it is difficult for any member in that church to rise above the pastor. Whenever an individual completes an apprenticeship, they should ask for their blessings and move out on their own. Remaining after an apprenticeship is like a woman refusing to marry and leave her parents' house after reaching marriageable age. It is the duty of the parents to give her out in marriage to another man by the way of tradition. Most people still cage the souls of their sons, daughters, employees, and servants after they have served faithfully and should be set free. Men who are independent should work for themselves and not for someone. When we serve other people in the dream, we have given our destiny to that person to progress. For success to be achieved on earth, we must work for it physically or in the spirit realm. There is nothing that comes for free on earth.

Judgment: "All a man's ways are clean to himself; but the Lord puts men's spirits into his scales" (Proverbs 16:2 KJV). God sends every soul to earth for a temporal time, and at the end, He takes their records and appraises their suitability for reincarnation. We are permitted to use only one body to live in every life opportunity. "You've been weighed on the scales and you don't measure up" (Daniel 5:27 KJV). In the book of Daniel, when the disembodied hand wrote on the wall, it revealed the judgment that was to come upon King Belteshazzar, who had been weighed on the scales of God's judgment and found wanting.

"And as it is appointed unto men once to die, but after this the judgment" (Hebrews 9:27 KJV). This means that you can't use the same physical body to live more than once in any civilization on earth. After death, the living soul returns to God, who decides if the soul deserves another chance at physical life. Some souls will wear angelic bodies, some supernatural bodies, and some mortal bodies, depending on the grace extended by God.

PART K

Key: The key is a symbol of a solution to a problem, the answer to a question, freedom from slavery, open doors in the face of hindrance, failure, and success, and something hidden being revealed.

Whenever you dream of a key, please search for the padlock. If you are given a key in the dream, it means you have been given the solution to a particular problem. It can also mean that the solution to your problems is in your hands. It's very good to see a key and the padlock together; it means the problem is known and the solution has already been released.

In my personal experience, I once dreamt that I was looking for my shop, which was close to one that belonged to my uncle and his wife. When I finally found the shop, I noticed my uncle had locked my shop long ago. Fortunately for me, I found the key and the rusted padlock used to lock my shop. In that dream, I was pleased I found the shop, key, and padlock, and since that dream, my business has been progressing well. My uncle was actually responsible for my stagnated progress for a long time. Thank God for His deliverance. If you see the padlock alone, you have identified your problem but not the solution. It is preferable to see the key rather than only the padlock, but it is better you see them both.

Kill: Killing in the dream means the end of existence of a thing. Killing in the dream does not always mean death. When something is prevented from happening, killing can be used to illustrate it. A lot of people have been killed in the dream, and yet they are presently living. Killing can represent a change of personality or an upgrade to a new phase or stage of life of an individual. It can also show an attempt on the dreamer's life that won't be fatal.

When you kill someone in the dream, it means they will never be a threat to you again.

Kidnap: Being kidnapped in the dream is a bad omen. It could be a warning of physical kidnapping or an indication that the dreamer's soul is caged by a spiritual entity stronger than the dreamer. Kidnapping can come in the form of an arrest by unknown uniformed men or a gang of people. When a dreamer is kidnapped in the dream, it means the dreamer's spiritual defense is weak (i.e., their guardian angel isn't strongly connected to the dreamer). Whenever any spiritual entities come to arrest or forcefully take custody of a person's soul in the spiritual realm, the guardian angels of the dreamer ought to prevent or resist the attack. If the intruders succeed in arresting or forcefully taking the dreamer's soul into their custody, it means the dreamer is not in a good harmony with their guardian angel.

The dreamer might see themselves already kidnapped or forcefully taken into custody and start planning how to escape or escape from their custody entirely. Any soul caged or taken into custody must fight to liberate their soul from such a situation. Sometimes our guardian angels reveal to the physical body the state of our soul so that we can take physical action on earth to liberate the soul from bondage or prison in the realm. If any soul is complacent seeing himself/herself in a servitude, isolated, kidnapped, or kept in custody, it means that soul is caged without immediate remedy, and the soul is compromised. That soul has surrendered to the will of the captors.

When an individual is guilty of an offense and the offended person takes advantage of the situation and summons the offender before a strong deity, the demons in charge of that deity will go to arrest or kidnap the offender's soul without resistance. Whenever our soul is guilty, it becomes docile, weak, and susceptible to attacks, especially when we willingly committed the offense.

If a person enters into a covenant with an occult organization willfully and they contravene the rules and regulations of the organization, the occult police can come in any form to enforce the rules without resistance from that person. So when we are forcefully taken without resistance, it shows our soul is truly compromised.

King: King represents royals or noble personalities. It symbolizes authority, power, dominion, ruler ship, and chain of command. Any events associated with kings represent societal, communal, or collective power and authority. When a king visits a dreamer or a dreamer is welcomed or accepted in a king's palace, it means the dreamer will progress in that land and be favored. It is a very good experience to dream about kings. If someone dreams of becoming a king in the dream, it means the dreamer will surely be a leader. The person has royal blood and leadership qualities. Dreaming about kings is a good dream that reveals a big vision.

Kingdom: Kingdoms are spiritual geographical spaces that have existed or exist in a particular time with attached events. Whenever kingdoms manifest in the dream, there are important events or information that need to be revealed to the dreamer. Every piece of event or information should be noted for interpretation. When a dreamer visits other kingdoms, it shows that dreams have matured, or the dreamer is allowed to be part of that kingdom.

Kiss: This is a sign of attraction and love. Whenever or whatever you kiss in the dream shows a strong attachment to that object or image in the dream. When a person kisses you in the dream, it means that person is in love with the dreamer. It's a sign of love and not harm. However, most kisses in the dream are a crafty deception to attract a dreamer's soul in order to harm the dreamer, pass on a spell, or lure them into spiritual fornication.

Knock: It is to create attention or to put out a strong signal demanding the dreamer's attention to awaken someone's soul or to ask for attention or acceptance.

Knowledge: This is the degree of consciousness or knowledge a dreamer possesses in their subconscious mind. All the events and experiences a soul has gained in all its existence from one civilization to the next is stored in the soul's mind. In each dream experience, those stored events and experiences become part of the knowledge the dreamer's soul possesses in the dream world. Most time, our present knowledge stored in our brain memories distorts the assimilation of new information or knowledge revealed in the dream world. If a dreamer is projected to the future time in the dream world, they may find it difficult to comprehend the new knowledge they receive there because it's a new knowledge not existing in their subconscious mind. The things you can interpret and understand while dreaming already exist in your soul's mind.

PART L

Lab/laboratory: It denotes a healing process or procedure. It is just a direct revelation concerning solutions to ill health. If a dreamer dreams about a laboratory, it means they will seek or find a solution to the ill health.

Label: Picture is a mark of identity in the realm. It is also an established thing that cannot be changed. Whatever you see on a label is already known, decided, or established. Labels can be likened to pictures. If a label of someone is on your car or anything, it means the dreamer is strongly attached to whatever is on that label. Anything on a picture or label is hard to change in the dream realm.

Labor/work: Labor, work, or jobs are any activities you are involved in that would lead to a reward or wage. Hard labor represents slavery or servitude. Work, labor, and job means success and progress, but when it becomes hard to bear or is done under compulsion, then it becomes spiritual slavery (i.e., working without seeing any success or progress). For instance, if a dreamer finds themselves picking fruits or harvesting farm produce of their own free will with joy, it could represent various things. For a married woman, it could be a sign of pregnancy or conception. For a man, it could symbolize success and progress in his endeavors. Harvesting fruits or farm produce is a symbol of an immediate gift of God to the dreamer. In a short while, the dreams will start to manifest in the physical realm.

When a dreamer is planting, working, or doing a job that requires time to reap the benefits, then such good things will manifest after a length of time. For example, if a man sees himself planting a pumpkin seed, it means the dreamer's blessings will manifest in three-quarter a month's time, which is the time it takes a pumpkin to mature in the physical realm. But if someone is dreaming of plucking mangoes or harvesting pumpkin vegetables, it means the dreamer's sowing stage is over and they will soon reap a blessing.

Lady: The image of a lady represents an institution, organization, or the soul of a woman. Women represent earthly institutions, deities, or organizations. The appearance of a woman or lady in the dream reveals the content of the message for the dreamer. If the lady is pure in appearance and she is bereft of any sexual attraction, such a lady is a clean spirit that has manifested for a divine assignment. This type of woman always dresses in white, looking divine in appearance. They don't smile easily or act romantic toward the dreamer.

Every woman in the physical world has an organization or kingdom she represents in the realm of the spirit. The appearance and mode of manifestation of the lady tells the dreamer what her assignment in this life is. Many ladies who manifest in our dreams are seductive demons from the kingdom of darkness. Some are evil spirits using the appearance of a lady to destroy a man's life. On the other hand, the guardian angel of a dreamer can use the faces of trusted women, like one's wife or mother, to reveal something to the dreamer. The following appearance of woman means the following; see *mother*, *wife*, and so on.

Language: Language in the dream is the best way to describe a geographical location of an event, whether in the past, present, or future. If you can understand any language spoken in the dream, it is easy for the dreamer to know the place of the event. The human soul in the dream can read minds, so they don't need to understand any language to comprehend. So when a dreamer understands a language in the dream, it also means the dreamer has lived there when such an event took place—or will live there when such an event will take place. The focus of the dreamer should be the people or race who own the language and the meaning of what is being said.

Last: Being last means backwardness, setback, or difficulty. It can be an advantage in events like death and sickness. In good things, it is not good to be last, but in bad events, it's good to be the last one standing. Some years ago, my sibling dreamt of seeing me in a queue, and when it was my turn to be attended to, my trousers fell off my waist. I left the line and ran away to dress up properly. When I returned to the same line, he saw me at the back of the line. That was exactly what happened to my earthly experience in succeeding in life. When I was about to make it big in life, things turned around to be worse for me. I couldn't pay my rent. It took me more than a decade to return to the road to success again.

Laugh: When people laugh at you in the dream, it's an indication of shame and mockery. The dreamer should be careful not to engage in anything that can bring shame and dishonor to them. When the dreamer is the one laughing or laughing with other people, then it's a sign of a good thing that will happen to the dreamer. Laughing can represent mocking but also victory and joy. It depends on the circumstances of the dream experience.

Lamb: "Behold the lamb of God who takes away the sin of the world" (John 1:29 KJV).

The image of the lamb symbolizes purity, innocence, innocuousness, harmlessness, sacrifice, remission of sins, cleansing, reconciliation, obedience, exchange, life settlement, salvation, redemption, and intervention.

Animal traits or characteristics could be used to describe a person's personality, behavior, and purpose. In the other words, a person could be given animal names likened to that person's personality. When we describe Christ in His nature of innocence, purity, harmlessness, sacrificial nature, and obedience to God, we use term the Lamb of God. When we refer to the kingship of Christ or His position of authority, we call him the Lion of the tribe of Judah (Revelation 5:5 KJV). When names of animals or other nouns are used to call a person, it only describes or qualifies that person's purpose and traits. For example, when we refer to God as a consuming fire (Deuteronomy 4:24 KJV, Hebrews 12:29 KJV).

A lamb as an animal is a specially chosen animal for spiritual work. The soul of a lamb is equal to the soul of a human. It's the perfect replacement of a human's soul. Lamb is usually used to exchange the life of a human. "The soul that sinneth, it shall die" (Ezekiel 18:20 KJV). Before the death of Christ, God instructed the Israelites to give a yearly sacrifice, which cleansed them of their sins. "And ye shall offer one he-goat as a sin offering and two he-lambs of the first year for a sacrifice of peace offerings" (Leviticus 23:19 KJV). In exchange for our lives, a lamb can symbolically be used as a sacrifice during the mosaic period for sinful sacrifice.

It's not good to kill a lamb without reason. Lambs are preserved for spiritual sacrifice. The blood of a lamb appeases spirits. When a lamb manifests in our dream, it's a sign of divine visitation for intervention, for settlement or appeasement. Do not bury a lamb alive in your family, except under God's direction to do so. Lamb is a great spirit for appeasement. "Your lamb or young goat shall be perfect without blemish or bodily defect, a male a year old, you may take it from the sheep or from the goats ... Moreover they shall take some of the blood and put it on the two doorposts and on the lintel of the houses in which they eat it ... For I the Lord will pass through the land of Egypt on this night and will strike down all the firstborn in the land of Egypt ... The blood shall be a sign for you on the houses where you live; when I see the blood I shall pass over you, and no affliction shall happen to you or destroy you when I strike the land of Egypt" (Exodus 12:5, 7, 12–13 KJV).

If a dreamer practices traditional religion and sees a lamb in a dream, it means they need to perform a sacrifice. It's a divine sign to accept salvation of God.

Law: There are basic principles of life in the physical life and in the inner world of humans. When we dream about the law, it is a word of caution to be principled and law abiding. The law represents the particular part of our life that needs attention. To a lawyer, someone who works in the court, or a clergyman, it's a normal dream. The laws we see in the dream hold an important message for our moral life, our daily work life and engagements.

Lead: When a dreamer sees himself/herself leading a people or leading in an event, whether sports or exams, it is a symbol of blessing, success, and favor. The most common meaning is leadership. It takes a reader to lead in anything in life.

Learn: This means acquiring knowledge. It is a good experience for the soul and spiritual growth. Most things we usually learn in the dream are always strange. These things are past or future experiences of the soul. A dreamer could be learning a knowledge known in past civilizations, thousands of years ago, which this present civilization is unaware of. And a dreamer could be projected into the future to learn a new knowledge not known to this present civilization.

Learning in the dream is a good experience for the soul. Whatever we learn in the dream exists in the dreamer's subconscious mind. Sometimes it's very difficult for the dreamer to remember or develop it. There are some people who always learn in dreams, and they are destined to be great teachers, holders of knowledge, inventors, or creative minds. Most things humans create today were inspired in a dream state.[40] Many great songs sung in this world are learned in a dream. In the dream lies the past, the present, and future events, including inventions. Whatever you hear or learn in the dream is the key to many earthly problems. Desire to learn new things in the dream and in the physical realm. "Poverty and shame shall be to him that refuseth instruction: but he that hateth reproof is brutish" (Proverbs 13:18 KJV).

---

[40] www.rd.com/list/ideas-that-came-from-dreams/.

Land: This is a separate world that holds life, the ancestral home of humans. When lands manifest in the dream, it means the dreamer has a case with a deity spirit of the land. Land to a non-Christian is a deity that represents land gods. To a believer, land represents possession and productivity.

Land is also form of defense. When land arises in the favor of a dreamer, it means the dreamer's enemies will possibly die.

Land also means home coming. When it manifests, it could mean impending death of the dreamer.

Life: This refers to anything that is presently existing. Life can manifest with various images, including a living tree with fruits, yam, or animals. And its interpretation depends on the cultural background of the dreamer. When life manifests in any form, it means long life, productivity, children, and prosperity.

Light: Light is a timed event that reveals things. It is also the beginning of manifestation (i.e., it activates things to begin to manifest). When timed events are on lock mode, pause mode, or hidden away from everyone, those events are in the thick darkness.

Whenever the light is activated, everything hidden away will start to manifest according to time. When God commanded light to manifest on earth, everything hidden by darkness in the world began to manifest according to God's command. "And the earth was without form or void and darkness was upon the face of the deep ... And God said, Let there be light and there was light" (Genesis 1:2–3 KJV).

Any matter or thing whose time has come must manifest on earth. When light is put off in the world, everything is on pause mode again. Every dream is shown with light; without the light, we can't see any image or motion pictures. Whenever we find ourselves in the dark in the dream, it means the information our soul is searching for is a deep secret whose time hasn't come to manifest. Additionally, evil entities like to operate in the dark because darkness covers them up. Darkness means secret or certain things have been hidden away from the dreamer.

Our prayer is for God to cast His light unto our pathway to help us succeed in whatever we set our hands to do. Without light, which directs vision guardians, no person will succeed in anything. God is light, and light brings understanding and wisdom. "Thy word is a lamp unto my feet and a light unto my path" (Psalm 119:105 KJV).

"Then spake Jesus again unto them, saying, I am the light of the world, he that followeth me shall not walk in darkness but shall have the light of life" (John 8:12 KJV).

God said, "Ye are the light of the world. A city that is set on a hill cannot be hid" (Matthew 5:14 KJV).

"For so hath the Lord commanded us, saying, I have set thee to be a light of the gentiles that thou shouldest be for salvation unto the ends of the earth" (Acts 13:47 KJV).

This is the mandate of God upon our lives as believers and followers of Jesus Christ. We ought to be the light of direction, vision, understanding, and wisdom to the entire universe. When light shines in your dream world, God is with you. In time, good events, understanding, and revelation will come into your life.

Father, make us a light to our generation and the ones to come. Amen.

Limit: We are limited in the realm of the spirit by the level of our faith. We operate according to our knowledge about God in our minds. It is in the mind that we build thoughts, inspirations, and dreams. The things stored in our subconscious mind are the pillars of our faith in the dream realm and in the physical world. From the substance or evidence of things in our subconscious mind is where our faith in God is built and exercised. As humans, we are limited on earth and in the dream realm by our faith and the existing knowledge we possess. To go beyond our natural limit, we must increase knowledge to our present civilization.

"Faith comes by hearing and hearing by the word of God" (Romans 10:17 KJV). As we live on, we learn great testimonies about God and store them in our mind, and it becomes a part of us. In the dream, in this world or the next world to come, we will be functioning according to the faith we built while on earth now. Before God, there are no limits. All are equal before God but not in our abilities and faith. There are people who will rule with God in the next new world order, while there are ones who will just live on earth. Now is the time to feed our souls with God's words, which are spirit and life. In the dream realm, our true selves manifest better. Whatever we do in the dream, we can achieve in the physical realm unless we have been projected into the future or past to learn certain things.

Always remember we can do all things by God's grace, whether in the dream or on earth. If you want to fly in the dream, you can; if you want to walk on water, you can. What you can do in the dream with ease is a part of your soul's personality forever.

Listen: Listening is a strong channel of communication in the dream realm. Whenever your ear is open to hear something in the dream, your senses in that region have drawn in more energy to hear or get information from afar. In this instance, distance, walls, space, and time are not a barrier to the dreamer to hear secrets.

When our sense of hearing is used to pass information to the dreamer, it means such information is direct without codes or images. The dreamer doesn't require an interpreter or deep wisdom to understand the message. The ear is also used to decode conversations that have been discussed in secret. When we talk, our voices are recorded in waves and stored forever. It can be recalled for another round of listening like a CD or cassette. When certain secret conversations or evil plans are stored up in dream waves, God can recall it to the hearing of the dreamer. It is just like a leaked voice recording. Even King Solomon identified that there is nothing that can remain hidden under the sun. All information gotten in the dream by listening is for the dreamer's information unless he/she is instructed to pass it on. Some people's ears are open in the dream and in the physical world. They can hear God talk to them directly, though most of the times God speaks to humans, it is in the dream state. You have vision as a dreamer, and some vision happens while the person is awake.

The first time God wanted to speak to the people of Israel, they couldn't withstand the direct communication with God. God can use earthly elements to communicate to humans in a vision or dream; breeze, wind, or air can transform information from current form to vocal form. These natural things can dilute the currents, vibrations, and powers in

God's words to softer vocals humans can easily decipher. God uses a lots of methods to communicate with humans, not direct voice communication. Whatever you listen to in the dream is very important. The human ear is telepathic; it can discern information from afar. The ear is part of the human sensory organ designed to communicate things to the brain. Hearing or listening in the dream is a special gift from God.

Some prophets of God can hear human hearts thinking but can't see visions. Some can hear, see visions or dreams, and have the wisdom to interpret what they can hear and see. I pray all prophets have all the gifts in the ministry to do their job. Every dream, vision, or hearing needs wisdom from God to use it to work.

Live: This refers to your place of dwelling, a place you take shelter and do the business of life. In the dream, wherever we live is only an illustration or symbol.

You may see yourself living in a big, well-furnished home while you are living in a single room. Where you live in the dream is an object of interpretation. When a dream wants to reveal a block house or iron house, they may use wood to represent the house. Living in a gutter or dejected place in the dream may be a way of communicating with you that you need to change your status of living and personality. You may see a mud house in your village manifest to you as your home. It means you should consider building a house in the village. You may see yourself live in a mansion in the dream. Such a dream is revealing your blessings to come. Where you see yourself live in the dream tells you something about your status.

Load: Carrying a load in the dream represents a mantle of great responsibility on the dreamer. A load can also mean a curse. When a dreamer is carrying a load that represents curses, the challenges they are facing have no cure or solution.

Another meaning of a load in the dream is slavery and suffering. If someone is caged by a wicked person, it isn't uncommon for them to dream of carrying a heavy load and walking aimlessly. Any dreamer who sees themselves carrying a load in the dream should pray for deliverance immediately.

The content of the load is the major sign to know whether a load is a blessing or a curse. If the load is filled with treasures, money, gold, or food, the dreamer's endeavor will pay off or be blessed. If the load is stone, iron, or condemned objects, it is definitely a cursed load.

One day, I dreamt I was carrying a lot of items on a lonely pathway. In my mind, I knew the load contained good things, but it was big and burdensome. I was also afraid that bad people would attack me and dispossess me of the load. Suddenly, tall, evil spirits in the form of humans walked toward me to take away the load in my possession. Seeing that I was helpless, I lifted the bag and threw it down to the earth, knowing fully well that I was in the dream state. The plan was that if I threw the load out to the earth, the evil spirit couldn't come to the earth to take it. I would be left alone to fight with them without losing the load. I succeeded in throwing the load to the earth first, then faced them in a fight. The fight became so fierce I forcefully disappeared from there back to earth (i.e., I woke up). When I slept again, my soul went back to that same place and continued fighting with them until the battle was over. This dream was a good dream. I took back my blessings that the devil had seized long before. Those evil people were demons in charge of seizing my good fortune. God went with me in spirit to take it back to earth.

If your wealth is not released to the earth, you can't enjoy it. Your prosperity can't manifest on earth until it is released to the earth. There are a lot of people whose destinies and blessings are trapped in the realm of the spirit. In the dream, they drive the best cars and spend good money, but on the earth, they are busy trekking on foot. You have to claim your destiny. It is the will of God for you to possess your possession. Amen.

Local: Local things in the dream refer to past events and our present living standard. It is rare for divine entities to use local things to represent the future. Local could symbolize the origin of a thing or the primitive nature of an event or information. Local things are also symbolic representations of past and present things in our lives. You could see a local house in the dream representing the place you are currently living. The mud house you see in the dream could represent a block house here on earth. A wood house you see in the dream could represent a glass house on earth. Things that appear local in the dream could represent a good thing in the physical. It only describes your present status of living.

Local also represents your present geographical location. When local things are used to talk to you, it must be objects, locations, or things you are very familiar with.

Location: Location in the dream realm is different from the way we understand it in the physical realm. Every dreamer uses the mind or the subconscious mind to navigate at will during a dream state. Whenever the mind leads us is where we would go. We can be in different locations using one subconscious mind. You can sleep in the first dream and dream dreams, and you can sleep in the third dream and still dream dreams with one mind in different locations at the same time. Anywhere our mind directs our soul to journey to get information is a location.

Location in the dream is an imaginary place created for communication. It can be like a drama scene or a theatre stage. It could be just pictures, images, or life experience. So location is the foundation upon which we get information or we communicate with another world. There is an invisible hand that directs our mind to locations in the dream. We might not see the hands of God's angels in our dreams, but they are very active. Sometimes our guardian angel can be disguised as personalities in the dream to help us. They could take up different faces or personalities to play various roles in the dream realm.

Location (part 2): Location in the dream as an actual representation of a geographical location. In the dream, you could discover that a place you know as a road in the physical realm is a market in the dream. It could mean any of the following:

- That location is a suitable location for a market.
- The location was a market in a past civilization.
- The location is conducive for successful business transactions.
- The location is blessed because it attracts people of like minds.

Location in the dream is the best search engine to determine the original places or things. A lot of things are misplaced on earth. Some places that were lands in previous civilizations have now become oceans. If God wants to show a dreamer something relating to the time of Noah, he may discover where an ocean was previously. Location changes in the dream mean there is a paradigm shift or time gap.

Lost: To get lost in the dream is to be distracted or lose sense of direction in the physical world. Anytime you get lost in the dream, it reveals you have lost your sense of direction in the journey of your life. Anyone who year in, year out remains the same without improvement or achievement is lost. When you realize you are lost in the dream, quickly begin to retrace your steps. It is a nice revelation that tells the dreamer to return to the basics.

An individual could be advancing in their professional career or business, but they are lost already. Where they are headed is not their destined destination, and all their endeavors will end up in failure at last. Whenever you are lost in the dream, observe where you are going. If it is what you are doing, please go back to the drawing board with prayers and ask God for a sense of direction. Now if your belongings get lost in the dream, it's a sign that you may lose something very important, depending on the symbol of what you lost.

Lose: To lose something in the dream is a bad omen. For example, losing a person in the dream means death or demotion of the person in the family, workplace, or position of authority. Whatever you succeed in losing in the dream has a strong possibility of occurring on earth. Most things we lose in the dream are forewarning to take precautions. Others are for the dreamer's information. Try not to lose money, a phone, or important objects in the dream.

Love: Love is just a magnetic field of attraction to the things our physical and soul bodies desire. Whatever we are involuntarily attracted to on earth or in the dream is love. Love in the dream is an energy that pull us toward something without the ability to stop it. Relationships build love or attraction in our souls.

If we dream of people we are in relationship with, whether brother, sister, relatives, parents, or friends, we are likely to feel safe and naturally attracted to them without fear. These energies of love or attraction can also be formed around habits. Whatever we are addicted to on earth we usually see ourselves doing in the dream involuntarily.

Our inner, suppressed desires create love or attraction to those things in the dream world. There is no deceit in the dream world. Our hidden natures and desires are easily exposed and manifest clearly in the dream. Our desires create attraction in the dream world, especially the ones we crave to experience. Whatever we love on earth manifests as our weakness in the spiritual realm, which evil people can use to harm us in the dream. The things we love can be used to ascertain the nature of our true self and personality. It can be used to measure the level of an individual's spirituality.

For example, a man who loves womanizing or is addicted to sex can easily be exposed in the dream whenever a woman manifests in his dream. The speed at which he gravitates to the woman to have sex measures his carnality to sex physically. If someone with evil intentions wants to poison such a fellow, all they need to do is send a demon to manifest in the form of a woman to execute those evil plans to a dreamer. It takes the intervention of God or a distraction to save the situation.

Some dreamers eat in the dream, and some drink beer. All these attractions to things we love are great danger of the flesh. We should learn to resist the desires of the flesh in the dream. We should not create loopholes or weak points for the enemy to strike us. Most sicknesses, diseases, and problems we face were sown in the dream state. Resist the devil, and he will flee from you. We can't make our bodies the habitation of the devil. Demons are more powerful to attack in the dream realm than in the physical. It is needful for every dreamer to be alert and wary in the dream to resist temptation and evil attack.

Luck: When you have luck in the dream, it is a sign of unmerited favor that will soon come your way. It is a direct message of incoming success and prosperity. If a dreamer is allergic to managing secrets, their guardian angel may use luck to reveal being unlucky. Opposite meaning of an image can be used to protect secrets from a dreamer.

Any dreamer who doesn't know how to manage secrets or information will always dream the opposite meaning of things. If the true side of secret information is given to such a dreamer, it will endanger them and negatively affect the fulfillment of the dream or information.

Lunch: See *food*.

Lion: This symbol represents power, authority, supremacy, leadership, royalty, dominance, fearlessness, and commanding influence. The image of the lion represents a strong personality.

If an individual dreams of a lion, they are likely going to be promoted at work or be selected to be placed in a position of authority. It shows that the dreamer has leadership qualities they can use to influence others to do their wishes. The lion is synonymous with domination and supremacy. Anybody in the dream you see as a lion is a leader, a fighter, a goal getter, a warrior, or a hero. You can work with them, but you can't force them to do anything against their will. They are very powerful.

Lineage: This represents the circle of life in a family. Life is in a cycle that can be likened to the earth's orbit around the sun. Our lineage is the natural home or geographical location of each human soul on earth. Our lineage on earth can be terminated or changed if our soul is transferred to other higher worlds. When we are living as a person on earth, we are strongly attached to our family lineage, and when we die, our soul is also strongly attached to our family circle or lineage in death or the world of the dead. The dearly departed souls in a particular family are what traditionalists call ancestors.

These statements describe the strong bond of family, and its effects leach into the spiritual. Our lineage can be traced using a family tree, and it is important in our journey of life. When we die, our souls return to God and join other members of our lineage who have departed before us. If God wants to reincarnate any soul, God chooses that soul from within his family circle. When God allows a soul to transmit to heaven or other world, that person loses their family circle or lineage on earth. They will be joining another lineage suitable for their present personality.

In heaven, the kingdom of God will be divided into the twelve tribes of Israel. There are twelve lineages of the human race that form the basis of the nations of the heavenly world. These souls will be chosen from all of humanity, not only from the twelve tribes of Israel.

Any soul that God wishes to return to the earth based on earthly records or what we call God's judgment will divinely return to their natural lineage unless God decides to swap that soul to another family lineage for good. When you encounter any ancestor in a dreams, please pay attention to what they say or the circumstances around the meeting. The message they have is a very important message from God to the living. Using the image or symbol of your lineage means the message is important to your life journey.

The family lineage is a decider of our destiny. God has a purpose of bringing people together to form a lineage or family tree. Every person is a nation. We are channels for other souls to emerge into the world. We must fulfill our purpose in our family lineage. When we don't fulfill the things God requires of us, we might return to the same lineage to complete our unfinished business. When we live above earthly boundaries by doing what God commanded us to do, we are automatically heavenly candidates. We no longer have business with the world.

Lamp: It's a symbol of light reduced to a person. Lamp means sense of direction. It's a sign of someone whose presence illuminates the world. Other organizations call it illuminati (i.e., a light bearer). A person who can command a crowd is a visionary and has a special intellect to understand things can be symbolized as a lamp.

God gives us lamps to guide our footsteps and direct us to successes, riches, and good fortune. Every lamp will need oil (i.e., God's grace, anointing oil) to keep it burning. "Ye are the light of the world. A city that is set on a hill cannot be hid. Neither do men light a candle and put it under a bushel but on a candlestick and it giveth light unto all that are in the house. Let your light so shine before men, that they may see your good works and glorify your Father which is in heaven" (Matthew 5:14–16 KJV).

Library: This is a hallmark of knowledge. Whenever you see yourself in a library, there is new knowledge has been made available to you by God. In a little while, it will start manifest in your inspiration. To have access to a library means you have been chosen to have a special insight into divine knowledge.

List: A list contains decided things or names of people for a particular event. A list in the dream world is difficult to influence in the physical world. Whenever you see someone's name on a list of school admission or employment, that person will likely succeed.

Loan: When you dream of giving loans to people in the dream, it means God has placed you in a position to assist others. It might not be fiat money; it can include anything of value. Giving out loans in the dream is a good omen.

When you receive loans in the dream, it means whatever you are seeking you will find, and you will obtain favor from people. When you receive a loan in a dream, you must repay it by doing good deeds to others. Not all our blessings are intended for our personal use. God can use us as a channel to pass on the blessing.

Lonely: This is a sign of abandonment, disappointment, or the loss of a loved one. Whenever a person is lonely, it shows that a tragedy is about to befall the person. For example, standing alone in the rain means eventual death, controversy, or trouble without solution. Loneliness suggests helplessness. It should be strictly avoided.

Look: This is a medium of perception of the soul in the dream realm. Looking measures the level of the soul's awareness while dreaming.

Lottery: This reveals that your endeavors are a game of chance. However, if you win a lottery in the dream, you will soon get luck. Dreaming of a lottery is not encouragement to gamble.

Loyal: Having people loyal to you means you are in charge. You are in a total control of yourself and others. It's a symbol of confidence, stability, and self-esteem. It means you are on the right track. You have been empowered by God to take absolute control of your situation in your family, your organization, or wherever you find yourself.

When you are loyal to someone or people in the dream, it means you require patience, humility, and loyalty to get what you are looking for or to achieve your goals. It could also mean you are a servant to another person. However, when loyalty becomes servitude or slavery, it becomes a bondage to the soul.

Loyalty means you honor and respect someone else to direct you in the affairs of life.

Luxury: Dreams about luxuries are fantasies.

PART M

Master: Any master or teacher you see in the dream is your guardian angel. They are divine beings appointed unto us by God to help. Angels come in different forms and appearances. Part of the duty of angels include the following

- They guide us (Exodus 23:20 KJV).
- They do the will of God and help us accomplish God's will (Psalm 103:19–22 KJV).
- They encourage and minister to us (Hebrews 1:14 KJV).
- They act as conduits for God's messages to us (Luke 1:13 KJV).

They can bring inspiration, wisdom, and healing. Any problem they solve is solved forever. Always appreciate God by giving an offering of thanks whenever you see them in your dreams.

Match: See *gamble.*

Mother: When you see your earthly mother in the dreams, she could be representing your guardian angel. Any demon wishing to deceive a dreamer's soul will not manifest in the appearance of a dreamer's mother. Demons of seduction do not use the image of a mother to appear to a dreamer.

However, other kingdoms of darkness like witches can use a mother's image to destroy a dreamer's soul. They will use a mother image to gain the trust of the dreamer and make them let their guard down. It takes the intervention of God to escape an attack from evil men when they use a dreamer's mother as a disguise.

Majority: It means total support. Whatever you have the majority, support in the dream is already established.

Manifestation: This refers to the appearance of symbols and images that are used to pass information to the dreamer.

Manipulation: This refers to illusions used to influence a soul in the dream. We are always being manipulated in the dream by supernatural beings. They define our dream experience by manipulating our subconscious mind in the dream. We are servants to whatever we yield ourselves to. If we yield ourselves to God, He will guide us for our own good. But those who yield themselves to the devil are manipulated by the dark realm, except when God has a message to deliver to that soul. Such dreams are usually very strange and remarkable. In the case of King Nebuchadnezzar of Babylon, he had multiple dreams that were forewarnings of judgment upon him (Daniel 4:4–37). It is a good practice to hand over your soul to God in prayers before sleeping.

Manners: This refers to the body language and behavior of the dreamer in the dream. Manners are physical attitudes or characteristics a dreamer possesses in their subconscious mind. They showcase our true personality in the dream realm.

Manners could be obstacles or hinder us from receiving communication from angels when we dream. This is the reason our angels manipulate us to give out information. It's like a child in the hand of the parents or adults. Children will always throw tantrums, but the parents or adults will find a way out of love to manipulate their manners to achieve stability.

Market: The marketplace symbolizes our business life on earth. The location of a market in the dream shows a geographical place conducive for business. That location is endowed with an aura that attracts people for transactions.

When a dreamer is marketing a product or services in the dream, such a product will gain customers' acceptance. If a dreamer dreams of visiting a market to buy goods, it is a sign of impending blessing. It could also mean the dreamer is rich. We require value to obtain something of value in the dream. When a dreamer is the one selling in the market, it means the dreamer's kind of business would receive patronage. Just like in other public spaces, it is not good to be disgraced in the market. The marketplace symbolizes money, merchandise, and the ability to make wealth. Those who interact with it are rich and wealthy.

Marriage: Marriage is a human activity strongly recommended for the physical world. Dreaming of marriage could be a direct message of marriage for the dreamer. These types of dreams are good for single people, especially when they are in a serious courtship with someone. That dream is an affirmation that they are on the right track, unless the opposite meaning of the dream is used to reveal a secret to the dreamer for some wise reasoning.

Marriage in the dream can be used to direct a man or woman to someone to marry. When a person who is ripe for marriage, or someone is praying for God's direction to get married, and the person gets married in the dream, it means the request, prayer, or person's desires will come to pass. In the case of the man, the personality, physical appearance, and family background of their wife-to-be could be revealed in the dream. This would make it easy for the man to locate his wife from that dream description. Chances are the dreamer can find the woman he got married to in the dream. A lot of married people have dreamt of getting married to their current partner before they ever met. Many times, they would only recollect the dream after some years in the marriage.

The danger in getting married to strange people we are not familiar with in the dream is that evil people and even your heart's desires can manipulate dreams. When evil people manipulate marriage dreams, they can give out a dreamer's soul in marriage to strange spirits, demons, or deities. If this happens, that person will be unable to get married physically. This phenomenon is popularly known as spiritual husband/ wife.

It is not good for a married person to get married again in their dreams. It is a sign of initiation into an occult or demonic association. It could also mean that the person you got married to is not your destined spouse. If a married man sees his girlfriend or mistress in his matrimonial bed or home, it means that woman is wishing to get married to the man. Anyone you dream of marrying is truly in love with you.

Marriage means relationship restricted to people the dreamer truly loves. It is not good to do it with strange people unless it foretells of a future lover.

Meditation: In the dream, it is a level of spiritual growth. When we meditate in the dream, it means we communicate deeply with God without vocal prayers. At that level, the dreamer can pray with only their mind. Meditation shows spiritual maturity in one's knowledge of God and self-awareness.

Membership: It's a circle of people a dreamer belongs to. Whenever you find your membership in the dream, it is your true place. One day while dreaming, I couldn't get access to a place where I wanted to have a meeting. David Oyedepo of Living Faith met me and gave an ID card that granted me access to that restricted venue. I hung my ID and was able to gain entrance. That ID card he gave me marked my calling to service as a minister of God. Do not despise the role of mentors and senior colleagues in your life. Their wealth of experience and connections can grant you access and membership into hidden places.

Memory: Memories are stored experiences of the human soul. Memories are generated in our subconscious mind. When it is generated, it becomes symbols, images, and motion pictures that tell a story. Our memory can predate our current civilization, although you might be unable to recognize the symbols or images.

Everything we see in the dream has actually existed or will be made manifest in the future. When dreams look strange, it is possible our memory is dragging us back to ages past or our soul is projecting us to unknown future events.

Mind: The human mind is an abstract part of human intelligence that remains with an individual throughout their life's journey. When we die, our physical brain memories and body decay in the ground, but our mind and soul personality go back to our Creator God. So our mind is the brain box that remains forever. The human soul is eternal; it cannot die. The soul without the body is useless and vice versa. It can be likened to how a memory card and a phone work. The memory card is useless until it is inserted into a phone. Our soul with our mind remains inactive when separated from the physical, intelligent human body. But whenever life returns to our physical body, the soul is revived and starts synchronizing our memories and knowledge with the senses attached to the body.

When Christ was born on earth, He had no memory of His true self as God. While the fetus, the Holy Spirit of God, created, grew, and was born from the womb of Mary, He was like every other child needing care, love, and affection. It took twelve years for Jesus to come to the realization of Himself. The Bible reported that Christ grew in strength and in the knowledge of God. He began to recall who He was when He was twelve years old (Luke 2:42–52 KJV), and at thirty, He knew He had come into the full realization of Himself and His purpose on earth as the Son of God (Luke 3:23 KJV).

As we grow in our physical bodies, we ought to grow in our knowledge of our souls and understanding of our purpose. "Man, know thy self" is a popular saying that encourages us to reflect on our true selves.

Mental: These are waves of thoughts existing in the physical and spiritual realm that can be tapped into by any pliable mind.

Mistakes: Mistakes are warning signs, cautions, or prevention signals. They can also be showstoppers or modes of prevention. When mistakes are made in the dream, it means the planned action or the manifestation of the dream has been suspended. Whenever a mistake is made, the whole exercise is in futility.

Money: This is the essence of value used in exchange for something else. Money in the dream refers to your wealth or riches. When we encounter a foreign currency like dollars or pounds in the dream, it means the cash in question is worth a lot of physical money on earth. A person's purchasing power is measured by the units of money or value a person possesses in the invisible world.

Every soul has an amount of money stored in their favor in the spiritual realm. Human souls originate and are given a destiny by God. All that soul will ever be has been written from the beginning. Heaven begins to release value to us from the time we are born on earth. Some people's value is released ahead of their birth and kept in custody of their parents, from whom they eventually inherit wealth. Generally, most people come into wealth as they grow in knowledge and begin to work. Wealth and the power to make wealth belong to God, and He gives it freely to whomsoever He wishes. Our prayer to God should be to receive intact that which He has destined for us.

Christ admonished us to save our treasures in heaven, where moth and dust cannot corrupt it and thieves cannot steal it (Matthew 6:19–20 KJV). Saving money in heaven simply requires you to sow seeds of kindness, humanitarian works, goodness, and selfless service for God and humanity in order to build savings in heaven. The good works you do today for God and humanity, including using your talents, gifts, and professional career for His glory, count toward your savings in heaven. In the next world, in heaven or on earth or other worlds, God will use that savings to measure your unit of money in heaven. Every person on earth is worth something; nobody is valueless.

"He that is faithful in that which is least is faithful also in much. He that is dishonest in the least is also dishonest in much. If therefore ye have not been faithful in the use of earthly wealth, who will entrust true riches to you?" (Luke 16:10–11 AMP). When God releases money to us by His grace, God will evaluate our ability to manage the money for further blessing. To whom much is given, much is expected (Luke 12:48 KJV). If we have been blessed with talents, wealth, knowledge, time, and the like, it is expected that we benefit others. When you join God in distributing the wealth of the nation to His children, you become one with God, and you will always be richer. "He that giveth unto the poor shall not lack but he that hideth his eyes shall have many a curse" (Proverbs 28:27 KJV). For our resources to manifest on earth to us, we must do some work. Working for what belongs to us to come to us is the law of nature on earth. The natural principle of life according to Christ is you reap what you sow. But for you to reap your money or resources, you must work for it. There is nothing like free money on earth. There is a curse placed on humans to work before we get what has already been given to us (Genesis 3:17–19 KJV). That curse is holding our physical bodies on earth, but in the realm of the spirit, we can get our money without work. It is easier to be in possession of money in the dream. You can buy whatever you like in the dream, drive expensive cars and planes, and live in a mansion, but you can't do the same on earth without work and time. So work is just the finishing touches you need to perform to get your money on earth.

When you possess money in the dream or live a life of luxury in the dream, it means the dreamer is rich. A soul can use dreams to know their original status in the dream. Whatever you see yourself do in the dream is you, and you can achieve the same thing on earth.

There are many obstacles that stand against God's blessings and purpose in our life—family foundation, curses, and choices we make. Wrong marriage or associations can stand against God's blessings in our life. Some people are working so hard without success. When we get things right and walk with God like Abraham, heaven will unleash unquantifiable blessings to us. "But seek ye first the kingdom of God and His righteousness and all these things will be added unto you" (Matthew 6:33 KJV). We can change our destiny by giving our lives to God.

There is a simple law of abundance God revealed to Moses. If you give God 10 percent of your income as tithe, God will give you an increase. When you assist God to distribute human resources on earth among people, God will fill your storehouse with wealth. God said there would not be room enough to hold it. May this be my experience in the name of YESHUA, I pray. Amen!

Mood: These are discerning images or symbols to determine someone's state of mind. If a dreamer's mood is bad in the dream, it foretells a bad situation they will encounter. When a dreamer's mood swings to good mood, they will soon get good surprises.

Movement: Movement in the dream is just changing from one stage of dream to the other or changing from one scene to another scene with the mind. We could walk with our legs and hands, crawl, fly, drive cars or boats, or fly planes at light speed. Every location we find ourselves in the dream has its own way of movement. There are places you can only walk on water, and there are some places you need light speed to move (i.e., appear and disappear).

Mystery: These are unknown revelations to the soul. It requires God's intervention to make known mysteries. Mysteries belong to God alone. Mysteries are things or events that time has not yet made known to a human soul.

Mad: To be mad in the dream means to lose consciousness in the dream world. It is not a good experience. The dreamer will not remember anything that happens under that circumstance. Madness in the dream can be like a seizure of the soul body. The emotional body of the soul will appear to be frozen or inactive. The thoughts and signals in the mind will jam or fluctuate.

Unconsciousness in the dream can occur when a soul meets evil personalities in the dream. The bad spiritual vibrations from the evil personality can make a dreamer to get shocked, leading to temporary insanity or loss of memory.

When a soul encounters an evil attack or has a nightmare, the dreamer's body receives the shock waves in the physical world. The dreamer might wake up feeling disoriented and weak. To avoid memory loss and temporary insanity in our postdream experience, it is a good practice to meditate on the Word of God at night before bed and in the morning when we wake up.

When you wake up from a nightmare, don't immediately stand up and go about your day. Remain in your bed in the same position you slept, close your eyes, and start meditating to recall the events of your dream. Then gradually open your eyes and stand up.

Encountering a mad person in the dream is a warning of possible insanity in your actions. What the mad person is doing is the key to the proper interpretation of the dream.

Magazine: (See *calendar*.) Pay close attention to any image or written information in the magazine, as it is a direct message for the dreamer. Anything captured in a picture or writing is already established. The dream only serves to reveal the information to you.

Magistrate: (See *court*.) It's a sign to be lawful and follow the due process of the law. It's also a sign of possible disagreement that may likely lead to litigation. If a dreamer works in a court of law, it is not abnormal to dream of their place of work. For them, the dream would have more to do with their career than someone who does not work in the law court. The key to understanding the dream depends on the activities and events going on in the court.

Being in a magistrate court could also mean the dreamer has been summoned before a local deity for judgment or vindication from the witchcraft, occult organization, or local deity.

Magnet: (See *attraction.*) This signifies the force of attachment and affinity a soul has for something or someone.

Mail: It's a message box. If you can read the mail, you get a direct message that does not need interpretation.

Maize: Represents fruitfulness, growth, and success, especially when you see a field of maize with seeds.

Mall: See *market.*

Map: It is a detailed direction to a place on earth. A map guides one on a journey. Pay attention to any map given to you in the dream because it is the key to your success. When you see a map, it means your journey will be successful. A map means a sense of direction has been given to someone in whatever they are doing. It can be likened to a solution to a problem. Whatever you are doing, you won't be misled or lose your track record of success.

Marine: See *water.*

Mask: This means hidden secrets.

Medicine: This means healing and restoration have been administered to a dreamer. Whenever a dreamer takes medicine in the dream, they will surely recover from an ailment.

Menstruation: This is a sign of fertility and relates to a woman's sexual life.

Military: Military men in the dream can refer to the armies of heaven, government institutions, or any person charged with the responsibility of maintaining law and order. It also means enforcement of laws or executing a decided commands. Military men can mean heavenly intervention for a soul. Whenever army or military manifests in your dream, a rescue operation will have commenced for the dreamer.

Mock: See *laugh*.

Mob: This means public condemnation of an activity. When a mob appears in your dream, it is revelation that you are committing an abominable act. If the mob catches the dreamer in an act, it means that soul will never commit a similar act again. It is a strong warning to a dreamer to desist from doing things that are not culturally or traditionally acceptable to a people.

Moon: This is a heavenly body that regulates events. The moon determines the timing of events in the world. Dreaming about the moon indicates a worldwide established event that will have global significance. Seeing a moon in the dream is a divine revelation about things to come.

Mountain: A mountain signifies responsibility or something that requires work and determination to achieve. A mountain also refers to a sacred place of worship. Being at the apex of a mountain is a sign of overcoming tribulation or elevation in an individual's life.

When a person dreams of climbing a mountain, it means their endeavor requires effort. Praying on a mountain is a sign that a soul needs to pray to God. Falling from a mountain is a bad omen!

PART N

Naked: Nakedness means humiliation, shame, disappointment, surrender, submission, to make a covenant, to make open declaration, to seal an oath, prayer, or covenant, or to open a secret. It could also mean to be cleansed and accepted. The different meanings can be applied depending on the circumstances in the dream.

In my personal experience, I dreamt of myself in a long queue, waiting to be attended to. As I approached the front of the line, my shorts loosened from my waist, and I found myself naked. I was embarrassed, and I left the queue to put my clothes in order. When I came back to the line, I had to rejoin at the end. In this context, my nakedness signified disappointment and a rise and fall in my life. Everything happened as I dreamt it.

If a dreamer finds themselves bathing naked privately, it means sanctification or cleansing of the soul and spiritual baptism. When you see yourself walking naked in the dream, it means shame and humiliation. To cover someone else's nakedness is to cover that person's shame and disgrace.

Name: There are codes of information embedded in a name. Names only describe the characteristics of a thing. The names we hear in the dream may be symbolic and not the actual earthly name of an individual. If you meet someone who wants to help you overcome a situation in the dream and they tell you their name is Godswill, it means that your problem is in God's hand. Do not think your friend Godswill in the physical world will help solve the problem.

God gives name to some people before they are born. "Your wife, Sarah will have a baby, a son. Name him Isaac (Laughter)" (Genesis 17:19 MSG). Some people's names are given by God at birth or before their naming ceremony. Names can describe historical circumstances upon which someone is born, and names can envision the parental expectations and wishes for their child. In a spiritual home, names describe the personality trait of the child and the office of the child or their spiritual calling. In summary, names foretell the prophetic nature of a person.

When names are mentioned in the dream, it describes a situation and reveals a message of hope, an answer to prayers and the key to problems. Names ought to be given by God's inspiration and not mere human thinking. Before a child is born into any home, God usually reveals it to the parents. The revelation will also reveal the name of the child. Every great person born in this world received their names before they were born. God foretold the names of great men in the Bible like Isaac, Moses, and John the Baptist.

If your parents give you a carnal name, please pray to God to give you a heavenly name. Names hold a lot of secrets about a person. The name we hear in the dream actually exists in the world or has existed in the world. The problem with most people is not bearing their true names from God. In the dream, they could call an unfamiliar name to the dreamer, but that strange name may be the dreamer's father's name. We are disconnected in many ways from the spiritual realm. You may know someone with a particular name, but their true name on their birth certificate is not the same. So if someone mentions the name on the certificate, people who know them with the other name will not understand. That is what happens in the dream most times. Desire to know your real name. Read meaning into every name you hear in the dream.

Narration: See *revelation*.

Narrow: Narrow means coded information, regulated activity, and a strict way of life or a direction that leads to a particular destination. Most narrow paths lead to death in the dream. Ancient, narrow paths leading to a junction reveal ritual practices. Narrow path is a spiritual route that leads back to earth or to the underworld. It's a route for the spirits. Narrow paths lead to ancient or old secrets.

Whenever you find yourself on a narrow path, something great is about to happen. Narrow paths are ancient or secret ways.

Nature: Represents the physical world and its rules. Images, symbols, and motion pictures can be used to represent natural things. Everything on earth existed in God as thoughts and visions before He spoke the words that brought the world to being (Genesis 1 KJV).

Nature is a virtual prototype of a building or a drawing designed in the mind of God. The first stage of creation of the universe began in the mind of God. Its final execution was the actual physical creation of the universe. You can feel wind, but you can't see it. The true origin of nature lies in the realm of the spirit.

There exists a shadow world called the virtual world or abstract world. The abstract world is the mother of natural world or the physical world. The metaphysical world is the source of all things on earth. So natural things are the physical manifestations of the invisible or spiritual world controlled by God. Nothing manifests on earth without God's express authority.

From the day God commanded, "Let there be light" (Genesis 1:4 KJV), He began the birth of the natural world, and from that day, natural things have been manifesting according to their time. All natural things are subject to the laws of birth and death. Everything has its time of existence on earth. When things die, they only change their physical forms. God can bring forth a river where there is none. He has them inside Him, and all things can come forth at His command. The speed of God's command can't be measured by human eyes. The execution of God's command works with time, but in our eyes, it feels like lightning speed.

In the dream realm, we see nature in different forms. Natural things in the realm of the spirit look different from their physical forms on earth. And that is why images and symbols are used to represent nature.

Nest: Represents business, prosperity, success, and a comfortable life. In most places, it is called long life and prosperity. It is a very good thing to see a nest in the dream.

Network: It's the power of God that connects humanity as one people. Networks are waves and currents that link and connect us to people and things. In the dream realm, these waves are everywhere. It makes it possible to hear, see, and perceive things from thousands of miles away. Networks connect our physical body and our soul with the help of neurological pathways in our physical body. Without our nervous system, our brain will not coordinate the different parts of our body to work properly.

While dreaming, if your phone, computer, or any electrical device you possess doesn't have a network, it means you have been cut off or denied access to your destiny helpers in the physical realm. Pray to God for a network to eat with kings and princes.

News: This is direct information for the dreamer. Whatever you hear in the news in the dream is beyond the dreamer's control.

Night (darkness): This represents a state of inactivity. It can also symbolize a thing whose time of manifestation has not arrived. Night and darkness are used to divide the day from night. It also shows the times of the day when the moon or the sun should stand in the sky. Darkness represents night, while light represents day.

Secret things are hidden under the covering of darkness. Evil and occult worshippers choose darkness to operate because it covers their secrets. If the work of evil is done in the open, it loses its potency. In this way, darkness also represents evil.

If you find yourself in the darkness or in the night, it means you are already surrounded by evil people, and they are ready to strike. When things are revealed to you at night, it means the information is classified or secret. Whatever you see at night, in most cases, are things that will happen with time.

Notice: (See *news*.) Notices are established information given to a dreamer for their private knowledge. The content of the notice is the subject of interpretation to the dreamer.

Nurse: This is a symbol of healing. Dreaming of a health care professional is a revelation of one's health status. Depending on the circumstances of the dream, it can be a sign of a dreamer's need to visit a hospital for checkup. When nurses appear in our dreams, we have been healed. Amen.

PART O

Obituary: It's a message of death for an individual or problem. An obituary is an already decided event by spiritual hierarchies or evil organizations. Whatever is printed for public consumption in the dream realm is hard to reverse on earth. Obituary notices are a direct message to the dreamer concerning them or others. It is a bad signal of events that could lead to death. When evil people kill someone in the spiritual realm, they like to place the person's obituary in the realm of the spirit so that chances of their survival will be minimal. Whenever you see obituary notices in the dream, object in prayers and tear them down.

Occupant/occupy: This is a sign of possession or takeover. It's a revelation that someone is claiming ownership over your property. It is also a sign of strangers or visitors.

The most common meaning of this revelation is that someone is sharing your assets, such as your spouse, unknown to you. If a married person dreams of a strange individual occupying their home or matrimonial bed, it is a sign their spouse is having a serious extramarital affair.

If you see someone occupying your land, property, or business, it is an indication to be wary of trespassers, land grabbers, and hostile takeover in business by competitors.

Oil: This is the God-given measure of grace bestowed on every individual on earth. It is this oil that keeps you shining and succeeding in all that you put your hands into. Oil is a revelation of a big treasure for the dreamer. You are about to make it big-time. Your riches will flow like oil, serving and enriching others.

Oil also represents long-lasting business that will bring intergenerational riches. Oil can symbolize royalty when it is used to anoint the dreamer. Oil means you have been chosen and anointed for a position.

Old: These are the things of the past that link us to the present. Whenever we see old things, it reminds us of things in our past that may have direct influence on us now.

Open: Anything done in the open or in the public eye in the dream has been established (i.e., difficult to reverse). Public notices in the spiritual realm can be likened to a court case where judgments and sentencing have been given.

PART P

Palace: Palace is the habitation and residence of royalty. It symbolizes the seat of authority. The activities done by the dreamer are the subject of interpretation.

Padlock: Represents problems, obstructions, or hindrances. It can also mean preventing something from happening. Padlocks prevent a person from receiving their blessings. It also keeps success and progress at bay. Every blessing, favor, and destiny that is locked in the spirit cannot manifest on earth. It is better to padlock your problems than to lock away your blessings. Whatever is locked in the padlock is the object that requires opening.

Whenever you encounter a padlock, please endeavor to search for the key or find a way to break it. If you find a padlock in your dreams, it means your problem is known and exposed, but it requires your effort to free yourself from it. A problem known is half-solved. Unless it is an undesirable item, it is not good to lock something in the dream and lose the key.

Pain: This is a signal of physical harm in the spiritual realm. Some sleeping positions may cause harm to the physical body. In this case, the brain will send pain signals to awaken the physical body to adjust itself. There are some injuries that occur in the dream realm that lead to physical pain as well. The human soul can also feel pain. Many things that happen to the soul while dreaming can affect the physical body on earth.

266

Parrot: This reveals the spirit of backstabbing and gossip. The physical traits and characteristics of an animal can be used to reveal information in the dream realm. Anyone who sees themselves as a parrot in the dream must realize that their weakness is loquaciousness.

Party: Or gathering, it suggests any event that will draw a crowd to your house. It is usually a sign of celebration. Parties can be used by evil men to execute their evil plans, like poisoning a dreamer or initiating them into an evil organization. Parties in the dream should be avoided. It's a good channel to enchant a dreamer.

Passport: ID card. It means permission, access, authority, belonging to, acceptance. Wherever you see yourself with a passport, you are welcome. That place is your home. Whatever you do there will work and be accepted.

Pastor: It is a sign of a call to serve God. If you see yourself as a pastor, you have been anointed and called to serve. But if you encounter a pastor, you need deliverance or prayers.

Path: This refers to directions in the dream.

Penis: When a dreamer dreams of the male sexual organ, it symbolizes a sign of an adulterous, evil spirit. The male sexual organ can also appear to a dreamer to reveal information about their health status or other incidents surrounding them. If you dream of a sickness or injury on your sexual organ, it is a direct message that you will get an infection soon if you are not careful.

If your penis is weak or completely missing in the dream, it means you have lost the vitality and strength of your sex organ. The male sex organ is a direct message relating to a man's sexual life and health. But when you see a woman with a manhood or another man's manhood, that person is associated with a ring of homosexual and adulterous demons.

People: Water, fish (represent the clergy people), and animals of various kinds can be used to represent people. In fact, there are people who transform into animals while dreaming. There are people who have souls of animals as part of their earthly life journey, so they change into such animals in the dream.

For instance, there are people who can shape-shift into a cow, lion, or tiger in the physical realm. So it's very common for such a person to use the image of those animals to dream. Some animals we see in the dream realm are actually human souls.

Wherever people gather in the dream, the events and decisions there are always binding. The presence of people in the dream realm brings lasting solutions to problem or events.

Petition: A petition means a soul has been summoned before a deity or an organization for justice. If a dreamer receives a petition, someone has summoned the dreamer. But if the dreamer is the one submitting the petition, it means the situation requires a higher authority to judge.

Photograph: A photo is a piece of a message or information for the dreamer's notice. Whatever image or thing you see on a picture is true and permanent. The image captured in a picture is already decided and cannot be altered or changed. It's a way of telling a dreamer that a particular message or information is true and permanent.

When a dreamer takes pictures in the dream, it means their life and their decisions are in their hands. If other people take a picture of the dreamer, it means that the dreamer's life is in the hands of others.

The content of the photograph is the subject of interpretation. For instance, wedding photographs mean a marriage will take place and stand the test of time.

Pig: This is a symbol of uncleanness or a demonic manifestation. Most unclean animals represent evil deities. Animals can be used as a symbol or representation of deities, kingdoms, dominions, organizations, and authorities.

Pill: (See *drug.*) It symbolizes healing or an antidote for poison, snake venom, and so on. When a dreamer swallows pills, it means God has intervened for their healing. It can also mean that the dreamer might be sick soon.

Pit: It is a sign of problem, controversy, sickness, and death. When you fall into a pit in the dream, you will soon fall into a temptation. The size of the pit determines how big or problematic the matter will be. And how the dreamer falls into the pit is instructive on how to escape or avoid the problem.

The ability of the dreamer to come out of the pit is also relevant in determining how serious the problem may be. If a dreamer falls into a very big, deep pit and is unable to come out of the pit, it means the problem will almost consume the dreamer. This can result in the death or permanent disability of the dreamer. When a dreamer falls into a mighty pit filled with deadly animals like snakes, and they overpower the dreamer, it is revelation of impending sickness, which could lead to death. It takes the grace of God to deliver such a dreamer from such a problem.

Place: This refers to any geographical location in the dream that your soul wishes to visit.

Placenta: To a pregnant woman, this is the key to her survival during childbirth. So when the placenta appears in the dream, it is a warning or information regarding labor. It is a strong indication that precaution and care must be taken. The events and circumstances surrounding the appearance of the placenta are the object of interpretation to the dreamer.

Plague: A plague is a direct judgment from God. It is divine punishment for evil committed against God and humanity. When plagues manifest in the dream, it tells the dreamer that God is angry and may punish the iniquity of the dreamer. It's also God's way of judging evil altars or deities.

When a plague attacks or visits your enemy, it means God has intervened on your behalf.

Plain: This part of the spiritual realm can usually be accessed in first-sleep dreams. First-sleep dreaming usually happens during light sleeping like daytime naps.

Plane (airplane): This represents air transportation, including international business connections and local or foreign travel. When a dreamer boards a plane, it means they will travel soon or get a visitor soon.

Planes also symbolize control or dominion over powers in the air and below it. A person flying in the sky as a pilot or plane has received authority over earthly powers, destruction, or charms. The dreamer's spiritual growth has given them authority over the marine and earthly kingdoms. Any dreamer that can turn into plane and fly with passengers is a spiritual leader, high priest, bishop, or spiritual commander.

During the COVID-19 lockdown that cut across the whole world, I had a very interesting dream. On April 24, 2020, I landed a very big cargo plane. I took a bottle of wine from the plane and shared with my friends. Meanwhile, I had bought some oil tools for supply, awaiting in Dubai since late February of that same year. I couldn't fly them because of the worldwide COVID-19 lockdown. When I woke up from the dream in the morning, I told my wife that Dubai had relaxed their lockdown, and cargo international flights would soon start. That same day, I heard Dubai had lifted their lockdown, and very soon, our goods would be on the way to their final destination. Dreams don't lie. Drinking wine from the plane was a symbol of us celebrating a successful endeavor.

Pocket: This is a box of treasure belonging to a dreamer. Whatever is in your box is yours and must be guarded jealously.

Poison: Poisons in the dream are evil energies that take the form of food, fruits, sexual orgies, drink, mutual interaction,

sharing to pass on to a dreamer during a dream. Most food we eat in the dream is poison to the soul. Any sickness associated with food poison in the dream is difficult to cure with our orthodox medicine. Evil projects poison with the use of image symbols that may appear as something we like in the physical world, to poison our soul in the dream. So eating, drinking, and sex should be avoided in the dream.

Police: When police appear in the dream, trouble is imminent. Police could represent the local authorities who maintain law and order in a community. Police presence signifies trouble that needs justice. To a native person, police means someone has summoned the dreamer to a native court for justice.

Some people usually invoke people or summon somebody in their local deity for revenge or retribution justice. When this kind of thing happens, police will appear to arrest the dreamer in the dream. Police could represent dark forces and good forces in the realm of the spirit. When police are arresting other people or your enemy, it could mean literal policemen (i.e., direct warning to stay away from trouble).

Pornography: Every aspect of pornography is associated with adulterous demons (see *naked* or *nude*). Porn in the dream can help a dreamer to send sexual signals to the physical brain on earth to release sperms or sexual energies from the human body, called a wet dream. This reduces excess sperm or pulls of sexual energies in the human body. So the brain can generate porn images in the dream to help the sex organ free itself from swollen sexual feelings.

Possess: When something inhabits a dreamer's soul beyond their control, it can be called possession. Anything that prevents you from expressing your freewill is best described as possession. Evil spirits can possess someone's body and suppress their soul.

Poster: (See *photo* and *picture*.) Any information written on a poster is established and very reliable. It is like a notice (i.e., just for the dreamer's knowledge). The information is beyond the dreamer's control.

Poverty: Poor. It describes the dreamer's state of living on earth. Someone could be poor in the dream but very rich in the physical world. What it means is despite the dreamer's present living standards in the physical world (rich), they are poor in the realm of the spirit.

If a rich man sees himself as a poor man in the dream, it means he has not reached his peak or true potential. They want him to work harder to attain his true status on earth. It is not good for a poor man to see himself poor in the dream. If it happens, the dreamer should pray for a change of destiny. That person isn't doing enough to grow.

Praise: Songs of praises in the dream are messages to God. They are prayer points and songs that celebrate and extol the qualities of God. Praise helps to build our faith in God. It holds answers to our prayers. Praises are the guidelines to link to God. The best prayers in the dream are done when we give praises. Whatever we ask God in praises is answered. David prayed in praises. The entire book of Psalms are words of praise to God. Prayers in brokenness also move prayers faster. "A broken and a contrite heart, O God, thou wilt not despise." When you praise God in a dream, continue with that praise when you wake up. It's very powerful to destroy Satan.

Prayer: Prayers are powerful, important conversations between humans and God. When someone prays in the dream, it means that a soul needs prayers. The things you pray for in the dream are the things you need from God. Praying in the dream reflects the level of spiritual maturity of an individual. Praying in the dream is like praying in the spirit. In the dream, you use spiritual tongues to pray to God. It's a good spiritual exercise to pray with your soul in spirit. Prayers in the dream are prayer points and prophetic pronouncements about your problems.

Pregnant: Pregnancy is a sign of fertility. The meaning of pregnancy in dreams is contextual (i.e., depending on the status of the dreamer). If a menopausal woman finds herself pregnant in the dream, it simply means one of her daughters or someone close to her is pregnant. It can also be a sign of unfaithfulness on the part of the woman. It doesn't mean the woman is physically pregnant.

When a single lady sees herself pregnant in the dream, it foretells of her future marital status and her fertility status. But the primary meaning is the single lady could be giving birth to her children in the spirit. A woman having this kind of dream is married in the spirit and has given birth in the spirit realm. It's difficult for this kind of woman to have children physically on earth.

President: King, ruler. Represents the powers that be in the land. The authority that regulates the ruling of any kingdom, society, place, or people rests on the ruler, king, or president. When you meet a president in the dream, it means the dreamer is in that status, depending on the circumstances of the encounter with the president. When a president visits a dreamer in the dream, it means the dreamer will be favored. It could be a job position or contract by the government. Whenever you meet any ruler king or president in the dream, something good from that land must come to the dreamer. It also means the land or society the dreamer is a resident of will prosper. That land accepts him and will favor him. Any stranger in any place he may see himself should endeavor to meet the leaders, king, and rulers of that place in the dream. It's the sign of acceptance and prosperity.

When presidents, kings, and rulers appear to a dreamer, the dreamer is part of the kingdom in spirit, and he can make libations or perform rituals in that land as if he is the son of the soil.

Presence: This means someone is alive, available, or in existence. Anybody missing in a dream is likely to die or stop existing. It is better for our problems and our enemies to go missing or be absent. Our enemies should not be present.

Press: Whenever the press is involved in a situation, it means that thing requires publicity. See *media* or *news*.

Price: The value of anything in the dream is the price. When we see prices of anything in the dream, it means those things have their worth or value in earthly currency. There are things you buy or receive in the dream with the exchange of money in the dream. What it means is that you must work to earn that thing, or it will cost you something to achieve that thing. Whenever prices are involved, it means that item demands effort or sacrifice to get it on earth. There are things we must sow seeds on earth to achieve.

Priest: Clergy, pastor. Anyone who has the oracle of God is a priest. If you see a priest in your dream, you need a priest to solve your problem. You need God's divine intervention to get out of your problem. If you are the priest in the dream, then you are a priest by nature.

Prince/princess: These are signs of royalty, including a palace and kings.

Prison: It is a revelation of a life of slavery and servitude. It is more preferable that someone gets lost in the business of life than to be a prisoner in the spiritual realm. A prisoner in the dream has no rights or self-will. The person's soul has been possessed and is forced to follow their commands. When an evil person uses the anointing or destiny of another person to grow rich, it automatically turns the person into a prisoner.

A soul that has been imprisoned will experience stagnation and be unable to resist womanizing, drunkenness, and so on. If you see yourself in a prison, it is important to pray for yourself without ceasing.

Profit: This is a sign of imminent good fortune in the life of the dreamer.

Publish: This means to make a thing known to others. If you see yourself publishing anything, please speak out to people about that thing. Don't hide it or keep it privately so that things don't hurt or affect you later.

Protest: This is a sign of objection or condemnation of something a dreamer is doing or about to do.

Protect: It's a sign of divine protection. What you are doing is sacred. Go ahead without fear. God is with you.

Pursue: Anything that is pursuing a dreamer is after them. The thing chasing the dreamer is the object of interpretation (e.g., if a dog is pursuing a dreamer, it is a symbol of the organization or the person seeking to hurt the dreamer).

Purity: This means something holy, divine, without blemish, or perfect.

Prophet: See *priest/pastor.*

Project: A project represents what the dreamer is engaged in now. The circumstances in the dream will reveal to the dreamer the true picture of things. The dream can also show the future prospects of your project.

PART Q

Qualification: Merit. The symbols of qualification are prizes, certificates, results, gifts, and so on.

Quarrel: It is a revelation of disagreement, division, and misunderstanding between people. Whenever you quarrel with someone in the dream, it is an indication that you will have a difference of opinion that may lead to disagreement or quarrel.

Queen: See *king*.

Query: Warning of impending trouble in your place of work or business. When one receives a query in the dream, it is a sign that you are doing the wrong thing.

Quiz: This means an upgrade to another stage of life. See *exams*.

Quote: Kind advice in words. Direct wisdom intended for the dreamer.

PART R

Race: See *lineage*.

Radio: It's a strong channel of information for the dreamer. It just symbolizes information of public knowledge available to the dreamer. When you see a radio in the dream, it has information for the dreamer. Whatever is heard from the radio is already known; it's not secret.

What you hear on the radio is a general message for people of like minds. Such information is meant to be shared and not to be kept secret. Always listen attentively whenever you see or hear from a radio in the dream.

Rail: Way—a means of traveling, impending visitors.

Rain: It is a divine sign of intervention and also a divine trouble for a dreamer. Rainfall with strong winds is like a knife or fire to a dreamer. If rain is falling on someone alone in an open place with nowhere to take cover, it means the dreamer will get into a problem that will possibly claim their life or overcome them. If rain falls with a strong wind amid a celebration party or gathering where the dreamer is involved, and it scatters the occasion or disrupts the event, such rain is a divine intervention for the dreamer.

Whenever rain stops an evil ritual from progressing where the dreamer is involved, the rain is a divine help to rescue the dreamer. In most cases, rain depicts something beyond the control of the dreamer.

Rank: This is an indication of a position of authority, command, title, privilege, right, and power given to a soul. It is also the hierarchy of spiritual power given to a soul. To whom much is given much is expected. Although we are equal before God as humans, we do not have equal abilities. "And he gave some apostles; and some, prophets and some prophets; and some, evangelists and some; pastors and teachers; for the perfecting of the saints for the work of the ministry, for the edifying of the body of Christ, till we all come in the unity of faith, and the knowledge of the Son of God, unto a perfect man, unto the measure of the stature of the fullness of Christ" (Ephesians 4:11–13 KJV).

Receipt: This is a sign that something has been paid in full on behalf of the dreamer. Whatever item is contained in the receipt rightly belongs to the dreamer. It is difficult for a dreamer to lose something given to them in a receipt in the dream.

Reception: A receptionist symbolizes a gateway or gatekeeper to treasures, knowledge, secrets, or certain privileges. When you see a receptionist in the dream, it means the dreamer has been inducted into a new circle. The dreamer will be adopted into a special place or office with certain rights and privileges. When a receptionist turns a dreamer back or refuses to attend to the dreamer, it means the dreamer is not qualified to enjoy the privileges of the new position or circle.

The position of a receptionist or gatekeeper in the spiritual realm is manned by angels. They are the people who grant or deny access into hell or heaven after life's journey.

Recognize: Whatever you recognize in the dream is familiar to the dreamer. This means that whatever is familiar in the physical realm will be recognized by the dreamer's soul in the spiritual realm. It takes inspiration and interpretation by a divine being for a dreamer to recognize things they are unfamiliar with on earth.

Nevertheless, whatever we see hear or perceive in the dream exists and is known by the dreamer's soul via the conscious mind or physical intelligence.

The reason we don't always recognize things in the dream realm is due to memory loss during rebirth or conception. During conception in the womb or the initial journey of life, everybody loses the memory of their former existence. As the child grows, some of the thoughts or stored information in the soul will start synchronizing with the physical body through thought waves, inspiration, perception, intuition, and dreams. After this process, the dreamer will begin to recognize most things in their mental intelligence and subconscious mind in the dream.

Record: This is a divine file where everything about our life history has been recorded. Everything in the universe has records. We have a special angel is in charge of keeping these records while we live on earth and responsible for closing and submitting it for judgment when we die. "And is appointed unto men once to die but after this the judgment" (Hebrews 9:27 KJV).

People like Lazarus, John 11 (KJV), and the saints of old who died and later resurrected after Jesus died on the cross also died twice (Matthew 27:52–53 KJV). Some people like Enoch (Genesis 5:24 KJV) never tasted death before they were judged and raptured to heaven. Every individual's record is very ancient (i.e., our records as human souls precede our present existence on earth). In Jeremiah, God said, "Before I formed thee in the belly, I knew thee" (Jeremiah 1:5 KJV). He knew us and all we are ever going to be.

Our records from the past determined who we became in this present civilization. In the new world to come, it is the record of the life we live today that will determine who we shall be in the next world. In the dreams, our ancient record manifests in the form of images, symbols, motion, and pictures that are strange to us. When our past manifests in the dream, it is usually a strong warning not to allow history to repeat again or a call for the dreamer to repent. So when we have strange dreams, it is usually our records coming face-to-face with us. Whatever you see or meet in the dream is part of you. some of the strange faces of people we meet or encounter in the dream are us. Anytime our present soul detests or hates our records and past sinful life in the dream, that dreamer's former sins are forgiven. When we no longer enjoy a former lifestyle, it's a perfect way to know we have truly changed for good.

I had a friend who would dream of fighting wars. It was so scary it became nightmares. After he shared the dream with me, I perceived it was something in his past records haunting him. He professed that he now hates fighting and war. After that, I advised him to pray to God for forgiveness and ask for a new destiny in Christ. Today, he doesn't have those dreams anymore. Anything that haunts you or causes nightmares is a part of your records that you need to settle with God.

Read: The ability to assimilate and the power to understand when you read a thing in the dream means you have been given permission to have access to privileged information or secret knowledge.

On the other hand, you might encounter written symbols that you won't be able to read. This clearly means you have not been given the authority or permission to know it. Sometimes the writing will look blurry, be placed in a dark place, or be in blinding light, making it impossible to read. This symbolizes that you have been restricted from viewing that piece of writing. Anything you read in the dream starts to exist in your subconscious mind. After some time, it will start manifesting in the physical intelligence of the dreamer on earth.

Recover: (See *restored*.) Whenever you salvage or recover a lost item belonging to the dreamer, it means that anything that was lost to some evil people or due to personal mistakes has been restored. It's only a matter of time before the restoration will start manifesting physically on earth.

Red: This means settlement, sacrifice, or war. The opposite of red in the spirit is white. The opposite of what white represents is what red symbolizes.

Refuge: Needing help. This is an indication of disaster, war, or bad events that can render someone homeless. When we take refuge in the church or in a deity, it means we need divine intervention to solve our problems.

Refuse: This means resistance; it is a refusal impulse generated by our soul. To protect us, our guardian angel can generate a refusal impulse in our subconscious in the dream to defend or reject certain evil plans. Whatever we refuse in the dream is a divine intervention to save us, and such a thing shouldn't be accepted in the physical world. If someone gives you food in the dream and you refuse, it means that food is poison or harmful. In real life, we shouldn't accept food from such a person if we can interpret the person well.

Register: A register is a book that has a definite purpose. Registers can be used to log the members of an organization. Whatever is contained in a register is already established by God. A register can be likened to the book of life and book of death. When you see a register, take note of its purpose.

Regret: Anything that causes you to regret in the dream should be strictly avoided. The feeling of regret is a direct message to avoid the cause of the regret. The natural impulse to reject, regret, or refuse things or situations in the dream is a strong sign to avoid that thing.

Reject: See *regret* or *refuse*.

Relation: There is a natural impulse to be drawn to people you have a strong emotional connection to. When this happens in the dream, it simply means your physical body is attached to the person you relate to in the dream. It's a good sign to maintain strong ties with the people you already know in the world. When you relate cordially with people, friends, relatives, a wife, children, and so on, it is a strong sign that the relationship is good. When you relate with people you are not familiar with in the dream, they are your future friends, relations you will relate with later in your life. The people you meet in the dream are all your destiny helpers or people you will encounter on earth. You might recognize some of them, although you haven't met them yet.

Have you ever had a sudden memory about a friend, where it feels like you've met them before? The strange feeling you get when it feels like you've encountered a particular situation before is called déjà vu. The human brain has records of our dreams, but we tend to forget them. The memories of some dream can just pop up suddenly and remind us of forgotten things we have dreamt about. A lot of people have seen or met celebrities they have heard about from a foreign land but in their dreams. It means in the course of their life here on earth, they will meet a person having equal status and personalities in their life. So dreaming about relationships with kings, presidents, elite class, ruling class, noble people, and celebrities is good. In fact, you know yourself or who you are from the kind of people you relate with in the dream. Tell me whom you relate with in the dream, and I will tell you who you are!

Religion: Religion is represented in dreams based on the kind of offering, rituals, or worship a dreamer experiences in their dream. Whatever you believe in with all your heart, are loyal to, and make sacrifices for without being coerced is your religion. When you are religious or diligent about something, it means that thing is sacrosanct.

Different religions have doctrines and practices that are peculiar to them. The manifestation of a particular practice in a dream serves as the object for interpretation. For example, if a Christian dreams about the tithe box or paying an offering, God is reminding them to pay tithes and contribute to the church purse. Whatever religion a dreamer associates with is the religion from which a dreamer receives instruction and manifestation. "Yes, people are slaves to anything that controls them" (2 Peter 2:19 ERV).

If you dream of a strange religion, it is a warning to the dreamer that their name has been given to strange religion's altar in order to indoctrinate the soul into a new religion. If you notice a different religion manifesting to you, that is where you belong. Every soul has a religion that fits its existence on earth.

Repeat: See *repetition* and *dream*. When dreams are repeated, it is a clear indication of the importance of the dream or message to the dreamer.

Report: This is information compiled for the dreamer. The contents of the report are not intended for the dreamer's personal benefit. The information ought to be released to a third party. When things are reported in the dream, the dreamer needs to bring revelation and understanding to the people the information is meant for.

Request: These are prayers we make in our dreams. While dreaming, the things we wish and pray for are our actual needs. The dream life usually highlights the things we need to resolve in our physical life on earth. Dreaming is a direct channel of communication between humanity and God. This is why the requests we make in our dreams are the best for us.

Rescue: Rescue is the defense mechanism the soul initiates to save itself from harm. The soul can willfully cut short a dream experience in order to return to earth. When having a nightmare or other unpleasant dream experience, the dreamer will suddenly wake up in reality. This is called rescue.

Additionally, the soul can command weapons to manifest for attack or a fight. To dreamer's soul can run away from danger or escape at will from evil to rescue themselves. The dreamer's soul can fly, run, and swim in an ocean to rescue the dreamer from evil.

Whatever means the dreamer's soul activates to return to reality, the soul and physical body must quickly synchronize to allow the dreamer to feel fully functional and live a normal life. If a dreamer feels disoriented after waking from that dream experience, they need to fall asleep again to allow their body and soul to realign. When the soul and physical body are not aligned, it creates gaps. These gaps can cause forgetfulness, memory loss, inability to focus, and lack of willpower. Some people are not doing well today because of this problem.

Any soul that is improperly rescued is at risk of harm. The dreamer remains trapped unless prayers are said to help the dreamer. Many times, the dreamer will notice that when they fall asleep, the same dream continues to ensure a successful rescue.

Rest: It is relaxation of the soul. The human soul sleeps and relaxes in the dream. Experiencing dreamless sleep is a good indication of the soul resting.

Result: Certificate.

Restriction: This means access denied, not permitted to, unworthy, or disqualification. If you experience resistance to anything like a revelation, place, or situation, it means the dreamer has not been given the authority to receive the knowledge, experience, or thing.

Many years ago, I dreamt that my soul traveled to the first heaven. It looked like another world above the earth. A solid, opaque substance restricted me from entering. I was only allowed to peep through a hole in the walls to see inside the celestial city. Everywhere looked fresh, clean, and sanctified. The men and women walked around in peace and looked undefiled. I strongly believe that the Garden of Eden is located above our present world.

There are various elements that form a barrier of restriction, including water, space, doors, windows, and fire. These banners usually serve as a restriction to protect the dreamer in the dream. A dreamer could see themselves separated by distance, space, or any element from a relative or friend who is dead in the dream. Such restriction saves the dreamer's soul from interaction with the dead.

Reverse: (See *aback*.) When you reverse from a situation in the dream, it means you should withdraw or stop whatever project you are embarking upon. Dreams can be reversed to show the dreamer how important the information is. Reversal could be a sign of danger ahead or a venture that is too risky to continue. Reversal emphasizes how critical a message is to the dreamer and the inherent risk or danger ahead of the dreamer.

Revolution: This is a gradual transformation of the situation of a people, country, or nation. A revolution is a spontaneous, collective experience that triggers an eventful change of things by circumstances beyond the control of the people involved. It's a natural way the world improves and encourages the evolution of events, people, and places on earth.

Whenever oppression reaches its climax, the people affected will become dissidents to rules and begin to protest over a slightest provocation. If you dream of a revolution that cuts across tribal boundaries or the dreamer's geographical boundaries, it means there will be a national revolt or disagreement among the citizenry.

Revolution could mean change of leadership, government, or a trending thing. The size of the revolution will indicate the scale of the revolution. To a leader, dreaming of a revolution is a strong sign of public rejection.

Rich: Riches refer to the personal possessions of an individual. This includes physical cash, fiat money, paper money, things that have monetary value like coral shells, silver, gold, precious ornaments, or jewelry.

Eggs, refuse dumps, and human waste also represent wealth and riches. Trees that are bearing fruit symbolize riches. When you are in possession of any of these symbols, you are a rich person in the making. Sometimes these symbols foretell the arrival of untold riches in our lives.

Riot: See *revolution*.

Risk: This means danger ahead. In situations involving risk, the dreamer's soul triggers a feeling of doubt, uncertainty, and fear to make the dreamer alert and watchful in the dream. The circumstances surrounding these feelings should be noted for the dreamer's interpretation.

Rival: Rivals are a sign of competition and opposing factors that could make you fail. The presence of rivals in the dream is a revelation that there are people equally interested in your area of business or career. It is a warning sign to the dreamer to be alert and watchful to defend their interests in their place of work, worship, or business. Rivalry suggests enemies of progress.

The character traits of people we see in our dream tell us of the kind of rivals we should expect. Rivals can be members of our family, friends, workplace, or business. Dreams of rivalry should not be taken lightly.

River: Rivers represent daily activities in a human's life, including work and business in a particular geographical location. The events surrounding the river are the subject of interpretation. For instance, if you dream of walking on a river, it means you are in charge of your career or your business without rivalry. When you swim in the river without sinking or struggling against the tide or current, it means you will have ease doing business. On the other hand, when the dreamer has difficulty navigating the river due to strong currents or turbulence, it means a big problem beyond the dreamer's control will emanate from the place of work.

Road: This tells the story of traveling, visitors, and the general journey of life. Roads reveal the destination and trajectory of a dreamer's life. When a dreamer loses their way, it means the dreamer has lost a sense of direction, focus, and vision. From that point, whatever they do will not yield any success. When you travel successfully by car or trekking, it means the project you are embarking on will be successful.

One day I was trying to board a bus to a particular location, and without warning, the bus moved and left me behind. I chased the bus till I woke up. I was practically running after the vehicle. It was an embarrassing indication that I wouldn't succeed in the venture I was embarking on. God was preventing me from suffering and toiling in vain.

Rocket: When you travel with a rocket in the dream, it means your soul is going out of this planet for a special experience. When the souls in Christ shall arise from the death to meet with Christ in heaven, they will move or will be lifted up like a flying jet or rocket. Rocket symbolizes celestial expedition to celestial worlds. Rockets travel at light-speed, so all the people who went to heaven with their physical bodies moved upward like rockets. The chariot of fire that zoomed Elijah to heaven was a rocket in its primitive nature (2 Kings 1:1–11 KJV). It's an unusual dream experience.

Room: Room symbolizes privacy or hidden things; it shows a dreamer's private life, those hidden traits and activities that are not publicly known. Certain abominable or immoral acts the public does not accept or support are done in the privacy of the room. Rooms cover atrocities, while things done in the public are exposed to all. Any activity that is successfully done in a room usually comes to pass in reality. Evil people usually hide under the cover of a room to commit evil.

Just like our physical body, the soul requires privacy to do the wrong thing. So in the dream realm, demons can deceive the soul to be comfortable in a room to commit certain evil practices. It is easier for the dreamer's soul to have sex in the dream than in public.

Root: It's a personal revelation for medicine and healing. Anyone who usually sees roots in their dreams is gifted in healing. Roots have healing energies that help relieve the sick. They usually manifest to a healer. If a sick person sees roots in a dream, it means the person will receive healing or a solution shortly.

Royal: King.

Run: Way of escape from danger in the dream. The speed at which you run shows how quickly you will escape from the danger. If the dreamer is not running fast, it means they might not escape the trouble. The event or activity that makes the dreamer run is the object of interpretation. For example, if a dog pursuing a dreamer gets hold and bites the dreamer, it means evil thing that has been planned will succeed. Anyone who has this type of dream should be praying for grace, healing, and salvation from evil. On the other hand, if the dreamer escapes, it means the attack will be unsuccessful.

Running is a way of escaping attack. There are times a dreamer runs without any motion, and the pursuer nearly catches them, but suddenly the dreamer wakes up. This means the problem is already attacking the dreamer, and it will take God to deliver the dreamer. It is preferable to stand and fight the source of trouble than run. Running is a sign of spiritual weakness and should be used as a last resort.

PART S

Safe: This is a zone where the soul feels comfortable. When the soul relaxes and does things in the dream without fear or threat, we can say the dreamer is safe. The things we do safely in the dream are things we are comfortable with on earth.

Salary: Salary is a means of income. If a dreamer receives wages or a salary in the dream, it means they will soon receive blessings or will succeed or be rewarded in the activity they are doing.

Sale: Making sales is a sign of a successful business. Whenever you successfully make sales in the dream, it's direct information that good business will come your way. Additionally, sales of a particular item tell the dreamer to dispose of those particular goods. If you are in the dream and sell your car, it means you should place your car on sale. Selling is an exchange for value; whatever you sell in your dream should be taken note of, as there is a special message concerning that thing.

If you constantly find yourself buying and selling in the dream, it is clear indication that your chosen career is business. The dreams will help you define what aspect of business you should engage in.

Salute: To salute someone in the dream means to give due respect to them. It's an indication that the person deserves honor and deference. When people salute you in the dream, it means you are an important person, deserving of honor.

Sand: Sand is used to signify the uncountable nature of a thing. "That in blessing, I will bless thee, and in multiplying I will multiply thy seed as the stars of heaven and as the sand which is upon the sea shore and thy seed shall possess the gate of his enemies" (Genesis 22:17 KJV).

Sanitation: Sanitation indicates a need for spiritual cleansing and rededication. If you are performing sanitation in the dream, it means you should set yourself apart for spiritual cleansing and dedicate a time of praying and seeking the face of God.

Within the period of your sanctification, you should not corrupt your body by engaging in activities that can defile your body. Waiting on God by fasting and prayers would be beneficial to the dreamer.

Save: The dreamer is advised to save whatever income they receive within that period. When a dreamer saves money in the dream, it means God will bless the dreamer and require them to save it for future use. The power to make wealth belongs to God (Deuteronomy 8:18 KJV), which makes Him the best adviser on utilizing the wealth. Money doesn't come by accident; there are things God intends for us to accomplish when He gives us increase.

The issue many dreamers face is lack of direction and vision from God due to not spending enough time with God. When we misuse His blessings, it becomes difficult to progress. All money we receive is meant for a purpose in our life.

Scent: Every living being has a distinct scent. Our scent can announce us even after we have left a place. Our scent can be used to trace us. The scent of anything in the dream tells the dreamer where that thing is coming from. "The beast was taken and with him the false prophet that wrought miracles before him, with which he deceived them that had received the mark of the beast and them that worshipped his image. These both were cast alive into a lake of burning fire and brimstone" (Revelation 19:20 KJV). Anything that smells like brimstone, which has a sulphury scent like rotten eggs, is definitely coming from the pit of hell.

Scholar: To be scholarly shows an advancement in knowledge. To be a scholar in the dream means the dreamer is a genius.

School: School symbolizes a learning stage of life experience. It is used to teach a dreamer something that is a key to their success in the future. School could be used to reveal to a dreamer their struggles or achievements in the present or future. If you see yourself in class or a school environment you left long ago, there's an event your guardian angel is recalling; you need to take precaution to succeed in what is before you. You could see yourself writing an exam or taking a lesson. Remembering what happened in your former schools when you wrote an exam or were taking lesson will help you learn something to succeed. If you find it difficult to write an exam in school, it's a clear sign your challenges will be difficult for you to overcome it. If you feel you need assistance or seek help from other students, it means you need other people's support to overcome your challenges. Now when you realize you're in that school and start questioning what you are doing in the school you finished long ago, you will know you will overcome that challenge with ease. In this case, such a problem is underfoot. But the warning there is to be looking as usual so that your problem will not drag you back. Whenever you are in school in the dream, be very careful of what you do there. School holds a lot of lessons for a dream. It's your past that guides you to the future. When you see yourself in a higher school of learning higher than the one you attended, it simply means you are assailing higher academically. You have more to know in whatever you are doing, whether school or business or politically. It shows you have a promising future in what you are doing.

In the higher institution, what you are doing there tells you the challenges you will face in the future of your business or career. The kind of personalities within the school tell your next level in life. School is a place of learning and progress in life. When school manifests in the dream, it has something important to teach.

Sea: See *river*.

Seat: This is representing a position of authority that a dreamer exercises. It's good for a dreamer to always take their rightful seat in the dream. If a dreamer is at the steering wheel driving, it means the dreamer is in control of the situation or in charge of their life or business. But when a dreamer is in the passenger's seat in their own car, it means they are no longer in control. They will lose the control of the business to another person. The dreamer could be living another person's life or be under the influence of someone.

However, it is not a bad revelation if the dreamer is being driven smoothly, relaxing in the owner's corner. It is a sign to delegate menial duties while the dreamer takes the responsibility of overseeing everyone. If a king sees himself in the back seat while leaving his throne, it means he will be dethroned. A dreamer should always see themselves in their proper seat in the dream realm or in reality.

Scream: To scream in the dream is to initiate an emergency alarm. It is to alert the soul to react to save itself from harm. When a scream is initiated by the soul in the dream, all the defense mechanisms in the human intelligence are on a red alert. Every action the soul and the physical body take will be an emergency response mode. Sometimes a scream can wake the dreamer physically on the bed. Whatever makes a soul shout in the dream is a problem beyond the dreamer's ability to handle.

Nightmares are not always caused by evil activities, but due to unfamiliarity with the things of the spirit, a dreamer can be easily frightened. The cause of screaming can be a scary revelation or the manifestation of symbols or images that are frightening to the soul.

Selfish: It's the primitive nature of a dreamer.

Separation: Means disagreement or exclusion. If someone is dead, they are separated from the living. In that case, the dead soul is excluded from the living. When a person is dead in the dream, what strongly separates you from them is the realization that they are dead or a barrier or some circumstance between you and the person. If a married person is separated on the bed, it means disagreement loading, especially when one partner is facing back. Anything that separates you and someone is a sign of exclusion or a sharp quarrel, trouble, or controversy looming in the dreamer's life.

Servant: A servant personifies loyalty, humility, and obedience to their master. If a head of department, boss, director, or chairman dreams of becoming a servant, two things will happen to that man:

1. He will be demoted from his position of honor to be a servant. There are people who are destined to be servants forever in this world. They will always honor, respect, and serve others; they will serve them till they depart from this earth. If someone is a servant, he should see himself as a rich man in his dreams. A servant being a servant in the dream means they will always be a servant. It's a strong warning for the servant to make moves to grow up or risk remaining at that level. So when a man of honor who other people are serving becomes the servant, it is a bad revelation.

2. Additionally, such a dream acts as a reminder for the man to humble himself like a servant unto his people. "In your relationships with one another have the same mindset as Christ Jesus; Who being in very nature God did not consider equality with God something to be used to his own advantage; rather he made himself nothing by taking the very nature of a servant" (Philippians 2:5–7 NIV).

Sex: Having sex in the dream is one of the ways our emotional body cleanses itself of romantic thoughts or disturbing images that fill up the mental body. The body expunges certain disturbing thoughts and images in the mental body by recreating the experiences via dreams. For example, there are movies and news in the media and in the environment that can trigger unwanted feelings and emotions. To help our minds get rid of these things, the mental body recreates the movie or news into a dream to burn it out.

There are people who have filled their minds with pornographic material, videos, and media news, and over time, those thoughts start influencing their character. For people who cannot control their sexual urges, it affects many aspects of their life, including career and family life, because of their thought pattern. Thoughts are very powerful. "He went on 'What comes out of a person is what defiles them. For it is from within, out of a person's heart that evil thoughts come- sexual immorality, theft, murder, adultery, greed, malice, deceit, lewdness, envy, slander, arrogance and folly. All these evils come from inside and defile a person'" (Mark 7:20–23 NIV).

In Proverbs 23:7, Solomon proclaims that as a man thinketh in his heart, so is he. This means that thoughts can be creatively harnessed and channeled to create the life we want.

When sexy thoughts permeate our soul and we can't clean them out physically, the mental body will find a way to purge it out or satisfy it. As teenagers, it was a common thing to have sex in a dream; in fact, wet dreams are listed as one of the symptoms of puberty and adolescence. At that tender stage, the body is extremely sensitive to sexual suggestions, with little self-control.

On the negative side, having sex in the dream is a means for diabolical people to enslave and poison a human soul. Evil men can use sex to manipulate a dreamer. Sex is a direct channel from our soul to the physical body. Sex creates a strong, magnetic connection between physical bodies. It is the only way two individuals become fused together. We have not yet fully understood the implications and dimensions of sex. When sex manifests in the dream, it takes the grace of God to save us. The moment your soul is trapped with sex in the dream, your entire soul and your physical body on earth are wholly connected to it. When you wake up from the dream, you will notice you are also messed up.

You could fly a plane in the dream or do strenuous and energy-consuming work in the dream, but your physical body on earth will be quiet and calm on the bed. On the other hand, the moment your soul is having sex in the dream, your physical body on the bed will start showing signs of doing something exciting in the dream. The person's sex organs, lips, and facial expressions will start responding until the sex is completed. This is a simple illustration of how powerful sex is and the resultant connection to the physical body. It becomes easy to use sex to poison or to pass on a disease from the dreamer's soul to the physical body of the dreamer. Diseases that are passed on to people from the dream usually defy medical solutions.

Sex in the dream is a spiritual attack through which evil men can retrieve a lot of information from a dreamer, such as the following:

1. Personal information. They can suck a dreamer's luck or anointing oil to succeed in business of life. Our spirit sperm or seed of creation is our oil that keeps us shining and winning. When the load of our anointing oil is depleted, we can easily lose a job interview, contract, or business. A woman can lose her pregnancy during sex in the dream. A man can lose the strength of his sex life in the dream. When demons plug their penis in a person's private parts and vice versa, it is like connecting a computer cord to a demon server. With that connection, they can download data from your systems, or they can own the information in your system and manipulate it. They can send a viral attack to your system. They can do anything they want to do with your body. Sex is a perfect agreement between the dreamer and the demon or invader. During such mutual agreement, the demon is at will to project evil unto the dreamer.

2. Demons will always use the faces of people we are in love with to launch their attack. They can use the faces of people we have soft desires or fantasies about to launch the sex attack. When they succeed to create a harmony or permission during sex in the dream, they quickly execute their plans. Many times, God will save us halfway into the sex. In that case, the mission is aborted midway. People can be possessed by demons while having sex in the dream. The spirit of whoredom and adultery has been injected into the soul of many people during sex. The more the dreamer has sex in the dream, the more he flirts

around with women in reality. He can't fulfil his sexual urges, and such a person becomes a slave.

3. Sex is also a sign of marital or mutual relationship between a human soul and unclean spirits. When people are in a marital relationship or mutual affair with demons, they have sex to renew it. When a man or woman is having sex in the dream, it means that person is married to a demon. If a man loses his wife mysteriously due to a demonic incantation or invocation, the demon can use the image of the dreamer's deceased wife to be having sex with him and vice versa. If there are so many unsettled curses upon a man due to his alliance with women in his past life, strange women will be coming to have sex with the dreamer. Anytime you are having sex with a strange woman in a dream, you know you have a case or relationship with your past to settle.

4. Sex can be used to check a person's level of carnality or vanity. When a man or woman starts rejecting sex in the dream, it means their primitive nature is under control. When sexual dreams stop, it means that individual has been delivered from the shackle of evil manipulation. Anything you do in the dream that can affect your physical body on earth, like food or sex, should be strictly avoided.

Shadow: This is a reflection of a main object. Shadows in the dream are duplicates of the soul in the same form or in another form. While dreaming, we might see ourselves in the dream but with a different appearance or dream of ourselves while another version of us watches like a spectator. The soul has the ability to multiply into different bodies and act as a variety of things in order to teach the dreamer something important about their life.

Shame: This is a disgraceful act that can bring disgrace on the dreamer. Anything that brings shame in the dream should be avoided. Shame can be used to save a dreamer from trouble. A dreamer can refuse to do something that is harmful to the dreamer because of shame.

Shine: Shine is to make yourself known to people. Don't hide who you are from the public. Due to high crime rates, a lot of people are hiding themselves because of fear of the unknown. When you see yourself shine in the dream, it means you shouldn't hide. It's a reminder for the dreamer to help others and to be a source of direction and vision to lead others.

Ship: This is a symbol of merchandise and goods on an international level. It's a sign of the business of buying and selling of goods. When you see a ship, it means a business will soon come your way.

Shock: These are vibrations that disrupt a dreamer's sleep. Shock can be as a result of revelations that the dreamer's soul can't stand to see or hear. In Revelation 1, "In His right hand He held seven stars, and from His mouth came a sharp two-edged sword [of judgment]; and His face [reflecting His majesty and the Shekinah glory] was like the sun shining in [all} its power [at midday]. When I saw Him, I fell at His feet as though dead. And He placed His right hand on me and said 'Do not be afraid'" (Revelation 1:16–17 AMP, Daniel

8:1–18 AMP). This is an account of John in a vision that terrified him and caused him to become unconscious. It was the intervention of the angel guarding him that brought him back to life.

Shoe: This is a sign of traveling or migration. If you plan on moving in search of greener pastures and you dream of your legs, foot, or shoe getting destroyed, amputated, stolen, or missing, it is a clear indication that the journey will not favor you. Shoes represent our feet and legs, which are symbols of movement or advancement in life. When our shoes or legs are harmed in the course of an adventure we want to embark on, it is a clear warning that it will be unsuccessful and probably harm us along the way.

Shrine: Dreaming of a shrine is a not good omen. It can mean that a diabolical person with evil intentions has taken the dreamer's name before a deity for judgment. However, you can't be summoned to the shrine in the dream when you are not associated with such an oracle. If a shrine manifests in a dream, the dreamer has a case to answer or has familial links to that deity. Dreaming of a shrine is a demonic manifestation with no hidden meaning.

Sickness: This is a sign of poor spiritual well-being. It is an indication that the dreamer's soul needs renewal or healing, and it has the ability to affect our physical health here on earth.

On the other hand, there are illnesses that have been written into our destiny. The illness could be fatal to our mortal bodies, but God allows our soul to suffer only in the dream to enable our physical bodies survive. Our soul is strong and can withstand shocks or vibrations better than our physical body. For example, a lot of people dream of themselves having a fatal accident, which they wake up and pray against. Then in reality, that dreamer gets involved in an accident but escapes unharmed. The dream was just a revelation to the dreamer that God intervened and allowed their soul to absorb the brunt of the accident.

Slave: This is a clear sign the dreamer has been enslaved by someone else. The dreamer is in bondage and must seek deliverance immediately.

Sleep: To sleep in the dream means the dreamer has traveled deeper into the spiritual realm to get hidden information. Just like precious gems are found hidden deep within the earth, sensitive information and deeply spiritual experiences cannot be experienced in first-sleep dreams. For example, someone who wants to visit hell will have to use second- or third-sleep dreams to gain access there. Because the human soul is a spirit, it can multiply itself at different vibrations to visit some places. There are places the dreamer's soul would have to shape-shift into an animal to enable them to visit there. All these things happen at various degrees of sleep.

Smoking: Reveals a dreamer's bad habit. It's usually a warning for the dreamer to stop that old habit.

Smile: Facial expressions reveal the emotional status of the soul. A true smile shows that the dreamer is at peace and has a stable mind.

Snake: This is a symbol of temptation, trouble, controversy, and sickness. Whenever you see a snake in the dream, please kill it. Snakes are enemies of one's progress. Whenever snakes appear in your dream, trouble is at your door. The details of a dreamer's encounter with the snake is the subject matter for interpretation.

In the dream realm, snakes and snake bites are dangerous. They mean an evil plan has succeeded that will require prayers and the intervention of God for the dreamer's deliverance. The snake bite can foreshadow a deadly illness, accident, or unprecedented bad luck in the dreamer's life. If a dreamer encounters a green snake hiding in green grass, it reveals betrayal from a close friend or family member. The dreamer discovering the snake means the enemy will not succeed, although they will make an attempt. When the dreamer kills the snake, the attack is aborted. When the dreamer makes a serious attempt to chase or kill the snakes, it means the dreamer will catch the enemy at the beginning of the problem and deal with it victoriously.

The appearance of the snake, such as the color, gives the dreamer more insight about the situation. Wild snakes that are not commonly seen at home indicate that the dream is about people, business, or places we are unfamiliar with. But snakes we are familiar with around us represent household enemies, colleagues, or friends. Smoking them out early means their plot will be exposed, and they will not succeed. When rare, deadly snakes like a python catch, kill, or try to swallow the dreamer, it is a direct attack from a spiritual power, deity, demon, or Satan that has come to kill the dreamer.

The manner of approach the dreamer adopts to conquer any snake they encounter in the dream is how they should deal with the problem on earth, unless they are defeated. A snake is a bad omen. Sighting one in a dream is a serious warning to the dreamer to be alert.

Soul: Every individual is made up of three entities—the body, the soul and the spirit of God. "The Lord God formed man of the dust of the ground and breathed into his nostrils the breath of life and man became a living soul" (Genesis 2:7 KJV). The intangible consciousness of a human (i.e., what makes them think, speak, and be) is the soul. It can't be touched like the physical body; however, it is a living being. The physical body and the soul are intrinsically connected; without a soul, the physical body dies. The human soul is our spirit personality that God breathed into Adam to live. God didn't just put oxygen into man's nose, but He put life, a human soul, into Adam's body. At death, our physical body returns to dust, but our soul goes back to God. So our soul uses our physical body to operate.

During the day, our physical body is switched on by the soul to live and work, while at night, our physical body is shut down for the soul to live and work in the spiritual realm. The physical body can break down or eventually die if we don't rest it or shut down when we are tired. But the soul lives on. The soul is our real personality that lives within our physical body. It is that body that will be given a physical or celestial body to live again after the resurrection of the dead. It is the soul that God will judge and not the physical body that will be lost to dust on earth. Everything we do with our physical body on earth affects our soul. "Watch and pray so that you will not fall into temptation. The spirit is willing but the flesh is weak" (Matthew 26:41 KJV). Additionally, the soul acts as a representation of us in the dream world. Although the soul can assume many shapes and looks, often, it takes on the resemblance of our physical body, which helps us recognize ourselves. As a spirit being, the soul can multiply itself into other faces or personalities while maintaining its indivisible soul status as one person.

There are things our soul would like to achieve, but our physical body is weak. We must be determined and disciplined to overcome the weakness of our physical body on earth. Everything we dream with our original person is possible to achieve on earth. Whatever we plan is achievable, but our greatest challenge is the limitation of our physical body.

Watch and pray to help every believer overcome. Listen to your soul experience and follow it with your physical body. Follow your dreams.

Spend: To spend in the dream means to invest money or wealth into meaningful projects. Always check what you are spending your money on in the dream. Just follow your dreams. You can't be wrong. If you see yourself spending on building materials, it means you should invest in a home project. Before God gives you money, He will reveal to you what to use it for. Whatever you find yourself spending on a car, invest it in that thing. It will be well with you, so spend. All you need is a direction on how to invest or spend your money. One thing to note is that every event has a time of fulfilment.

Star: Stars are heavenly bodies that foretell time and world events. "Where is He who has been born King of the Jews? For we saw His star in the east and have come to worship Him" (Matthew 2:2 KJV).

God constantly used stars to measure the unquantifiable nature of His blessings.

"Remember Abraham, Isaac, and Israel, Your servants to whom You swore by Yourself, and said to them, 'I will multiply your descendants as the stars of the heavens, and all this land of which I have spoken I will give to your descendants, and they shall inherit it forever'" (Exodus 32:13 KJV).

"The LORD your God has multiplied you, and behold, you are this day like the stars of heaven in number" (Deuteronomy 1:10 KJV).

From the times of old and across various cultures and belief systems, stars have helped astrologers, wise men, and oracles predict events and time. Whenever we see stars in the dream, they appear to prophesy about events that have global significance.

People read stars in the old times to understand seasonal changes, calendar cycles, navigation, and more. With the advent of astronomy, we now use a satellite to read weather conditions, communicate, monitor earthquake, and so on. Stars represents divine events encoded in the existence of the earth. When you dream of stars, heaven is interested in you. The nature of the encounter is the point for interpretation.

Status: This is the appearance of things in the realm.

Steal: This means to deny an individual of their rightful possession in the dream. Being stolen from in the dream is an indication of being deprived of a right, blessing, or opportunity by evil forces. In John 10, Jesus explains, "The devil comes only to steal, kill and destroy. I came that they may have life and have it abundantly" (John 10:10 KJV). The destiny, greatness, success, and prosperity of many have been stolen by the devil. Pray to recover recall all good things the devil has stolen from you. May God protect our blessings. Amen!

Steel: Wood or any other object could be used to describe iron or steel in the dream. Original form of the raw materials (e.g., black soil, ore, wood, etc.) could be used to communicate steel in the dream.

Storm: A storm is trouble on a large scale. Dreaming of a storm is a revelation of impending communal hostility, riots, wars, and violence of a great magnitude.

The magnitude of the storm determines the severity of the trouble. When a storm occurs in the ocean or sea like a tsunami, it is a disaster on a global level. A storm in the river indicates the disaster is localized and of a lesser degree. On the other hand, a calm river or sea shows how peaceful the people in that locality are. Swimming in the water tells you how you will work with people you are involved with in your business life.

Student: Students are symbolic representations of learning and experience. Whenever school students manifest in the dream, it's simply something to do with learning, something concerning your business of life and your life experience you need to progress in. Please check *school* for more details.

Survey: It's a way of describing a geographical location in the dream. Check location. In the dream realm, a dreamer could encounter a site as a market, while in reality, the place is something else. The things we see in the dream realm can act as a symbol or a literal representation of something else.

Swear: To swear in the dream is to declare a thing as an undeniable fact. It's a way of mind searching. When someone swears in the dream, they establish what they swore. In this case, the spirit and humanity bear witness to the dreamer's declaration.

Swim: To swim in the dream is a reflection of how we relate with people in our life and business. Swimming easily reveals an ease of communication and noncontentious living, while a reverse situation reveals difficulty and unease.

The size of the body of water determines the height of success and publicity attached to your life and business. It's usually difficult to swim in smaller bodies of water. This indicates how difficult it is to face people you know. Another meaning of swimming in the dream are things relating to the marine world. People who usually find themselves in waters swimming, dancing, and so on are related to the water world. Whenever water appears to them, it means their people have come to interact with them spiritually.

PART T

Taboo: These are abominable acts condemned by society that attract stiff penalties. When a dreamer sees themselves committing an abomination in the dream realm, it is a revelation of a primitive nature and evil propensities. It is an indication that they are vulnerable and capable of committing such acts. It points to their sinful history as a fallen soul.

The location and circumstances surrounding the dream scenario are points for interpretation. When the taboo thing is committed in the comfort of one's home or a house with a public view, it means it is recorded in the archives of history, and the dreamer's soul is likely to repeat it. But when it is committed in the glaring eyes of the public and the person is caught in the act, condemned, and criticized, that person has been forgiven. It shows that the dreamer's soul has been set free from the urge to commit that act, and it becomes repulsive to their personality.

There are actions and sins that transcend our present life on earth. There were acts that the sacrifices of animals could not cleanse. In Leviticus, chapter 18, God lists abominable acts, including incest, homosexuality, and kindred marriages. For these acts, the perpetrators could face death or be ostracized from society. Committing a taboo is like a stain on one's soul that follows them even after rebirth to their next world.

Anyone who finds a thing distasteful will be naturally repulsed by it and will not indulge in doing it. If a dreamer dreams about doing something repulsive, they will wake up unhappy about the dream. Some dreams are a reflection of our past sinful soul that God uses to examine if we will still indulge in it. When we show disinterest, those acts will be deleted from the archives and won't be used to judge us. Our past life is the reason we are here on earth. We can use our dreams to know things we are capable of doing on earth.

Tax: This represents government agencies or authorities. When you dream about tax agencies or officials, it's a clear indication that you will soon receive the attention of government authorities.

Teacher: Teachers are custodians of knowledge. If you dream about yourself teaching in the dream, it is a direct indication that you are an educator, in possession of a wealth of information. Anyone who plays the role of a teacher in the dream has received a revelation that they are custodians of certain knowledge to give to the world. It is irrelevant if the dreamer is a teacher in reality or not; they will notice an inflow of inspiration in their life.

However, when a dreamer sees themselves being taught in the dream by a teacher, it means the dreamer should seek knowledge, advice, or counselling in the area of any present challenge. The dreamer needs a sense of direction and refining of vision by people who are highly skilled or knowledgeable. The symbol of a teacher in the dream is good. It indicates you are in a position to teach or advise others, or you are to seek ideas, knowledge, or direction from others to succeed in life.

Technology: The great King Solomon said, "That which has been is that which will be [again], And that which has been done is that which will be done again. So there is nothing new under the sun" (Ecclesiastes 1:9 AMP). Technology is not new on earth, but it changes forms. God's creative command is still in effect till the earth passes away. Things emerge and go to extinction, giving way for new ones to emerge. This circular flow of events will continue till the day God declares the earth closed.

"But you, O Daniel, shut up the words and seal the Book until the time of the end. [Then] many shall run to and fro and search anxiously [through the Book], and knowledge [of God's purposes as revealed by His prophets] shall be increased and become great" (Daniel 12:4 AMPC). The ability to understand things is not inborn in humans; it comes from God.

Technology is not new. From times past, humans have developed various innovative ways of doing things. However, the verse above shows that God increases the valve on humanity's access to knowledge as time runs to the closure of human history. All the things in the form of technology we see in the dream are real. They are just waiting for their set time to manifest on earth. Not even a battalion of soldiers can stop technology or an idea whose time has come.

I have seen a lot of technologies in the dream realm that are yet to manifest on earth. When technologies are revealed to a dreamer in the dream, it is for their information. God does not allow His people to be ignorant of things happening on earth. This is why He reveals them ahead of their manifestation. When we have foreknowledge of an event or technology, we begin preparing the mindset of our people to accept it or to manage the technology. God doesn't want us to be caught unaware of trends of events on earth. He wants us to be part of it. In fact, God wants us to take the lead in technology. If we can't manufacture new technology, we can develop the empirical knowledge leading to the actual designing program. We can even promote it or invest in it. Although we are not of the world, we are part of the world, and the world belongs to God alone, and we are His children.

Tension: Feeling tension in the dream feels like waves of violence in the air and is an indication of impending doom. It is a way the spiritual realm forewarns us of danger. Experiencing tension alerts the dreamer to be watchful and on guard.

Test: Whenever a situation or event is subjected to a test, it reveals that the situation needs to be double-checked before execution. In academics, a test is regularly conducted to ensure the student has understood what has been taught and can utilize that the knowledge for their success. Passing tests in the dream is an assurance that an individual will surely overcome life's challenges.

Thief: Thief in the dream realm symbolizes anything that can rob an individual of joy, achievements, life-changing opportunities, expectations, destiny, and visions. These things manifest in the form of any force or entity that wants to forcefully dispossess and trick the dreamer out of their possessions. In reality, physical appearance has little to do with thievery. Anyone, including family members, colleagues, and friends, can play the role of a thief. This is why the spirit of discretion is a strong tool in assisting the dreamer. Determine characteristics, activity, and more that will help identify the person.

Timetable: This is a schedule of events in the timeline of a dreamer's life. This timetable is unknown to the dreamer. "Before we were even born, he gave us our destiny; that we would fulfil the plan of God who always accomplishes every purpose and plan in his heart" (Ephesians 1:1 TPT).

"It is the Lord who directs your life, for each step you take is ordained by God to bring you closer to your destiny. So much of your life, then, remains a mystery" (Proverbs 20:24 TPT). Every activity in the world is predestined and known by God.

When God reveals things to an individual, it's that person's privilege to object or assent to it with prayers. "The Lord our God has secrets known to no one. We are not accountable for them, but we and our children are accountable forever for all that he has revealed to us" (Deuteronomy 29:29 NLT).

God revealing the hidden things to us enables us to be prepared and pray against it if need be. Any dreamer who is given the ability to see tomorrow has been given an edge to succeed.

Traditions: Traditions remind us of our background and origin. It simply depicts home practices, events or things that require an original or native approach to solve. When we see traditional things in the dream, we must question the symbolism those things represent in our background. This helps the dreamer channel the revelations to adequately fight their battles.

Traditions dictate the basic principles of life of a group of people and cut across our religious, political, economic, and social lives. Our conduct should be in compliance with our societal norms and ethical conduct. Tradition defines your true self. Being your original self is the best way to live.

Traffic: Dreaming of traffic reveals temporary delay or setbacks a dreamer or individual may experience when doing something or handling a project. Traffic does not mean total hindrance in life; rather, it is indicative of natural events that have the capacity to slow the speed with which an individual achieves certain things in life. Traffic in the way of a businessman or trader means, although great success lies ahead in their trade or business, they might experience hardship or a slow pace along the way.

Train: This machine represents our energy, power, and the determination we require to complete difficult tasks or execute a business idea. The motion and activities surrounding the train are points of revelation for the dreamer. Riding on a train means the dreamer is part of a successful movement or business. When the train journey is moving smoothly, it shows a successful and easygoing life. However, when it gets stuck or goes off the tracks, it is indicative that the business will not be successful. When the dreamer drives the train, it means they are the one in charge of that situation, and the success of the business is solely dependent on the action or inaction of the dreamer. Whenever it is revealed that a person is in charge of their own life and destiny, it means you are a leader whose life should be an example and a light unto others.

Trap: This is a sign of temptation or impending trouble. If a dreamer finds themselves caught in a trap, it is an indication that the person has been trapped by the devil. Traps are snares set by the devil for people to fall into. However, if a dreamer sees a trap in the dream, it means the dreamer will uncover the plot and escape it. Whenever we see a trap in the dream, we should be very careful.

Travel: To travel in the dream is not always a direct indication that the dreamer will travel; it can also represent the journey of life.

Travel in dreams shows the important places a dreamer will visit in life to enable them to achieve certain things on earth. These places are called destiny destinations. Whenever you travel in the dream, take note of the places you visit so that it is easy to interpret. Each person has a place of destiny. In Genesis 12, God said unto Abram, "Get thee out of thy country, and from thy kindred and from thy father's house unto a land that I will show thee and I will make of thee a great nation and I will bless thee, and make thy name great" (Genesis 12:1–2 KJV). If Abraham had remained in his hometown, he wouldn't have made it bigger. We need God's direction to know where to sojourn or travel for greener pastures. "Many plans are in a man's mind but it is the Lord's purpose for him that will stand" (Proverbs 19:21 AMP). There are people who are destined to make it big at home, but unfortunately, such people travel abroad and remain stagnant there for a long time. So traveling in the dream is a compass that directs our journey.

Some places are representative landmarks of other places. Recognizing Lagos in a dream could indicate a broad geographical zone of Western Nigeria. The activities you see yourself doing in Lagos can assist you in discerning the particular location in the west that does that kind of activity. For instance, mining is closely related to Osun State. Such dreams tell the dreamer that the western part of Nigeria will favor them. If one dreams of traveling abroad, it means the dreamer will certainly travel abroad for an important thing that will change their life. Traveling in the dream reveals a clear direction to follow to achieve greatness.

The mode of transportation is also foot, suggesting difficulty in the journey of life. When a dreamer travels with a car, train, plane, or boat, it's a sign of favor during your journey of life. The kind of transport device the dreamer uses to travels tells the dreamer the speed convenience at which events will unfold for the dreamer during the journey of life.

Treasure: Finding treasure in the dream signifies good fortune for a dreamer. Treasures are representatives of good fortune, riches, and wealth. When treasures manifests in the dream in any form, it means the dreamer is destined to be a wealthy person and is blessed. Treasures are favors from God, and when you see them, it means you have been chosen to possess them.

Treatment: Medical treatment is a strong message of recovery from ill health. It is a clear sign of divine healing. It is also a sign that the dreamer may be unaware that they are sick. Ill health can occur in the dream without manifesting in the physical world. In this instance, the dreamer's soul absorbed the ill health alone without manifesting in reality. Most sicknesses and treatments in the dream are a warning to be cautious of impending danger ahead. Whenever we find ourselves taking medical treatment in the dream, we should be medically alert about our physical health. If someone is sick physically and finds themselves taking medical treatment in the dream, it means the dreamer will be healed.

Trophy: This can be likened to a reward or award of excellence or special recognition. Awards of this nature represent success and progress in whatever the dreamer is doing. A trophy also means to be chosen for special things. It's good to get a trophy or reward amid a crowd or in the open. When activities are conducted in public, in the open, and in front of a crowd in the dream, it means those things have been established. For evil entities to change events that have already taken place in public in the dream is very difficult.

Television: In a dream, a TV represents a portal display of visions, prophecy, information, and messages. The television represents a media house in the dream world. Whatever you see in the television in the dream is direct information or a message for the dreamer. It does not require interpretation.

When God chooses to use a television to tell a dreamer something, He intends to simplify the information in writing and motion pictures for the dreamer. Information or messages from the TV are already established and known information. The information is not usually classified, and it's not for the personal information of the dreamer. Whatever you see on the TV is usually past and present things and cannot manipulated. Some prophets can see someone's problem with an imaginary TV in their eyes. God can use the symbol of a TV to play back an event that happened in the past without editing it.

Twin: Means an agreement that must come to pass. Something that is in pairs is sure of happening, and it shows how strong powerful that thing will be. It's like a repeated dream that shows emphasis and how important that dream is. Twins are sacred things that show a perfection agreement of purpose to manifest on earth. Anything that can appear in twins or duplicate itself in twin form is very powerful and sustainable.

PART U

Uniform: This is a means of identification of a particular profession or group of people. If you see yourself dressed as a nurse or appear in a medical doctor's uniform in the dream, it's direct information that the dreamer is a nurse or medical person in the making. Whatever uniform we find ourselves dressed in reveals our true personality.

Dreams reveal our original personality. Uniforms tell us about our potential, our talents, and our naturally gifted profession. Uniforms identify us better than our mere ambition. Uniforms direct us to the kind of work or profession to do in the physical world. It tells us about our character traits. Sometimes uniforms describe your behavior or character trait. It's a common thing to tell someone, "You behave like a soldier," or "You have the heart of a soldier."

University: The university represents the peak in an individual's experience and academic knowledge. Primary schools and secondary schools indicate learning points or curves, while universities show physical maturity and experience to face life's challenges. It is not unusual for one to dream of themselves back in primary or secondary school, experiencing early life. However, when one begins to dream about university, it shows exaltation, upgrade, and liberty to do greater things.

For dreamers over thirty years of age, universities represent their current achievements and accomplishments so far. For someone who didn't attend university in reality, it indicates spiritual growth, knowledge expansion, and future advancement. When we get to the prime of our years, it is good to dream of ourselves at that height of learning and intellectual improvement.

To whom much is given much is expected. God and the society need a dreamer who usually sees themselves in the university of learning. The activities of the dreamer are the objects of interpretation for their understanding.

PART V

Vacancy: A job vacancy is an advertisement of career opportunities available to the dreamer. If a dreamer dreams of their current job, then they are on the right track. However, if the dreamer sees a vacancy in another area, it is a clear sign for them to change their career trajectory or begin applying for job opportunities elsewhere. The manner of job advertised on the vacancy is the object of interpretation for the dreamer.

Valley: This represents the highs and lows everyone experiences on life's journey. When a dreamer is at the peak of the mountain, they are at the apex of their achievements. When they are climbing down or walking through a valley, the dreamer might be facing some tribulation and difficulty that will require patience, determination, and the grace of God to overcome. "Yea though I walk through the valley of the shadow of death, I will fear no evil" (Psalm 23:4 KJV).

Village: This refers to an origin, beginning, or background. When we see our soul in the village while presently living in an urban area, it symbolizes a revelation concerning our ancestry. Take note of the things you do while in the village in the dream because it is key to understanding the message. If evil is planned against an active dreamer, God can reveal it by transporting the dreamer's soul to the village to uncover their evil plans. Whenever evil people invoke the soul of a dreamer or project evil against them from the village, the dreamer will see themselves in the village fighting those evil forces. Village things in the dream are very dangerous. It's our cradle, and they know us better, including our weak points. Finally, village dreams should not be taken for granted.

Violence: It's a sign of trouble. Violence refers to trouble on a large scale, like insecurity rather than personal trouble.

Visitor: It's a sign of traveling or the dreamer receiving a guest. Take note of your visitor's personality and character traits so that you can discern the kind of visitor you are about to welcome or the kind of people you are going to visit. God usually uses faces or people we know to represent the visitor in the dream.

PART W

Wage: (See *reward*.) Receiving wages in the dream is a sign of good fortune both for an employee and a nonemployee. A wage is a sign of reward or trophy. It means what you are doing will be successful or rewarding (Leviticus 19:13, 1 Timothy 5:18b KJV).

Warranty: A warranty is a written promise that if you find a fault in a product, it will be replaced or changed. A warranty works like a guarantee; it promises the dreamer that a message or information can be trusted. A warranty is a symbol of trust and confidence.

Water: (Also see *sea/ocean*.) Water represents people of various backgrounds. In fact, water represents the earth or the world full of inhabitants. At the beginning of time, the world was made up of water only. "And God said, let the waters under the heaven be gathered together unto one place, and let the dry land appear: and it was so" (Genesis 1:2, 9 KJV). Up to 60 percent of human composition is water.[41] So the spirit uses water to represent the human race in dreams or prophecy.

Wealth: (See *riches*.) Wealth is not money; rather, it is symbol of assets that can produce money or cash for a dreamer (e.g., vehicle, equipment, property, etc.).

---

[41] H. H. Mitchell, *Journal of Biological Chemistry* 158.

Welcome: To be welcome in the dream is to accept someone's proposals, ideas, plans, friendship, and so on. To welcome someone also means to accept someone's request, demand, proposals, ideas, plans, or whatever the person may present in the dream for consideration.

Wife: When you see your wife in the dream, there is a special message God wants to reveal to you about your wife. Her activity in the dream is the symbol of interpretation. For example, if you are sleeping with your wife on a bed, and she faces her back to you, it means she is not happy with you. Dreaming of your wife helps reveal the health status of your marital relationship in terms of peaceful coexistence, faithfulness, health, family planning, finances, and other aspects of your social, religious, economic, and political life. Whenever your wife starts manifesting in your dreams, it is a clear sign of unity and oneness of your spirits. This unity can make her manifest as the symbol of your guardian angel in your dreams.

On the other hand, every dreamer needs the spirit of discernment as a guide because evil people can disguise in the form of a dreamer's wife in order to harm him. The dreamer can easily escape this deception if they know the peculiar characteristics and attitudes of their wife. The evil entities may be unable to accurately copycat your wife. For instance, if your wife serves you food in the dream in a manner that is unlike the way the dreamer's wife would behave in reality, the spirit of discernment can help the dreamer notice it and abort the deception. However, for nondiscerning dreamers, it is more difficult to escape such an attack. Thankfully, God usually intervenes to rescue the dreamer from the evil schemes. God can also reveal the infidelity of a dreamer's wife by using another woman's face, image, or hypothetical situation to represent that circumstance.

Generally, women have a feminine attraction to men. Their presence can change the chemistry and psyche of a man. When they manifest in a dream, their mission is usually a trap or a plot to catch the man's soul. When ladies or women start manifesting in a man's life, it reveals the kind of women the man will meet physically. Every woman represents a kingdom, and every man will encounter women at various times in his life journey. Demonic entities can use our girlfriends, concubines, mistresses, or lovers to project whoredom onto us.

Wild: The wild is an unregulated environment—the streets or jungle where one's survival depends on being the craftiest one in the room. Such dreams mean the dreamer should not play gentleman to overcome a certain challenge or situation. Occasionally, a dreamer can turn into a wild animal to travel or escape a trap in their dreams. Every situation has a winning approach. There are situations that need wild and rascal approaches. Any animal you turn into or you use or behave like is the same approach you require to overcome your challenges.

Win: To win in the dream is a sign of victory and success.

Wind: Winds connote troubling situations in life. The degree of wind indicates the extent of the trouble. If the wind becomes a storm or tornado, it means war or battle. Controversies and violence of great proportion are represented by wind. Cool breezes represent a peaceful approach/appearance.

Witch: A witch is a master of cunning and trickery and powerful in the art of witchcraft. Witches operate in secrecy to manipulate and initiate people into the coven. While they look innocent and harmless, they can disguise themselves as loved ones and family friends in dreams, which makes dreamers feel secure. A witch can be disguised as our mother to serve us food in the dream. They can be disguised as our wives to have sex with us in the dream.

Just like cats, they practice evil only in secret because they are rendered powerless and witless if they are exposed to the public.

Word: When things are written in words in dreams, it means that information or revelation is established and can be trusted. It is very difficult to change or erase. Written words are decided decisions or planned things that must come to pass in our life's journey.

Worship: Worship is a spiritual exercise for the soul. The exercise of worship calls for reverence and divine obeisance. When we worship God in the dream, we renew our soul and strengthen our relationship with God.

The soul that came from God needs consistent prayers and worship, which act as its food to be strong and connected to God always. When you see yourself in the dream worshiping God, it means you are connected to God. A dreamer uses worship to unravel the kinds of songs, prayers, and styles of worship that suit their relationship with God. Every praise song or worship we experience in the dream is remarkable and key to opening the doors of heaven in our life. Always use the dream songs or praises to connect to God physically. It will be an amazing experience.

Every child of God should experience worshipping in the dream realm on a regular basis. Jacob, while sleeping during a journey, wrestled with an angel on his way back to heaven and refused to let him go without receiving a blessing (Genesis 32:26 KJV). After the struggle, during which his hip was dislocated, Jacob was blessed, and God also changed his name from Jacob to Israel. It must cost us something to change our destinies. What happened to Jacob was a dream life experience that affected his physical life.

So when you find yourself praying, worshiping, or singing praises, please take advantage of that dream state to change your world. Bring down heaven to change your life. It's a life-changing experience to experience things relating to God in the dream. When we praise God, pray, or worship God in the dream, heaven has come down to us for a life-changing experience. Our life isn't supposed to remain the same when we have these experiences in the dream.

Write: Whatever you write in the dream is reliable information or messages from the spiritual realm that will assist you in succeeding. Writings in the dream are like a cheat code from the divine realm to help in the journey through life.

PART Y

Young/youth: The life of every person is like a journey that has different stages. Dreaming of a younger version of yourself connotes the past, while a dream with an older version means the future. Dreams of the past could highlight any past mistakes, shortcomings, or experiences that led a person to success or failure. Our appearance in the dream is a key to knowing whether the information we are getting is for present or future use.

PART Z

Zebra: In the spiritual realm, different animals represent different kingdoms, dominions, principalities, and powers with their attendant character traits and personalities.